UP *from* SOUTH PHILLY

Anthony A. Chiurco, MD

LifeRich
PUBLISHING

LifeRich Publishing books may be ordered through booksellers or by contacting:

LifeRich Publishing
1663 Liberty Drive
Bloomington, IN 47403
www.liferichpublishing.com
1 (888) 238-8637

Because of the dynamic nature of the Internet, any web addresses or links contained in
this book may have changed since publication and may no longer be valid. The views
expressed in this work are solely those of the author and do not necessarily reflect the
views of the publisher, and the publisher hereby disclaims any responsibility for them.

Any people depicted in stock imagery provided by Thinkstock are models,
and such images are being used for illustrative purposes only.
Certain stock imagery © Thinkstock.

ISBN: 978-1-4897-0145-9 (sc)
ISBN: 978-1-4897-0144-2 (e)

Library of Congress Control Number: 2014901833

Print information available on the last page.

LifeRich Publishing rev. date: 2/15/2017

This book is dedicated in loving memory to my parents,
Anna and Alfred Chiurco,
and
to the thousands of patients with pathology of the
brain, spine and peripheral nervous system
who entrusted me with their care.

PROLOGUE

Tony,

I love the fact you are going to write about being from South Philly. I still insist that I be introduced as a kid from South Philly. I do it not to brag about coming from a ghetto to a gated community, which is a fashionable story politicians like to use, but rather because I was privileged to come from a community that had real values. I always wanted my kids to understand the values of "la famiglia." One of my biggest concerns about Washington today is that people do not understand we can have differences even to the point of screaming and shouting, but we are a family and don't let anyone outside the family even think about touching one of us. I loved being in a community of real people where you always knew where you stood, where you stood up and fought for yourself and if you got your ass kicked you didn't cry!

— *Andy*

Andrew Von Eschenbach, M.D.
Commissioner, Food and Drug Administration 2006-2009
Director, National Cancer Institute 2002-2006

CONTENTS

INTRODUCTION

"You can take a guy out of South Philly but you can't take South Philly out of the guy..."
— *Philadelphia Proverb*

My name is Tony Chiurco. I am a neurological surgeon practicing for almost forty years. In my youth, I chose a profession more challenging than one could ever imagine, fraught with triumph and tragedy in the pathology that affects human life. Probably like most people, reflecting on my life, there are joys and sorrows, elation and disappointment, wins and losses, friends and foes as well as love and hate. I wanted to leave something for my descendants, something intangible yet substantive, which might be more valuable than any material remnants of my life. I wanted them to appreciate the era in which I lived, the evolution of the art and science of medicine in that era with particular attention to neurological surgery, the characters I encountered, the lessons that I learned and most important, I hope in some small way to influence not only their judgment but also their decision making in some aspects of life. There will be areas of this book that not everyone will be in agreement with and may be deemed controversial. It may provide a stimulus for further investigation into areas of my interest and pursuit. Also, it may be confrontational and discourage the reader from picking this book up after a certain number of undefined pages.

I leave it up to you, the reader, to think for yourself while perusing this work as well as to think for yourself in life. After all each of us is entitled to an opinion and I am entitled to mine. Having grown up in South Philly, if you do not like my opinion, go fuck yourself.

— *Anthony A. Chiurco, MD*

CHAPTER I:
ORIGINS

**"Dad, I have only been typing for thirty minutes
and already two people are in jail..."**
— *Jen Chiurco (transcribing interviews)*

It was a cool, brisk morning in early May of 1967. The sun had broken through a passing group of cumulus clouds and began to reflect as sparkles on the wing of the aircraft I was staring at through the window. The Boeing 707 had stopped on the tarmac as the jet engines began to whine, preparing for takeoff from Philadelphia International. My pulse began to climb almost in sync with the increasing RPMs of the engines. I had never flown. I was intimidated and apprehensive. I began to perspire as my mind prepared for an event that I imagined to be life threatening.

At the time, I was a twenty-five-year-old medical student, six weeks from graduating from The Jefferson Medical College of Philadelphia. Following four years of an intense medical education, I was fortunate to receive a terminal ten-week vacation beginning in March and ending at graduation on June 7. Of my own volition, I sought exposure to a field of interest in neurological surgery, which developed during my years at Jefferson. Exposure was negligible to nonexistent as a medical student. I subsequently arranged through a surgeon mentor for a four-week rotation as an observer with The Neurological Group of New London, Conn., at the Lawrence and Memorial Hospitals. During that time, I was invited to accompany Rocco Angelo (the original surname, Angelone, was shortened following immigration), the youngest brother of my mother, Anna Angelo, on a trip to Japan and Hong Kong over the next six weeks following termination of my elective. It was great fortune for me that Rocco (Uncle Rocky) had a peptic ulcer and his brothers, the Angelo brothers, thought it would be a good idea if I accompanied him on this particular journey. We were bound for Japan and Hong Kong for a six-week business trip for Rocco and an educational/vacation trip for me.

The aircraft engines continued in a progressively higher pitch in preparation for takeoff and I reflected on my childhood and adolescence growing up in South Philadelphia. I thought about my experiences and the rigorous educational requirements necessary to qualify for enrollment into a top medical school such as Jefferson. The engines wound to an extremely high pitch and the plane began its path down the runway. We were flying on Pan American Airways, seated in the first-class cabin. The stewardess addressed us by our surnames in a very proper manner, which is an aspect of flight unknown today. Then the jet engines were screaming and as the plane was flying down the runway my pulse exceeded 100 beats per minute.

When the wheels left the ground and the aircraft angled upward, I experienced the sensation of flight for the very first time. I became hypotensive at the sound of the wheels being retracted into the aircraft, a sound I did not expect. I assumed there could be something wrong with the plane. I saw structures on the ground moving rapidly, fading into the distance. I began to think about my life to this point, flashing in rapid sequence not unlike the speed of the aircraft. At that moment, however, I was reassured as to what was occurring by my worldly traveling companion, my Uncle Rocky, who gave me guidance on what to expect in flight, as well as over the next six weeks on our trip to California and Tokyo. I settled into my seat as my pulse gradually diminished, along with my respirations and perspiration. I realized how much of the world I had not experienced or visualized. Growing up in South Philadelphia, I had not traveled further north than New York or further east than Sea Isle City at the Jersey Shore. I had not traveled further south than Washington, D.C. The furthest west I had experienced was West Philadelphia and now since the onset of my terminal ten-week vacation, I had traveled to New London, Conn. One can only imagine the excitement and feeling of adventure to travel to and experience the West Coast of the United States, mainly California, and then on to East Asia, including Japan and Hong Kong.

My mother's older brothers, Uncle Tim and Uncle Stan, had started a small business, Angelo Brothers, after World War II on Snyder Avenue in South Philadelphia. Their father Stanislaus had passed away from cancer of the rectum at Philadelphia General Hospital, the county hospital for the indigent and uninsured. The business began as a paint store and slowly grew and expanded into lamp parts and then light bulbs. The post-World War II economy was one of the greatest business expansions in our economic history. This small family business eventually graduated to become the most profitable line of decorative light bulbs and was climbing the ladder in production, chasing G.E. and Philips. Manufacturing at the time was economical outside the United States and the company's current production was in Japan, where light bulb production had begun and developed. Uncle Rocky had made these initial contacts and was the emissary of the Angelo Brothers in foreign countries. I was invited to make this trip with Rocky, which was probably the most exciting adventure of my life thus far.

Rocky, like all of the Angelo brothers, was of medium height (around five-foot-ten), with male pattern baldness and terrific blue eyes. He was very slender and always dressed well, with wide-lapel suits that were popular in the '40s and '50s. Rocky had a high school education and went to Girard College in Philadelphia qualifying for admission as an orphan. He attended a short time before quitting. He would later say that he regretted his lack of a college education, but at that time of his life he was just too hedonistic and indifferent to stay in college. Nonetheless, Rocky was an intelligent man and an avid reader – but definitely a man with a wild side.

After we arrived in Los Angeles from Philadelphia, we checked into the Beverly Hilton Hotel, where Rocky spent several days conducting business with distributors and our sales force. The Angelo Brothers, at that time called ABCO (Angelo Brothers Company), had a large warehouse on La Cienaga Boulevard in Los Angeles. The visual beauty and contrast of California was overwhelming to me as an initial shock. I rented a car, a green Mustang convertible, and while Rocky was doing business, I motored myself through Beverly Hills, Bel Air, Malibu and surrounding visual sensations. I had actually never really seen a palm tree, to give the reader an example of my extreme naiveté and inexperience with the world by age twenty-five.

On the second evening at the Beverly Hilton Hotel, I wandered to Uncle Rocky's suite to check our plans for dinner. Rocky was on the phone, screaming at the other end of the line and cursing with words I was well familiar with, having grown up in South Philly. "Fuck him and fuck you. If he wants to see me, he can come to Tokyo. I will be there in forty-eight hours. Fuck him, too." This vitriol went on for several minutes and the phone call ended. He did not want to talk about the conversation and we went out to dinner. That evening we dined with one of his old Hollywood buddies, a man named Blake Edwards.

Mr. Edwards became famous subsequently for producing movies, among which of great notoriety was the *Pink Panther* series. Over dinner in a boutique-like Hollywood Italian restaurant, the stories emerged and they reminisced of the great fun in Hollywood after World War II in the late 1940s and early 1950s. On the car ride to the restaurant, the aroma of a certain cologne filled the car. That aroma is now familiar to me for almost fifty years – an aftershave and cologne called Acqua Di Selva from Milano, Italy, a Victor product. This was the "in" fragrance in Hollywood and what a surprise – the aroma was on Mr. Edwards as well. It was even more amusing forty-five years later, while watching an original *Pink Panther* movie featuring Peter Sellers, that I noticed David Niven open the medicine cabinet in the bathroom and a secret note about that evening's caper was stuffed behind a bottle of Acqua Di Selva. Now the reader must understand this is a very eccentric, relatively unknown fragrance, but after I began wearing it in 1967, I realized its potency. In the operating rooms in later life, it was rare for a nurse not to ask me what I was wearing. I would always respond in typical fashion that it was Acqua Di Selva and if she bought it for her husband, when she was in bed with him, she could think of me, a response reflecting the flamboyance of my youth.

We were approximately ten hours into the flight to Tokyo when I grew bored and needed conversation periodically. I asked Rocky what was the issue on the phone the evening I entered his suite, causing his tirade. He explained to me that the man on the other end of the phone was Bernie Bernstein, an old Army buddy, who now worked as Burt Lancaster's valet. Burt learned that Rocky was in town and wanted to get together. Burt, of course, should be well known to readers of my generation – a famous movie star, Academy Award winner and movie mogul, who was the first in Hollywood to write into his contract that he could make independent films. I knew there had been a rift between Burt and Rocky, going back to the late 1940s.

When I was a child, approximately age seven, Burt would visit our summer home in Sea Isle City because he loved my mother's cooking, with particular attention to lasagna. I remember Burt opening the icebox (refrigerators had not quite entered the average home and a daily visit from the iceman carrying a block of ice on tongs was a familiar site in the 1940s). Burt would eat the lasagna cold at times. He often carried me around on his shoulders – I recall one especially memorable event when I was ill with a sore throat, he threw me up in the air and caught me and was trying to cheer me up. It was not uncommon for Rocky and Burt to have a catch with me when I was a child, only I was the object being tossed. I have vividly in my memory Burt and Rocky walking me down to the beach on 43rd Street on their hands. It was amusing and attracted the attention of passersby, which may be the shock effect they were looking for, as well as amusing each other. Burt was tall and handsome with prominent teeth and a forehead full of hair, and very charismatic. One summer, Burt and Rocky had rented a house in Ventnor, N.J., along with my Uncle Tim and Aunt Isabel. We were invited to a Sunday dinner and Aunt Yolanda, wife of Uncle Emidio Angelo, picked us up in Burt's 1949 maroon Ford convertible. This was memorable because there were four children piled into the car with the top down and I remember sitting in the back of the car, enjoying my first ride in a convertible. The open air was unique and the pleasure of the sensation of apparent wind striking me would last a lifetime. I remember glancing at the speedometer. Aunt Yolanda was doing fifty-five miles per hour on the ocean drive, going over the Strathmere Bridge from Sea Isle en route to Atlantic City. What fun! We arrived and sat for dinner after Burt, his wife Norma, Uncle Tim and Aunt Isabel came off the tennis court. Dinner was eccentric. Burt's wife, Norma Anderson, would cook over the stove with a cigarette hanging out of her mouth. My mother has never stopped talking about finding a cigarette butt in the spaghetti sauce bowl on the dinner table. And in an even greater calamity, Burt's oldest son, Jimmy, sat on my new model airplane and crushed it! Total disaster!

At the height of World War II, Rocky enlisted in the Army and, as a soldier at age 18 with the American Forces, he participated in the American invasion of Sicily. He was wounded in that operation and was recovering prior to being sent into Special Services because he could not return to combat. Rocky was a singer and a dancer as a child, and they thought that he might be able to provide some entertainment for the troops in the Special Services Division. After the Allied Forces took over Italy, Rocky made a trip on furlough to investigate our family origins. He went to Sulmona, Italy, from where his parents had emigrated. Sulmona is a city and commune of the province of L'Aquila in Abruzzo, Italy with a population of around 25,000. It is in the Valley Peligna, a plateau once occupied by a lake that disappeared in prehistoric times. In the ancient era, it was an important city and is known for being the native town of Ovid, of whom there is a bronze statue in the square known as Piazza Settembre, located on the town's main road also under his name. Sulmona also is famous for production of confetti. Sulmona lies approximately 85 miles northeast of Rome in the mountains toward the Adriatic Sea. Sulmona's strategic position made it a target for air raids during World War II and much of the destruction has been mostly restored. Uncle Rocky told me that when he found the home of his ancestors, namely grandparents on the Angelone side, he knocked on the door and they opened the door, then slammed it shut when they saw an American soldier who was armed – after all, Italy was at war with America. His poor knowledge of Italian as he attempted to explain who he was, combined with his military dress, created a temporarily alarming situation until the family realized who he was and why he was there. Then he was embraced and established the connection that was to be enjoyed by Rocky's generation, as well as the next generation.

After Rocky arrived in the Special Services, he encountered Burt Lancaster, who was an acrobat, and they became instant great friends. They returned to the United States after the war and settled in the New York area. Burt had grown up in New York and Rocky in Philadelphia. They were living together and dating two women who worked in the same office building. Burt subsequently married one of the women, Norma Anderson. One day in route to meet them, Rocky and Burt were going up in the elevator when a gentleman in the elevator said to Burt, "Are you an actor?" His answer was "Yes, I am an actor," which of course he was not, but he thought it might be prudent to answer in the affirmative since the inquiring gentleman seemed to be well dressed and of some importance. The gentleman then suggested that Burt show up and try out for a part in a play that was being produced. Burt indeed showed up and actually got the part, and play opened in Philadelphia. The play was a flop, but influential audience members from Hollywood noticed Burt's great physical appearance and ability and his strong personality. One of the individuals in the audience was Hal Wallis, who then signed Burt for subsequent film production. Burt emigrated to Hollywood and along with him went Uncle Rocky. Burt subsequently made his first movie, *The Killers*, based on Ernest Hemingway's novel of the same title. Rocky also had a small part in the movie and was listed as Rex Dale, his show business alias. I remember seeing the movie many years ago, with Uncle Rocky sitting at a round table playing cards with Ava Gardner, among others, in the opening scene. Rocky had an affair with Ava Gardner during the making of that film, and he told me later that he succeeded in attracting one of Hollywood's most desired actresses through his sense of humor. He taught me an important lesson: The way into a woman's boudoir is to make her laugh — that was the secret. The last time Rocky encountered Ava Gardner was one evening in Madame Cherry's Copa Cabana in Tokyo an enchanting club where I was to dine on our sojourn.

When I pursued Rocky over the issue as to the breakup with Burt, he related to me that a movie was to be made entitled *I Walk Alone*, starring Burt, Lizabeth Scott and Kirk Douglas. Rocky related to me that he had a screen test for the film and was given a costarring role as the character Skinner. He claimed that another actor was having an affair with the producer's wife and that she interceded to get him the part that was promised to Rocky. Because Burt did not stand up for Rocky, the relationship fell apart. According to Rocky, *I Walk Alone* would have made him a Hollywood star because of the importance of his role. Later on in life, however, he did admit to me that his years in Hollywood were primarily hedonistic, whereas Lancaster was a serious student of film and would spend much of his spare time reading and studying in his desire to achieve. Rocky admitted that he did not really want to make something out of himself and did not possess Burt's drive and tenacity.

After the fallout with Burt, Rocky moved on and entered a show-business stage career as Rex Dale, teaming with a chubby comedian with bushy, curly hair named Marty Allen. They played the clubs in Las Vegas and around the country. Rocky would frequently bring show-business characters to our home whenever he was in the Philadelphia area so that they could experience one of my mother's home-cooked Italian meals. I remember having dinner with Marty Allen, Buddy Hackett and others who achieved great notoriety in the late 1950s and 1960s on stage. One particular comedian and actor was memorable, his name was Guy Marks, who did a classic sensational imitation of a fly. He was born and raised in South Philadelphia and a very close friend of Rocky. They wrote a song together, *Loving You Has Made Me Bananas*, which actually climbed on the charts. But Rocky's show-business career never really took off because he focused more of his attention on gambling, drinking and womanizing. I remember visiting Las Vegas and seeing him lose everything at the craps table — his brothers had to bail him out. While he was playing, big-name comedians like Alan King and Don Rickles would come up and greet him with a slap on the back, saying,

"Hey, Rex, how'ya doing?" He just waved them away because he didn't want to be bothered while he was gambling. But there were so many other times when I saw Uncle Rocky wrap people around his finger with his charm and sense of humor. He had a great charismatic personality and was a born salesman. When we arrived in Tokyo on my first trip overseas, there were ten cars full of his business associates waiting for him, greeting him with enthusiastic shouts of "Rocky-san!"

During our flight to Japan, Uncle Rocky recounted his history with Burt Lancaster and his early days in Hollywood as we were ten hours into our journey over the Pacific. The conversation then drifted to ancestry and what Rocky learned about our family after engaging our relatives in Sulmona. My mother's father, Stanislaus, was a baker in Sulmona. Stanislaus had a brother who was a banker. The banker had a son, Romolo, who served with the Italian forces in World War I and was made a Comandatore della Corona d'Italia. Romolo later came to America to acquire a Ph.D. in economics at Columbia University in New York. While doing so, he was following a famous murder trial carried on the front page of *The New York Times*. A lawyer, Julia Grilli, was defending a man accused of killing his wife. He was so enthralled about this woman that he had to meet her, which he did and married her. She was from Brooklyn. Romolo then went back to Italy and entered the Italian Diplomatic Corps, learning fluent Japanese with Mussolini. He subsequently became Mussolini's commercial attaché in Tokyo during World War II and was imprisoned when the Allies took over Japan. He lost his son at the time, the details of which are not known. When he returned to the United States, he invested in a new startup company called Hertz Rent-A-Car. He acquired founder's stock and became affluent. He moved to 88 Deerfield Drive in Greenwich, Conn., next door to Prescott Bush (father of future President George H.W. Bush). The baker, meanwhile, at the turn of the 20th century in his modest shop had a more difficult life in Sulmona. A man who visited the bakery shop on a regular basis would frequently proposition Grandmom Laura, Stanislaus' wife, until one day, he put his hand on Laura and Grandpop Stanislaus threw him in the oven. Then he was arrested for murder. He was subsequently released to come to America, where he and Laura produced seven children, namely Emidio, Stanislaus, Romolo, Rafael, Rocco, Lucy and Anna (my mother). Family synonyms for these seven individuals were in the same order: Uncle Midi, Uncle Stan, Uncle Tim, Uncle Pat, Uncle Rocky, Aunt Lucy and of course, my mother. (It should be noted that there are two Romolos mentioned – Romolo, the Italian ambassador, was the son of the banker; Romolo, known as Uncle Tim, was the son of the baker.)

As Uncle Rocky explained our family's history, over the Pacific, suddenly the engines of the aircraft made a different sound, again causing me apprehension and alarm, having no flight experience in my life. Rocky explained to me that "they reverse the engines" on such a long flight, which he knew from having done this round trip to Japan numerous times. The stewardess brought him slices of bleu cheese and crackers as a snack, and he asked me if I wanted to share. I was not interested. Rocky insisted, "You will love bleu cheese." I tasted it and I have been eating it ever since. First class at that time was sensational, with personalized service, and the stewardesses were well mannered and beautiful. One ordered from a menu and it was equivalent to flying in a first-class restaurant. I became a great fan of Pan American Airways, which is now defunct. As many events in life are ironic, it is of interest that one of my close personal friends today, Duke Wiser, is the son of the former chairman of Pan American Airways, Forwood (Bud) Wiser, who passed away from Alzheimer's disease in middle age.

Everyone smoked on board for the most part and the air was unhealthy because of it. The detrimental effects of smoking and secondary smoke were not well known at that time. Dr. Richard Doll of London made the association of cigarette smoke with lung cancer in 1950, but this epidemiology was only gradually accepted as a significant factor in the development of this carcinoma and number-one cause of death in men – a disease entity that eventually took the life of Uncle Rocky (Winston cigarettes) and Uncle Tim (Lucky Strikes).

Stanislaus Angelone, *circa* 1920   Laura Angelone, *circa* 1920

Rocco (Rocky) Angelo, *circa* 1942

Burt Lancaster, *circa* 1949

Rocky Angelo
aka Rex Dale, *circa* 1950

Burt Lancaster and Lucy
Angelo on the beach
in Sea Isle City, NJ

Romolo
(Tim) Angelo,
Isabel Angelo,
Annetta
Chiurco, and
Burt Lancaster
circa 1948

The flight to Tokyo was coming to an end. Getting comfortable in the seats despite the first-class cabin was difficult on such a long flight. I would frequently find two empty seats and stretch recumbent across both. Rocky did not make the flight less apprehensible on our path to the tarmac when he explained to me one of the great air crashes in history occurred coming into Haneda International in Tokyo, where a large jet had crashed with no survivors in the recent past. I am sure any reader would appreciate the first flight apprehension when traveling in an aircraft with unknown sounds and unfamiliar occurrence in a perceived dangerous venue.

We finally landed safely, much to my relief, and as Uncle Rocky and I exited the plane I found myself thinking about the lesson in family history I had just gained. I began to understand how far my family had come to start a new life in America. And as I looked out the windows of Haneda International on our way to baggage claim, I was acutely aware of how far I had just come from my old neighborhood in South Philly.

CHAPTER II:
EARLY YEARS

**"If you did not grow up like I did, then you don't know, and
if you don't know, it's probably better you don't judge…"**
— *Junot Diaz, from* The Brief Wondrous Life Of Oscar Wao

Growing up in South Philly always has been a point of both pride as well as ambivalence. I learned about family and community and that no one was going to hand you anything in life. There was no other formula than hard work to achieve success.

I was born on August 24, 1941, to Alfred and Anna Chiurco. My father was a commercial agent for Erie Railroad and my mother was a homemaker. I was named for my father's brother, Tony, who died suddenly of a myocardial infarction (heart attack) before I was born. At the time of Tony's demise, my parents were vacationing in Maine and had to return home for funeral services. To the best of my arithmetic ability, I believe it was more likely than not that I was conceived in Maine. I grew up in a row house at 1621 South 22nd street between Morris and Tasker Streets. We lived across the street from my uncle Tim Angelo and his wife Isabel, who lived at 1628 South 22nd Street, also a row house. The strict row house has a unique history in America that began in Philadelphia with Carstair's Row on what is now Samson Street in center city. The row was named after Thomas Carstair, who designed the homes for developer William Samson. With row houses a developer would purchase an entire block of plots, build a row of connected houses with a uniform design, and then sell the finished buildings. City plots could be developed in the most space-effective way as possible. As a result, row houses quickly became the urban house of choice. Because of their origins they were called "Philadelphia row houses" in the beginning.

My sister, Annetta, who everyone calls Annette, was born sixteen months before me on April 15, 1940. My father was eleven years older than my mother—she was thirty-six and he was forty-seven when I was born. My mother went into labor after eating dinner at Uncle Tim's and gave birth to me at 2:30 p.m. in the afternoon at St. Agnes Hospital, which was a moderate-sized catholic hospital on Broad Street, the site of the annual Mummers Parade which strolled down Broad Street every New Year's Day. It is ironic that thirty-four years later, I would be visiting the same hospital for the second time, only as a surgeon evaluating a patient with a self-inflicted gunshot wound through both frontal lobes.

My memory of my mother is that of an ingratiating, generous, loving and gregarious woman. She was of medium height and always overweight physically. Many Italian women eventually get obese and my mother was no exception. She was a traditional housewife, caring for the home and children. She had abundant friends and would bake cakes and cookies whenever the opportunity arose. She liked to make Italian cookies called pizzelles. She had a pizzelle iron and you would often see her in the kitchen making bags of these flat, waffle-looking items and distributing them to friends and family. Her oldest brother, Emidio, the artist, always enjoyed pizzelles with his coffee and would come over for such. My mother also was a talent at making ravioli and strawberry shortcake. Everyone loved Anna Chiurco. The first thing people would say to me was "How is your mother? Tell your mother we said hello." She had a big fan club because she was charismatic and compassionate. My mother, unfortunately, went as far as third grade in school. She could just get by in terms of her ability to read and write. She was born in Philadelphia in 1906, one of seven children of Laura and Stanislaus Angelone. Life was tough for first-generation Italians whose parents emigrated from the old country. In summers, Anna and her brothers would pick tomatoes in New Jersey fields to provide income and food for a large family of seven children. Attending school was difficult as she was left-handed and teachers would beat her left hand to force her to write with her right hand. My mother's other primary interest aside from cooking was the Catholic Church. She was a fervent Catholic who attended mass frequently and she encouraged my sister and me to attend church as well. The Catholic Church represented a source of comfort and she was a good client. Following my formal education, I gradually developed a strong and anti-religious sentiment that is reflected in my later life. However, in my mother's daily existence, I understand she sought out the church for solace. Sometimes, it was a way of dealing and getting through life. My mother and the rest of the Angelones were exceptionally good, fine people. There was not a mean bone in any of them.

I believe I was mentored toward academic interest because of my father who more or less molded me more than my mother. My paternal grandfather emigrated from Lucca, Italy, which is in the central part of the country, not far from Florence. My grandmother was called La Donna Annetta. I saw pictures of her and I must say she gave a whole new meaning to the expression "coyote ugly." Grandpop Chiurco was a tailor who opened a shop in Center City Philadelphia near Chestnut Street, which is more likely why my father was always well-dressed and left for work in three-piece suits. My grandfather Chiurco died when my father was a young man.

My father was born in Philadelphia in February 1895. It is astounding to consider that when my father was born, there were no automobiles, airplanes, television, or antibiotics for that matter. He stood about five feet eight inches tall and always had a protuberant stomach. He did not attend college; however, to have done so would have been exceptional for a first-generation Italian in 1911, the year he graduated from Southern High School. He did eventually take classes at the Wharton School at the University of Pennsylvania. My father was an athlete at Southern High, which I learned when I found several track and field trophies in the basement. He was a chief petty office in the United States Navy and served in World War I. He would occasionally take me to Franklin Field to see the University of Penn Football Team play. We also attended the

Army Navy football game, played annually in Philadelphia. His cousin, Saverio Brunetti, was a physician attending the game for the crowd of almost one hundred thousand in the stands. We would arrive in a police paddy wagon with the sirens and lights flashing and avoided all traffic going in and out of the stadium.

My childhood memory of my father is that of an older gentleman who would usually be seen sitting in a chair on the porch reading the newspaper or Reader's Digest or a book. He had pale blue eyes and wore round spectacles without frames. He was essentially bald except for small wisps of white hair, thin over the temples bilateral, and was usually quiet and intent on absorbing what he was reading. It would be difficult to interrupt him. Dad was a strict, intense, rigid, no-nonsense individual. His friends were educated. Most of those in the social circle were physicians, lawyers, and judges. Dad was not very communicative. He was reticent, but would have bouts of anger and could be verbally abusive. My father had angina from my earliest memory of walking with him and he would frequently stop and rest after a two-block ambulation. He was a strict disciplinarian and insisted on my return home at nine o'clock during my teenage years. I believe he was frustrated in his marriage, more likely than not due to an intellectual difference with my mother. His frustration was exaggerated probably due to concomitant biochemical depression. In that era, of course, there were no antidepressants. In retrospect, with my medical knowledge, I would say he was a twenty-four-carat depressive and he acted accordingly. He exuded misery.

I remember on one occasion when I was ten years old, my father was driving me to the Jersey Shore on a Friday afternoon. My mother was already there with my sister. We were riding through Hammonton, New Jersey, on the back roads before the Atlantic City Expressway or Garden State Parkway were built. All of a sudden, he pulled the car over to the side of the road. I asked, "Dad, what are you doing? Let's go. I want to get to the beach." He had the car in neutral and looked at me and said, "Son, promise me something." I said, "Yes, what? What's the matter?" He said, "Just promise me." I said, "What?" He said, "Promise me that

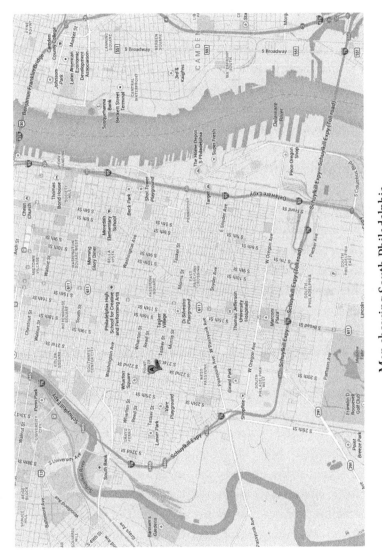

Map showing South Philadelphia

you will never ever get married!" I said, "Okay fine, I won't get married! Let's go, I want to get to the beach." So, I am sure if that was reflection of the marriage, it was a bombshell.

My father smoked a pipe and used Holiday tobacco. I would always buy him a can for his birthday or Christmas. I loved the smell of his pipe. Dad would come home, sit in his chair on the porch, and open a Philadelphia Inquirer or the Evening Bulletin. I believe the academic intelligence that was manifested in both me and my sister, who is a mathematics teacher, came probably through him, although the practical intelligence and the creative intelligence came through my mother.

My father provided as well as he could. He had an excellent character and he was forthright and honest. We were an average family and income was limited. My father did not make a lot of money even though he could have advanced with Erie Railroad. They offered him to be head of the Erie in Chicago, but he declined because he did not want to leave his friends and his Philadelphia roots. As a commercial agent, he was responsible for soliciting freight from manufacturing companies in Philadelphia and New Jersey areas to ship through Erie Railroad. The Railroad gave him a company car, always a two-door Chevrolet, which would be new every two years. He would solicit orders and once in a while he would come home in the company car if it was inconvenient to take the train, depending on where he was working that day. His office was in the old Commerce Building on Cherry Street in Center City, Philadelphia. We used to watch the Thanksgiving Day parade from his office on the fifteenth floor. My father did not impart business knowledge to me as I was growing up. He was laconic and not communicative. In later years, he encouraged me to have a profession. He suggested law or medicine, telling me not to work for someone, but be independent and self-employed. That was good advice, which I heeded. I do not believe he was ever happy working for Erie Railroad. His peak earning years were during the Great Depression in America. He was on the board of directors of Aetna Savings and Loan on Broad Street. He and two of his associates on the board would acquire foreclosed properties, rehabilitate them, and put them up for rent. However, during the Depression, the tenants

"Anna Chiurco" 24" x 30" oil on canvas by Emidio Angelo, *circa* 1955

"Alfred Chiurco, United States Navy" 24" x 36" oil on canvas
from photos *circa* 1918 by Anthony Chiurco, 2003

Anthony Chiurco, *circa* 1942

The neighborhood gang from left: Chubby Ricca, Jackie Egan, Annetta
Chiurco, Stanley Angelo, and Anthony Chiurco, *circa* 1945

Annetta and Anthony Chiurco, *circa* 1949

lost their jobs and could not pay the rent and the bank foreclosed. The latter occurrence was germane to my father not achieving financially. He did manage to purchase a modest summerhouse in Sea Isle City, New Jersey, in the 1930s for approximately $1,500 before his real estate interests began to suffer. Eventually, all of my mother's family came to Sea Isle City to vacation throughout my childhood.

While South Philadelphia is well known for being a tough, hardscrabble area, it was a perfect preparation for life, and thereby a favorable, but perhaps not optimal environment. It was the oldest ethnically mixed neighborhood in a big city in America starting with Swedes who settled in the area three decades before William Penn founded the city in 1682. As Philadelphia grew in size and reputation the south side neighborhood with stretches between Delaware and Schuylkill rivers became a patchwork of ethnicities. The generations of families living in tight row house lined streets meant that anyone growing up in South Philadelphia learned the value of community. You also learned the value of a good meal — places like the Melrose Diner, Pat's Steaks, and Red's Hoagies, not to mention Corona Di Fera, Ralph's, or Palumbo's Restaurant. These are South Philadelphia legendary institutions. I can still remember Uncle Tim buying me my first cheeseburger from the Melrose Diner on Snyder Avenue a few blocks from Angelo Brothers Company. It was the greatest thing I ever tasted. One day he brought me a cheeseburger with fried onions, which I declined. However, after tasting it, it was so outrageously good, I was sold!

We lived in South Philadelphia until I was ten years of age, when my father decided to move us to Overbrook, a suburb of West Philadelphia. My first memory of having any interest in the future medical career came around age seven or eight when I contracted scarlet fever and the house was subsequently quarantined. A sign was placed on the door because no one was allowed to come inside except for immediate family and medical personnel. My father had to get a nurse twenty-four hours a day to care for me. My pediatrician was Dr. Coppolino from St. Agnes, who visited me daily. He was a very distinguished-looking and well-dressed man in a three-piece suit with a mustache and he exuded a mystery of knowledge that would be responsible for someone's life. He carried a large doctor's bag, which was black with handles from which he would take instruments to examine me. I think the fascination that an individual could have such knowledge to take on such responsibility may have planted in me the seeds of a medical career, in addition to the influence of my father's cousin, Saverio (Sam) Brunetti, who was the chief police and fire surgeon for the City of Philadelphia.

When I reflect on the years growing up in South Philly, I have vivid memories of being three or four years old and playing with my peg set in the kitchen while waiting with great anticipation for pasta night (every Tuesday, Thursday, and Sunday), because I did not like anything else. It was not uncommon in later years as a practicing neurosurgeon whenever I was pounding a round bone plug into a cervical spine through the anterior approach following cervical disk removal to promote bony fusion between the vertebrae that I would have flashbacks of pounding the pegs in my peg set in similar fashion. Another strong early memory is the sound of sirens reflecting the air raid drills of the early 1940s during World War II. We would be awakened by our parents and had to get under the bed while my mother and father shut all the lights out in the house. The navy yard was nearby and in case the Germans ever bombed us by air, it was a standard precaution to have all the lights out in the city. Another clear memory is the vision of soldiers and sailors marching down Broad Street at the end of World War II. My mother brought me and my sister to watch the parade and I remember embracing my uncles who were marching in the parade who had served with United States Forces in World War II.

One actual disaster that my family survived was the Great Atlantic hurricane of September 1944, which devastated the Jersey Shore. As I mentioned earlier, my father was able to purchase a modest summer home in Sea Isle City. The house had no phone as well as no heating or air-conditioning or refrigerator. We had an icebox and every day the iceman would come by with his horse-drawn carriage carrying blocks of ice that he would carry in to the house with large tongs. The lack of a telephone was especially important because my father was away on business in Hornell, New York, and when the hurricane struck, he had no idea if his family survived. My sister and I had arisen from our naps and my mother and grandmother, Laura, were sitting on a brown leather loveseat in our living room saying the rosary. The water was just up to the porch — we had five steps up to the porch and luckily 43rd Street was the highest street in town. The water was about an inch or two from coming into the living room. My sister and I were laughing at the iceboxes floating down the street, as well as furniture, and other remnants of the storm. A fisherman came to our house in a boat and wanted us to get in, but my mother refused. The hurricane had clocked winds of nearly one hundred miles per hour and created waves twenty-five to thirty feet high. Hundreds of homes on the Jersey Shore were lost. At that time, there was no satellite weather forecast and with a nation at war, there was no dissemination of what could be considered strategic information, including the weather. We had no knowledge that a hurricane was coming. When it came — surprise! We either lived or died. Luckily we survived.

I attended St. Edmond's School, which was about six blocks from our house. One day during the routine school physical in third grade, the nurse did an eye examination and said I needed glasses. I cried for a week. I was devastated because wearing glasses meant that I could not be a jet fighter pilot, which was my dream at that time. As a child, I loved building model airplanes, which I would buy at a hobby shop on Snyder Avenue. I was particularly fond of jet fighter planes. I remember saving my money for two months to buy a model of the B29 super fortress aircraft, which dropped the nuclear holocaust on Hiroshima and Nagasaki in World War II. I saved the money from my income collecting newspapers and bagging washers for the Angelo Brothers. Home entertainment in the 1940s came from listening to radio as television had not entered households until about 1948. My favorite radio shows included *The Shadow* and *The Fat Man*, a detective series that opened up with a man entering a store getting on the scale weighing 320 pounds and then the announcer would say "The fat man." Listening to the Phillies and the Eagles was mandatory. When we bought our first television the screen was about ten inches and round made by Stromberg-Carlson with only the center part demonstrating a picture in rectangular fashion. It received three channels via rabbit ears on top of the TV box, which would have to be rotated to pick up optimal reception. The three channels were the major networks at the time: NBC, ABC, and CBS. I was immediately a fan of Howdy Doody, a freckle-faced wooden puppet with a big smile who interacted with the nasty Mr. Bluster and the Flubadub, an animal composed of nine different species. Princess SummerFallWinterSpring was a regular and the show was moderated by Buffalo Bob Smith and Clarabelle the Clown, who didn't speak but honked a horn. The children audience was called the Peanut Gallery, and to this day I can still sing with perfect memory the Howdy Doody theme song. The show came on at 5:30 p.m. just before dinner and my father would arrive home at the end of the show but frequently before the start of the next show at 6:00 p.m., which was *Frontier Playhouse*, a western and a daily show as well. My favorite cowboys were Hopalong Cassidy, Roy Rogers, Kermit Maynard and Gene Autry. Like other boys my age we enjoyed a crush on Dale Evans and wanted a white horse like Trigger. It was always a confrontation for me with my father in that I did not want to leave the television after the start of a good western to eat dinner unless of course it was pasta, which took precedence over most programs.

My boyhood friends included Jackie Egan, who lived across the street, next door to Uncle Tim. Jackie's grandmother made me my first Bologna sandwich with mayonnaise and tomatoes and I thought that was one of the best things I had ever eaten. Jackie and I also played with other children who lived across the street — Chubby Ricca and Al and Billy Gargani. That was our neighborhood gang — we would come out after school and play cowboys and Indians and we would flip baseball and football cards against the walls of the row houses. We all had cap guns and would buy a roll of caps for a nickel. One of the highlights of my Christmas was a beautiful gold gun and a black leather holster. This particular present sure surpassed others, namely underwear, which was common for me to receive at Christmas time. Another great gift was my Eagles helmet. I would wear that with my Eagles shirt when my father would take us to League Island Park, now called Fairmont Park, to have a football catch.

On our corner, there was a little store called Gumbo's where I would have to go to get cigarettes for my uncles and buy candy and ice cream. The cigarettes were fifteen cents a pack and they would sell them to me because they knew they were for my uncles. So in a way, I contributed to their ultimate demise from lung cancer.

When you went to Gumbo's, you would have to make sure to look up and down the street. You had to look out for yourself because black kids would travel in groups of three or four and they always carried sticks. The last thing you wanted as a white kid growing up in South Philly was to encounter four black kids with sticks because self-preservation is the first law of nature. You always watched your back. Fortunately, I never had such an encounter, but I did come close and ran before I was caught. One uncomfortable memory was a friend being run over by a car on Fernon Street and then the car backed up over his leg, which was a frightening, horrible sight to see as a child.

Our area of South Philadelphia was mostly a representation of an Italian neighborhood. I remember when someone died in the neighborhood, you would see a black wreath on the door. I recalled Grandmom Laura's wake, which was held in the living room of Uncle Tim's house at 1628 South 22nd Street across from our home. I was almost four years of age, but I do recall the coffin being against the window in the front of the living room and visitors coming through the front door with the coffin immediately to their right. Laura expired at St. Agnes Hospital following gallbladder surgery. The surgeon performing the cholecystectomy told my mother he felt it was the anesthesia that caused her demise. At that time ether was the predominant anesthetic and eventually was abandoned as newer anesthetics were developed. The problem with ether was the inability to determine how deep that patient might be causing physiological catastrophe not uncommonly. I remember that grandmom's face was covered with a veil. I did not quite understand the concept of death at such a young age, but it certainly became familiar in my career in neurosurgery. To see my parents and other loved ones crying in a less than hysterical fashion was upsetting to me as a child, as a chapter in our lives closed with the lid of the coffin.

If you have seen the *Godfather* movies, you may remember the "black hand" (La Mano Nera) who extorted the merchants. I remember walking with my mother and seeing an imprint of a black hand on the sidewalk corner next to a store. I asked my mother what that represented and she said she did not want to talk about it. She said, "That's bad, that's very bad." I am suspicious that this type of criminal activity was persisting in South Philadelphia neighborhoods during the 1940s.

When I would attend St. Edmond's School, it was not exactly a preppy clientele, so you had to protect yourself. At the time I transferred from St. Edmond's to Our Lady of Lourdes School in Overbrook, I was ranked third among boys in the fifth grade and I do not mean academic standing. Ranking was much like ranking in the World Boxing Organization, which occurred after a series of fights over a period of time. An excellent example would be the day a classmate Al Wasco wrote "jackass hole" on the cover of my copybook. I showed it to the teacher and said I wanted Al to erase it. She was dismissive and just offered a slight reprimand, which I felt was not commensurate with the offense I had endured. I went back to the seat where he sat next to me since the seats were designed to house two students. I said, "Are you going to erase that?" His answer was, "No." So, I hit him as hard as I could right in the nose. I broke his nose — he left class bloody. It was a major fistfight. He recovered from the first blow, but after that I got the best of him because I was bigger. I got him down on the floor and that was the end of him until it was broken up. Of course, we were both sent home. But that fight moved me into third place behind a tough Irish kid, Eddie O'Brien, and of course the number one ranked heavyweight, Artie Genoveve. Artie must have been twice his normal weight because he ate so much. His father had a hoagie shop. He had huge arms on him. No one ever got the best of Artie.

We did have girls in our class. In first grade, I had a major infatuation with the lass who sat at the desk in front of me. Her name was Rosemarie Gillingham, a cute English girl with freckles. In first grade we were caught kissing in the cloakroom. We were both sent home for that. Clearly, my sexual prowess was innate and got off to an early start. Four years later, the day before we moved from South Philadelphia to Overbrook, I had gone over to Al Gargani's house across the street. His mother happened to come in the room with a bra on and her breasts pushing through. That sight remained active in my memory indefinitely.

When I was not making model airplanes or carousing with my neighborhood gang, my mother had Uncle Tim hire me to do work for the Angelo Brothers. They used to wrap lamp parts in newspapers. Uncle Tim would pay me a penny for a pound of newspapers. If I could get one hundred pounds, I could make a dollar, which to a kid in the 1940s was a lot of money. I remember Uncle Tim would say, "Can you lift it?" And if I could not lift it, he would figure it was probably worth a dollar. Uncle Tim would put the newspapers in the back of his station wagon and take them to the store. I remember when Uncle Tim got his Ford station wagon with wooden panels on the side — they were called "woodies." I used to dream about owning a station wagon like that. My other job at Angelo Brothers was to put one hundred washers or sockets in a bag for a penny a bag. A lot of time, I would walk out with two or three dollars. The Angelo Brothers Lamp Store was around 20th Street on Snyder Avenue. As I mentioned previously, the business began as a paint store and expanded when Uncle Tim and Uncle Stanley started the lamp parts business. After World War II, Uncle Tim was thirty-four and Uncle Stan was twenty-eight. Uncle Stan had worked at a paint store before he went into the Navy, and Uncle Tim had worked his way up to managing "Old Man Cohen's Hardware Store." He worked throughout the war because an unstable knee kept him out of the armed forces and there was a shortage of many hardware items due to the war effort. Uncle Stan had access due to his service in the navy to liquidation pieces of tools and hardware items that the military was selling off. Uncle Stan had served in the navy in the Pacific in World War II and felt that he lost his hearing from the sound of the guns. He always had poor hearing in the years that I knew him. Uncle Tim took out a $3,000 mortgage on his home and they opened up a paint and hardware store. Uncle Stan got both of them into the surplus sale and they had a great success. The pricing was about ten cents to the dollar and it was fortunate how many products they had and how low the prices were. They bought hundreds of screwdrivers, hammers, pliers, etc. and parlayed the $3,000 into about $20,000. This was significant capital in 1945 and provided the means necessary to morph the business into wholesaling of lamp parts.

Angelo Brothers catalogue, *circa* 1950

New home of Angelo Bros. Co. in Philadelphia contains 130,000 sq. ft.

Angelo Brothers Company, *circa* 1960

The Angelo brothers (from left: Rocky, Stan, Tim, Pat, and Midi)

As the business grew on Snyder Avenue, Uncle Pat subsequently joined his brothers Tim and Stanley. Uncle Pat was in the army and would tell us terrible war stories about how he had killed Germans, but he would also at times tell us about how he would kill Japanese, and it never occurred to us that they were two different areas of the world. As we got older, we found out that he really never left the army camp in Texas! But as kids, he would get us all excited with these adventure stories because he knew it was fascinating for us. So he would fabricate these entire wartime episodes! Uncle Pat was terrific. He never married and lived to age ninety-six. I was with him the night before he died at a hospital in Northeast Philadelphia.

My time spent with the Angelo brothers was an important part of my upbringing.

As the Angelo brothers' business was thriving, the rest of the neighborhood around us was changing. By the time I turned ten, South Philly had started to grow a little more dangerous. My father felt that time had come for our family to move out of the old neighborhood to get us involved in better schools and surround us with a more genteel peer group. The family moved to Overbrook, west of Philadelphia, a move I resented at first, but one that helped to mark an important new chapter as I moved into adolescence.

CHAPTER III:
ADOLESCENCE

"Give me a lad by the age of seven and I have him for life..."
— *Jesuit Adage*

As my father's 1936 Chrysler rumbled down 22nd Street with South Philly fading into the background, I slumped in the backseat and stared dejectedly at my shoes. Moving out of South Philly and into Overbrook — leaving my friends and family — was a significant and very upsetting transition. Luckily, I had a very loving mother who ultimately made it easier for my sister and me to get through the move. We were the first members of the family to leave the neighborhood in South Philly, and I'm sure my mother was not happy about the move herself. But my father ruled the house, and this was his idea. Our house was a dictatorship, not a democracy, so outwardly my mother didn't put up much fuss.

I used to watch a lot of TV Westerns, and always wanted to see the West. When we were moving to Overbrook, which was west of Philadelphia, I created a fantasy that we were heading to the Wild West — that I would finally get to see some real cowboys. Of course it didn't turn out that way, but the move nonetheless marked a major change in my life. My father told us that Overbrook would be a better neighborhood for us to grow up in, and he was right. We lived in a more middle-class environment, in a row house in a tree-lined neighborhood. We never saw trees in South Philly unless we went to the park, but in Overbrook there were trees up and down the street and tree-lined islands in the middle of the neighborhood. Row houses were common in Overbrook, as they were in South Philly. The town was built in the early 20th century as an exclusive area for many middle-class Philadelphians who wanted to escape their crowded city neighborhoods, but who wanted to live in a setting that was still somewhat familiar. There were many row houses and duplexes on the east end of town, where we lived. The friends I made who lived on the west side — on Woodbine Avenue, and Overbrook and Sherwood Roads — resided in very nice single-family homes.

I was in the middle of fifth grade when we moved to Overbrook. I was enrolled in Our Lady of Lourdes, a Catholic school at 63rd Street and Lancaster Avenue (the actor Will Smith is the school's most famous former student). My first teacher was Sister Felicitas, whose face drooped on the left side and who talked through one side of her mouth, which I now understand was due to Bell's Palsy. As a youngster I found Sister Felicitas and other nuns to be a bit unsettling, because I thought to become a nun they had to have their breasts chopped off! I knew they were supposed to be celibate like priests and, because they always wore white garments that covered their chests, they didn't have the shape I was used to seeing on other women.

My classmates at Our Lady of Lourdes were mainly from upper-middle-class homes. I remember in particular the Noonan girls, Bunny, Peggy, and Barbara, who used to arrive in a black limousine because their father was CEO of Whitman's Candy. Then there was the Wolfington clan, who manufactured buses, particularly school buses, which are still seen today with the Wolfington name on the transom. Another prominent family was the McShains, who were national heavy construction magnates. Most of the kids in Overbrook were Irish, with a few Italians and WASPs. I found that the kids from Overbrook were nowhere near as tough as my peers in South Philly. I had no trouble maintaining my position in the class in terms of our fighting ranking — compared to where I had come from, these kids were milk toast! By the time I graduated from Our Lady of Lourdes in eighth grade, I was undefeated. I recall one kid who spit at me at the top of the stairs — I hit him so hard, he rolled all the way down to the first floor. It was terrible, of course, but that was the mentality coming out of South Philly: If somebody was in your way or gave you shit, that's how you responded.

I wasn't the only one dishing out beatings at Our Lady of Lourdes, as the nuns would regularly punish us physically. Sister Camilla, who taught eighth grade, had a big wooden paddle that looked like a tennis racquet. For any number of transgressions — laughing in class, saying off-color words or jokes, general misbehavior — she would call you up to the front of the room and whack you. We learned to pull our pants down low so the belt was across your ass and the paddle wouldn't hurt as much. When Sister Camilla caught onto that, she would pull your pants up to make sure you got stunned. In addition to the paddle, she had a triangular ruler that she used quite a few times to beat me on the hands. Corporeal punishment was routine.

I had a great interest in football so I joined the team at Our Lady of Lourdes. Lourdes had won the division title the season before I arrived. My most memorable moment came when I was playing fullback and scored the winning touchdown against St. Madeleine's — that was a tough team. I also remember getting our asses kicked playing against St. Rose of Lima. They played kids who appeared much older than grade school. Our team practiced at a place called the Hollow in Fairmount Park at 65th Street and Overbrook Avenue. We would walk there after school in our full pads, and in the fall we would smell burning leaves because everyone burned leaves on the curb. I later learned through neurological training that the olfactory tract for smell goes right to the medial temporal lobes, where memory is stored — so smell is an important part of stimulating memory from the past. Even today, when I smell burning leaves, I think about walking to football practice at the Hollow.

Two of my closest friends as a kid in Overbrook were Mike Callahan and Walter Amoroso, who have both passed from cancer in recent years. Another good friend, George Hills, was killed by a train in his first year of high school. I don't know why he was playing near the tracks. But I do remember that was the first time I ever heard a mother grieving aloud for her child, which is the worst thing you ever want to hear. In my career as a neurosurgeon, I heard that same cry many times — at trauma centers, in emergency rooms, in ICUs — due to children dying from injuries, brain tumors or other consequences. I vividly remember George Hills' funeral and the haunting sound of his crying mother— my first experience with death in a contemporary setting, which had a profound and indelible effect on me.

I played with Mike, Walter, George and other friends after school and on weekends during grade school. We often played a game called Ring Up, in which two bases were set up at end of the schoolyard with one guy in the middle to start. You would run from one base to the other across the schoolyard, and the guy in the middle would have to try to grab you. If he held you long enough to say, "One, two, three, ring up, you're my man," then you were in the middle with him. The player who lasted the longest without being caught was the winner. In addition to Ring Up, we played a lot of touch football year-round. In the spring, we would go to St. Charles Seminary, which was up on City Line and Lancaster Avenue, to play on the baseball field there. In the winter, we played ice hockey on a frozen pond at the Seminary. One thing that I remember vividly about playing ice hockey was the number of condoms scattered around the edge of the pond. At the time I could not understand how the rubbers got there — it was a seminary for Christ's sake! But knowing what I know now about the Catholic Church, I could probably figure it out. It does not really take a brain surgeon to guess what was going on there.

Starting in seventh grade, my buddies and I would meet up with girls from the neighborhood for what we called make-out parties. These were not necessarily parties for an event, like a birthday, but mostly just kids getting together because somebody's parents were not home. The guys would wear the coolest pegged pants (tapered at the ankle) and head to the parties, where there was a designated girl that you would hook up with — my partner was Rosemary in seventh grade, and Marie the next year. On Friday nights, we would go to a dance hall in the suburbs called Chez Vous with different girls. This was really the age when boys started focusing heavily on the opposite sex. When Sister Camilla found out about the make-out parties, she really tore into us, screaming and yelling that this was an occasion of sin and went against Catholic teaching, but of course none of us gave a damn about what she had to say about it.

Every Friday night in grade school and later in high school, we would meet at the Ryans' house at 64th Street and Woodbine Avenue. It was a large home with a full basketball court in the backyard. The Ryans were a family of nine children. The father, Tony Ryan, owned a bar and a beer distributorship. The oldest sibling, Joe Ryan, became an all-American high school basketball player at St. Joseph's Prep. His sisters, Mary Ellen and Khaki, were great basketball players, too — they used to come out and play with us as well. Then we would go to Howard Johnson's on City Line Avenue or to the Overbrook Diner for sodas, hamburgers and ice cream. And, of course, we were all smoking. I started smoking Marlboros probably at age twelve. Mike and Walter were heavy smokers, too. We were kids acting like little mobsters — with the emphasis on "acting." My father was a very, very strict disciplinarian. He had to know exactly where I was going and told me I had to be in by nine o'clock when I was in grade school. If I was not in by his curfew, my dad would be out looking for me. So I know that I had better come home on time because if he had to come out and find me, it would be embarrassing. He may have overdone it, but I think it was good parenting. He had to make sure that I was not going to get in any trouble. And, while we did the usual childhood pranks, such as removing Oldsmobile taillights in under a minute and hubcaps in less time, I never really did get in trouble.

Mike Callahan, whose father was a lawyer, would take his mother's car long before we got our licenses at age sixteen. Starting when we were thirteen, he would pick me up and we would go over to Joe Ryan's in Mrs. Callahan's 1953 Ford. Everything was a stick shift then and, thanks to Mike, we could all drive a stick shift by the time we were fourteen. One day, after Mike got his learner's permit, we were riding in the car with him driving and his mom in the car. We were going up Oxford Street, which had a big hill, and his mother was nervous because this was, according to her, Mike's first time driving the car. Mike was holding the car on the hill with the clutch, like he had already driven a thousand miles in the car (which he probably had!). His mom asked, "Where did you learn to drive?" Mike said, "Well, I read it somewhere," and when the light turned green, off he went, smooth shifting like he'd be doing it all his life. If I had tried to get away with that around my father? Forget it. If I had gotten caught, I would be wearing my father's foot in my rectosigmoid junction.

Aside from the early driving lessons, the important thing about my close association with Mike Callahan was his family's influence on my education. As a successful lawyer, Mike's father instilled in his son early on that a good education was paramount and that, in particular, St. Joseph's Preparatory School was the best high school in the area. St. Joe's Prep, an all-male Jesuit institution, was founded in 1851 in West Philadelphia, growing out of a small church created a century earlier in Center City by the Rev. Joseph Greaton. Mike Callahan emphasized to me that the Prep was the place to go if you wanted to be a success in life, which made a big impression on me. I told my parents that I wanted to attend the Prep, but they told me that we would not be able to afford the tuition, which was $500 in 1955, the year I graduated from middle school. So, being driven to succeed, I vowed to make the money for tuition myself by working over the summer. My father was opposed to the idea of me, at age thirteen, attending prep school in the city. It was just not affordable for him. My mother really stood up for me and encouraged me to pursue this dream.

I took the entrance exam — a written test that lasted all morning — and scored very well. Unfortunately my friend, Mike Callahan, did not do well and was denied admission initially. My father heeded my mother's wishes and went down to the Prep to inquire about my prospects. Based on my achievement scores and his income, I was offered a half-scholarship to enroll, so I only had to come up with $250 for tuition. That summer in Sea Isle City, I went into the Windsor Hotel on the boardwalk, lied about my age (you needed to be fourteen to get working papers), and was hired to wash dishes, bus tables and work behind the counter at the soda fountain. I worked nine a.m. to noon then six p.m. to midnight every other day, then noon to six p.m. on the days in between. This was hard work for a kid — I would be soaked from the steam from the dishwasher and from scrubbing two bathtubs full of pots and pans with caked-on food several times a night. Those pots and pans had to be spotless for the next day. For this work, I banked $39.72 every week, kept $2 for myself for spending money, and put the rest toward my tuition for the Prep. I held that same job every summer until I turned eighteen, when I got a lifeguard job at Somers Point on the Jersey shore for $75 a week.

St. Joe's Prep was at 17th Street and Girard Avenue in Philly — not a great neighborhood. Mike and I were among nine kids from Our Lady of Lourdes who enrolled at the Prep. Mike's father was a prominent lawyer who had graduated from Georgetown University and interceded to get Mike admission to the Prep. Most of us hitchhiked to school from in front of our church. Local businessmen going that direction knew we were kids at the Prep, so they regularly gave us rides. Sometimes my neighbor, Mr. McGowan, a severe asthmatic with chronic obstructive pulmonary disease, or my father would transport us. Leaving Our Lady of Lourdes and starting at the Prep was formidable because it was a very difficult school and a lot of students flunked out. The school demanded minimum of three hours of homework a night. My fear must have served as effective motivation. From the outset I always earned first honors, meaning you had to score above ninety in all of your subjects. In my second year, I was selected for the Homeric Greek class, for which only the best students were chosen. I worked hard for these accomplishments, as academics did not come easy to me. I think in a lot of ways intellectual pursuits come from the mother and, in my case, my mother had a third-grade education so I did not start with a lot of advantages. Then again, I did have two parents who stayed together and a mother who provided a lot of love in the home, which I believe is crucial for success. Both of my parents always encouraged me, and being the boy in an Italian-American home certainly helped, because the male child ruled.

At the Prep we wore jackets and ties, and always wore maroon and gray, the school colors. Our work focused on Latin, Greek and Mathematics. It was tedious, arduous work taught by no-nonsense priests or scholastics, i.e. Jesuits in training to become ordained. One exception was my freshman year homeroom teacher, Mr. Netter, a red-haired scholastic, who allegedly had come from an affluent family. Thirteen

Our Lady of Lourdes 8th Grade Gang (from left tor right): Jack Claffey, Lou D'Nunzio, Anthony Baionno, Mike Callahan, Walter Amoroso, Robert Flynn, Tony Chiurco, Tom D'Agostino

years later, I came upon an article in Life magazine that featured Father Netter. He was ordained but left the priesthood to elope with the secretary of Rudolph Bing, the head of the Metropolitan Opera! Our other instructors, as you might expect, did not offer such surprises. One teacher who epitomized the Prep experience was Father William Lynch, who taught me Latin and Greek for three years. He was a difficult taskmaster who demanded that you achieve or you would be expelled. Under Father Lynch I read Xenophon's *Anabasis*, *The Iliad*, and *The Odyssey* in the original Homeric Greek. I recall one lesson on the passage in *The Odyssey* in which Odysseus and his men escape from Polyphemus, the Cyclops, by driving a sharpened wooden pole into his eye as he slept. As Father Lynch explained the passage to us, he jumped up on his desk and jammed the window pole into the inkwell of a student in the front row — that's how intense our instructions in Homeric Greek were. I heeded the serious tone of our Latin and Greek instruction, to the point that I achieved the highest mark in all the East Coast Jesuit schools in the final Greek examination in my third year.

While our studies were serious, pranks at the Prep were common. A couple of students were even kicked out right before graduation after our "senior revolt," when the students commandeered the loudspeaker and took over the 3:15 afternoon broadcast that came from the principal. One of my classmates, Pat Sweeney, led the revolt against the dictatorship environment of the Prep. A core group wanted the rules changed, including being sent to "Jug," a detention classroom for even the slightest infractions. Another memorable prank was played on Father Aloysius Travers, who once pitched for the Detroit Tigers against the Philadelphia A's baseball team. On May 15, 1912, an ugly event occurred involving Ty Cobb and a handicapped New York fan, who was heckling the Detroit outfielder which led to the suspension of the "Georgia Peach." Cobb was suspended "indefinitely." His teammates did not agree with his suspension and refused to play further games. This was the first strike in baseball history. A Philadelphia sports writer tried to help and knew Al Travers, the assistant manager of the St. Joseph's baseball team. Travers recruited players from his neighborhood. On Saturday May 18th this "official" Tiger team took the field with Connie Mack's approval, who did not want to lose the gate receipts nor an opportunity to increase the reigning world champion's stats. Travers had never played any serious baseball and when he learned that the pitcher would earn twice as much he volunteered to pitch. With a 6-0 score the Athletics began to bunt on Travers and scored eight runs in the fifth inning. To his credit Travers even chalked up a single strike out as the A's had ten stolen bases, four doubles, and six triples, but not a single home run in their victory.

Aloysius Travers was always talking about impurity in young boys and imploring us not to masturbate. As a gag, a student put a condom over the end of the window pole in Travers' class. The first thing Travers would always say when he came into the classroom was, "All right, open the windows, let's get some fresh air in here." Nobody got up when Travers said to open the windows, so he grabbed the pole himself but couldn't get the window open. When he went to see what was wrong with the pole, he pulled the condom off. Seeing this old priest with a rubber pinched between his fingers, the class was in an uproar! Travers got red in the face, screamed and yelled and stormed off, dropping his books as he exited. He tried to suspend the whole class, but no one would own up to who did it, so the principal overruled him. Travers did not come back. They sent someone else for the rest of the semester.

In a Catholic school, confession was mandatory every Thursday and then Mass in the Church of the Gesu, which was attached to the Prep. I will admit that I had the same masturbatory fantasies that all the guys had in an all-male school where we didn't get to look at girls all day. And quite frankly, I didn't give a shit about confession. But I would go in because it was required, and one day I had Father Travers in the confessional, who said to me, "Well, it seems that your parents sent you here to major in impurity." I think I made a wisecrack to him stating that my mother thought I was smoking because she assumed they were nicotine stains on my underwear. I was rebellious then about the ridiculousness of the clergy trying to interfere with what I saw as natural, normal impulses. A lot of the students at the Prep went along with the program uncritically, and a lot of the brightest students did go into the Jesuits, but I never bought into the programming. It is noteworthy that in the recent past the Jesuit order settled abundant litigation in the Pacific northwest, namely in the states of Washington and Oregon for several hundred million dollars over child abuse scandals in just two states alone.

Excluding studies, high school was about girls and rowing. A lot of students at the Prep and in my neighborhood in Overbrook tended to date girls from Mater Misericordia Academy, a Catholic all-girls school in Merion, just outside of Philadelphia. There were some other all-female schools around where girlfriends would be found. My first girlfriend was Michelle, who lived in Overbrook and went to Mater Misericordia. Michelle was an attractive Italian-American lass who had a slight separation in her front teeth much like Ali McGraw. Her breasts had a college degree and with a pair of terrific legs, she was desirable. I would take her out on dates in my father's 1936 Chrysler and took her to my senior prom. This was also a time when I developed an affinity for movies. There was a theater in Overbrook on Lancaster Avenue called the Green Hill Theater, which showed primarily foreign films. I used to go by myself all the time to see these foreign films because I couldn't interest my friends to come along. I remember landmark movies such as *The Quiet Man* with John Wayne, and British comedies such as *I'm Alright Jack*, a farce about British labor. To this day, going to movies is one of my favorite things to do — it's the greatest form of entertainment next to the NFL.

The other lifelong love that emerged from my time at the Prep was rowing. I went out for football, and in my first year I was playing end and suffered a massive hit from behind in practice that ended my football career. I was carted off the field and walked several hours later. With football out of the picture, I needed to try something else, because you had to play a sport at the Prep. I had played sandlot baseball but never really played in an organized league, so I thought about other options. Since I loved boats from being down the Jersey shore, I thought I would give rowing a try so I went out for crew. I was fourteen years old the first time I ever sat in a shell, and I really took to it. I was already six feet tall, which was an advantage. I loved the vigorous exercise, and I've been rowing ever since. I remember sitting in the stroke seat in my first year, and John Quinn, who subsequently became a U.S. Olympic judge, was the coxswain. Like our schoolwork, it was a no-nonsense situation on the water. It was not intended to be fun — it was very physically challenging.

We rowed every afternoon on the Schuylkill River after school. We went down to Vesper Boat Club, where our coach at the Prep, Jim Manning, also coached. I can still recall very distinctly the beautiful smell of cedar and varnish, which greeted you when you walked in the clubhouse boat bay at Vesper. The shells were made of cedar in the 1950s by George Pocock in Seattle when I started rowing. Now everything is made from composites — carbon fiber, Kevlar, fiberglass — so that wonderful odor is gone. But I still get tremendous enjoyment from rowing. One of the highlights of living in Princeton, N.J., since the 1970s is being able to row my single on Lake Carnegie, which is one of the world's perfect rowing lakes.

Vesper Boat Club, where I got my start, is one of the most storied rowing clubs in the United States and the world. It started as the Washington Barge Club in 1865, about a decade into the emergence of rowing clubs on the Schuylkill, and changed its name to Vesper in 1870. Vesper Boat Club was located in the middle of boathouse row between the University of Pennsylvania boathouse and Malta Rowing Club. The Vesper eights won the gold medal at the first Olympic rowing regatta in Paris in 1900, and repeated the feat four years later in St. Louis and then in 1964 in Tokyo — making Vesper the only U.S. rowing club to win three Olympic golds. Vesper members cumulatively have amassed titles in more national and international races than rowers from any club in the country.

Names associated with Vesper are legendary in U.S. rowing history. I recall in my early years at Vesper John B. Kelly Sr. coming down and giving us a pep talk before a major regatta. Kelly had no time or compassion for losing or excuse for losing. If you lost a boat race by a foot or a length his attitude was you didn't want to win bad enough and therefore your mentality was that of a loser. Don't ever approach John B.

Kelly Sr. with an excuse. John B. Kelly Sr. was one of the greatest athletes in American history and the only American oarsman in the Olympic Hall of Fame to this day. He was denied entry into the elite Diamond Sculls, the singles event, at the Royal Henley Regatta in England in 1920. This occurred because he was a bricklayer who worked as a physical laborer, which was felt to be an unacceptable advantage in what was considered a gentleman's sport at the time. Also he did accept some travel expense money raised for him at Vesper to compete internationally which gave an excuse to label him as a "professional." Being denied at Henley, John Kelly was entered into the Olympic Games in Paris in 1920 and confronted in the finals Jack Beresford, who had won the Diamond Sculls at Henley the month before. Kelly beat Beresford by one second. The race took such a physical toll on Kelly that he writhed in pain for fifteen minutes after the finish. He then got up and went back to the starting line and rowed in the finals of the double sculls with his cousin Paul Costello and won a second gold medal, a feat, which has never been duplicated in the history of Olympic rowing. After receiving the Olympic gold medal Kelly sent King George of England a red brick in his green cap he wore while racing in retribution for denial of entry into the Diamond Sculls at Henley. When he returned a hero to Philadelphia there were over a hundred thousand people to greet him at the Philadelphia train station. The United States of America has never been able to duplicate a gold medal performance in the Olympic games in the men's open single sculls since John B. Kelly's victory over Jack Beresford in the 1920 games.

The son of John B. Kelly, John B. Kelly Jr. (Jack) became an accomplished sculler. Jack was a friend whose locker was next to my locker at Vesper boat Club. Jack was square-jawed, quiet, but powerfully built, much like his father in his youth. Jack went on to achieve what was denied to his father and won the elite Diamond Sculls at Henley in 1947 and 1949, as well as the US National Singles Championship. John B. Sr. once stated that one of the greatest moments of his life was the occurrence of Jack winning the Diamond Sculls and his daughter, Grace, winning the Oscar for her Academy Award winning performance in *Country Girl*. Jack Jr. could not repeat his father's Olympic gold medal achievement but did win a bronze Olympic medal, losing to Ivanov of Russia, who won three successive gold medals in Olympic competition in the men's open single sculls.

As Jack Kelly Jr. went on to become President of the U.S. Olympic Committee, his sister, Grace, entered a new career as Princess of Monaco. One afternoon the Prep Varsity Eight in which I rowed in the four seat, came into the Vesper dock after practice to be greeted by a local celebrity, Arlene Francis. Accompanying her was Grace Kelly and Prince Ranier of Monaco, who was courting Grace at the time. Grace was showing the Prince where her father had competed at Vesper, as well as her brother Jack. I met Grace Kelly as well as the Prince and shook their hands, as did each member of our crew. Grace was stunning in person, a true Hollywood beauty, appearing better than in her movies. A misfortune occurred when someone yelled for Eddie Davis, who was wiping off his oar with an oily, dirty rag, who turned around with the rag dripping on the end of the oar as it flew off and hit the Prince in the neck. The Prince took it well and smiled, perhaps not to react in front of his romantic pursuit.

Eddie Davis, now deceased, was the first prisoner of war to be released by the Vietcong after being shot down over Vietnam. Jack Kelly Jr. passed away at age fifty-eight in 1985 after jogging on the East River Drive, which now bears his name—Kelly Drive.

By getting my start in rowing in this environment, I was challenged to compete at a very high level. I gained a lot of technical skill in rowing very rapidly, and it was favorable that I was six foot two and one hundred and ninety pounds. As a sophomore at the Prep, I rowed in the four. In a four, as in the pair and the eight, the rowers are sweeping, meaning they use one oar. In a quad, as in a single and a double, the rowers are sculling, meaning they use two oars. The Prep quad won the national schoolboy championship twice while I was there; one of the members of that crew, Jimmy Heidere, became my dentist in Princeton later in life. The first time I went into his office he came in with a big syringe of Novocain saying, "Is that Tony Chiurco?" I said, "I hope you're a better dentist than a rower!" Jimmy just retired, and I sent him a note saying, "I think of you every time I get a toothache." By my third year at the Prep, I rowed in the varsity eight. We were undefeated in my fourth year winning both the Catholic League Championship and the Interscholastic Philadelphia City Championship. The final regatta was the National Championship, where we lost to Washington and Lee (they also beat us in the Stotesbury Cup, a venerable Philadelphia regatta).

By losing in the national championships in my senior year, the Prep crew missed out on the chance to compete in the Henley Regatta for the Princess Elizabeth Cup on the Thames in England, a world class regatta encompassing the European championships. My crewmates and I rekindled our bond in 1999, at the 40th reunion of our Prep class, when I entered our varsity eight in the Schuylkill Navy Regatta. I made the announcement the night before the event at a dinner at the home of Jimmy Nolen, who was the stroke man of that crew. They told me I was crazy, but I finally convinced everyone that they would have fun if we reassembled the eight and just paddled down the course. I told everyone to take two aspirin in the morning so we wouldn't have any heart attacks on the river, and we had a great time being back on the water together after a forty-year hiatus.

After the success of our reunion regatta, I told everyone, "Look, guys, we couldn't go to Henley when we were high school seniors. We lost the national championship, which ended our dream. Why don't we go now?" And I got the same response: "You're crazy." I told them we should enter the Henley Masters Regatta. The idea did not catch on, but then each year thereafter I hosted them in Princeton on Lake Carnegie, where we would reassemble the eight. Finally, by 2003, they were convinced. We lived all over the country, but everyone hired a trainer and we assembled the eight in Philadelphia twice in 2004 to row together. We entered the Masters Regatta in 2005, finally making it to Henley in our Prep blazers — albeit forty-six years later than we originally intended. Our athletic endeavor created sensational television and press coverage in the Philadelphia newspapers with photos of the eight both in 1959 and 2005. I had a nuclear stress test two weeks before Henley, to try to get some reassurance that I would not die. In the five-seat on the starting line, Phil Greipp, who is now a professor of hematology and oncology at the Mayo Clinic, turned up his pacemaker. In the six-seat, Ed McBride — who played football for Navy — was a concern for all of us because of his enormous size, pushing 300 pounds. But we all survived and, in fact, we advanced to the semifinals, where we lost to the Henley Rowing Club. It was a wonderful time. (As an aside, combining my love of movies and rowing, I recommend the film *The Social Network*, which features wonderful scenes of the Henley Regatta.)

The experience at Henley brought back memories of my last days at the Prep, a time when I looked forward to continuing my education and my rowing career. While I thrived academically at the Prep, I did not have many choices for where to attend college. First of all, my family had no money for me to go to college, so I was paying for it myself. I would need to find a school where I could make the tuition working over the summer, as I had done to attend the Prep. St. Joseph's University offered two advantages: The tuition was $850 a year, which I could make in a summer, and it was ten minutes from my house so I could live at home. The solution was very clear. So I enrolled at St. Joseph's College now renamed St. Joseph's University, where I would take the first steps on the path to my medical career.

CHAPTER IV:
COLLEGE AND ROWING

**"A man who dares to waste one hour of time
has not discovered the value of life..."**
— *Charles Darwin*

After graduating from the Prep in 1959, at age eighteen, I prepared to enroll at St. Joseph's College, and I needed to enhance my income. Working as a dishwasher and soda jerk at the Windsor Hotel in Sea Isle City allowed me to scrape together enough funds to cover tuition at the Prep, but the College bills would be higher and, as with prep school, the burden would be on me to cover those costs myself without the aid of a scholarship. My father had saved $750 for my college fund, which was not enough to cover the first year, but I would need to make up the difference. Noteworthy is the fact that I never touched that $750 until the beginning of my fourth year in medical school when for the first and last time I borrowed tuition money. Luckily, my godmother Sue DiPrespi had a contact with the manager of the Fairways Swim Club in Somers Point, New Jersey, who hired me as a lifeguard. For $75 a week and an additional $10 travel expenses, I worked three days in Somers Point and three days in Cape May. I used my father's 1936 Chrysler to travel between the jobs, and made sure to travel on Route 9, where the toll was fifteen cents, instead of the Garden State Parkway, where it cost fifty cents. This was a significant price difference in those days, when gas cost thirty cents per gallon and I needed to hang onto every dime for the $850 tuition at St. Joe's.

Hard work was nothing new for me, as I began working for the Angelo Brothers family business at a very young age. The experience of having to work for every penny that went into my education is one that I would never trade. My background was true preparation for life, because in the real world nobody hands you everything and pays your way at every turn unless you are among the financially elite, i.e. the upper echelon of socioeconomic status in America. I was privileged to be underprivileged — because I was ready for life. My background equipped me with the tools to pursue the most difficult, most intense specialty in medicine. After I graduated from medical school and decided to focus on neurosurgery, I would ask my classmates why they didn't pursue the same specialty. "Oh, I wouldn't do that — it's too hard," I would hear in response. "The surgery is too long. The training program is seven years. No way!" Well, they were students who had their tuitions paid for and, in many cases, had fathers who were doctors and earned much more than my father did. They came from privilege.

The Fairways Swim Club
Anthony (Tony) Chiurco, left, and Rich Gordon, *circa* 1963

Chiurco family photo *circa,* 1963

St. Joseph's Prep Varsity Eight on the Vesper dock, 1959 (from left: Jack Kelly, Jr., Jim Nolen, Bill Gummere, Ed McBride, Phil Greipp, Tony Chiurco, Dave Weston, John Graham, Stan Sarat, Coach Jim Manning with Jesuit moderator and foreground Al Duchnowski Coxswain).

St. Joseph's Prep Varsity Eight 40th Reunion Schuylkill Navy Regatta, 1999

Philadelphia Boat House Row

St. Joseph's Prep Varsity Eight off the starting line at the Royal Henley Regatta, Henley, England 2005. Henley Rowing Club Eight background.

"Mike Teti" 24" x 36" oil on canvas by Anthony Chiurco, 2002

"Shea Rowing Center of Princeton University" 24" x 36" oil on canvas
by Anthony Chiurco, 2003

Tony Chiurco (left) with Mike Teti on Carnegie Lake, *circa* 1990

Later in life I told my children that after they earned a college degree, they were on their own. Some of my kids had artistic pursuits, which is wonderful — but very rarely pays the bills. Eventually it sinks in that they might wind up living under a bridge unless they provide for themselves, because the free ride is over. I have tried very hard to teach my children about the value of hard work and the satisfaction and accomplishment of earning their own way in life. I always tell them, "Don't listen to what people tell you that you can't do. You are capable of doing anything you want to do. You just have to want it bad enough." I would say the same thing to most people, unless they are genetically impaired. Most people can do whatever they want to do, but you need tenacity and you need self-discipline. Those are the key factors for success assuming average intelligence.

Success in life can be a double-edged sword, because if you work hard enough to have financial rewards, as I have, your children actually can be hindered by being raised with money. It can be a handicap to come from privilege, and an advantage to come from handicap. In fact, there are certain indications that orphans go further in life. Coming from minimal educational and financial means, as I did, you learn how to deal with obstruction, challenges and difficulties in your way. You learn how to get around them and overcome them, because you have no choice. But when you come from a privileged background, someone is always there to take care of your problems. That is a fantasy life. The truth is, life is unfair. As the old saying goes, "Fair is where pigs win ribbons."

I told my children that after they received the best education money could buy, the world would owe them nothing. Nobody cares that you are a Princeton graduate once you are in a job, because a whole different set of skills come into play. What matters are your people skills; how you react to others; your interpersonal relationships; your desire to achieve; your self-discipline, ambition, creativity, tenacity, and most important your integrity — none of which you can measure on a SAT test! In the big picture, where you went to school is not the essential factor in success. Some of the most financially successful people I know never went to school—or they quit or were kicked out. Success on the SAT tests, in my opinion, is influenced somewhat on socioeconomic status. A kid growing up with uneducated parents is not going to hear polysyllabic words in the house. Nor will he likely be instilled with a desire to acquire knowledge—a crucial factor, which stands between the hereditable factor of IQ difference among individuals and socioeconomic factors. The hardware may be present but not the software programming. Academic achievement on the other hand heavily weighs on genetic input, effort, and less on socioeconomic factors, but doesn't necessarily correlate with the ability to succeed in life. If I had a dollar for every jackass I know that went to Harvard, Princeton or Yale, I could pay cash for dinner! This is not to say, of course, that there are not some extraordinary people who come from elite universities. But extraordinary people also come from public colleges, community colleges — and no colleges.

It upsets me to see young people's self-esteem destroyed because they did not get into an elite school for college. And I try to impress upon them that it doesn't really matter. What occurs once you exit the academic nest is based on a whole different set of skills. That the Ivy League diploma is great for level entry — obviously, a lot of businesses will take somebody who graduated from Harvard before they would somebody from Mercer County Community College, because that entry into an Ivy League school says a lot about your academic ability. But it does not speak for your personality, "emotional intelligence," people skills, and all the attributes necessary to achieve in the outside world once you leave the university. Personally, I would hire somebody who was preferably an athlete, who has self-discipline and knows the hardship of trying to win and the hardship of losing, who was at least a good student, who doesn't have to be top of the class but has a grade E for effort, who wants to achieve financially, and has a more than casual interest in sex. (Looks like I just hired myself!)

My own college experience was marked by two major factors: Excellent preparation for medical school and my chosen profession; and continued training and involvement in rowing, which is a source of passion that sustains me to this day. Both of these pursuits involved the hard work, physical and mental rigor in the form of self-discipline that are hallmarks of success in life. I entered St. Joseph's College as a pre-med student and between my studies in the sciences, which were very difficult there, and my obligations to the crew team for four years, I was extremely busy. I also was in the Air Force ROTC, which meant that every Wednesday I had to put on a uniform and attend class to learn about mechanics and flying planes. I held a fascination with planes since I was a young boy, so I enjoyed the Air Force ROTC classes.

I had serious misgivings about the Catholic education I had received coming up through elementary and middle school and the Prep, which I will discuss at length later in this book. As I grew up, I became more and more angry about the philosophical theology lessons I was subjected to, with which I disagreed profoundly. At St. Joe's we were forced to study the Catholic propaganda, a source of significant resentment to this day. From a class of thirty-five pre-medical students I was the only pre-med student who was a varsity athlete because the commitments of both pre-medical studies and varsity athletics were almost mutually exclusionary at St. Joe's. As a consequence, I didn't have much of a social life during college — it was all work and no play. I was taking courses in biology, analytical chemistry and physics, among the rest of my subjects. I had to be on the Schuylkill River every day for rowing at six in the morning and then again at five in the evening. We rowed between six and ten miles each session, lasting ninety minutes. I am proud that I was able to make the Dean's List and graduate with a bachelor's degree in biology in 1963, because the curriculum at St. Joe's was much more demanding than at other schools in the area. I know this because when I attended medical school at Jefferson Medical College (now Thomas Jefferson University), all of the students from St. Joe's were in the top 15 percent of the class — not just one, but all of us. The combination of my pre-med courses and rowing was considered suicide, but I thrived on the challenge.

I earned three varsity letters rowing for St. Joseph's College. I rowed for John McHugh my first year, and then later for Al Rosenberg, who coached the Vesper Olympic gold medal men's eight at the Tokyo games in 1964. I also rowed for Tibor McCan, a Russian immigrant. I rowed in the stroke seat of the varsity eight for Joe Toland, my senior year. These gentlemen were all renowned coaches in the sport. I also rowed for them at Vesper Boat Club. Bill Gummere, who remains a close friend to this day, and Phil Greipp were two teammates from the Prep who also rowed with me at St. Joseph's College.

The last race I rowed before beginning medical school was for a Vesper eight crew that Jack Kelly put together to challenge the Ratzeburg crew from West Germany on the Potomac. These Germans were world champions, coached by Karl Adam, and beat us by two lengths. I changed with these athletes in the Potomac boathouse — their arms were bigger than my thighs! I can't prove it, of course, but a steroid fueled crew was possible, especially knowing what we now know about German athletes in Olympic competition from that era. Eighteen months later, Karl Adam and the Ratzeburg crew were defeated by a narrow margin by the Vesper Boat Club gold medal eight in the final race of the 1964 Tokyo Olympic games.

My years spent on the Schuylkill River and along Boathouse Row were very formative ones. Rowing gave me another outlet to hone my work ethic and discipline and to find a competitive release. To compete in a boat race, you had to put everything out—win or lose. After the start, in well-conditioned athletes, the burning from ischemia in the muscles of the thighs and shoulders, brachii and forearms begins to take it's toll by the 1000 meter mark. As lactate continues to accumulate, the muscular pain can become unbearable in the last 500 meters. There is nothing like defeat in a boat race, when you can hardly breathe as you gasp for oxygen on the verge of losing consciousness at the race completion when you have put everything out to the point of physical exhaustion. When you have lost, especially by just a few feet, it's an awful feeling — but, you know, it's life. I am a major proponent of athletics for young people because it teaches you about life, particularly that you can't always win. I also think there is a difference in physically exhausting sports like rowing, swimming or track versus others that are not as physically demanding and reliant upon endurance. Take baseball, for example. Major league players are great athletes — their agility, sense of timing and reflexes are spectacular. But how physically challenged are they on the field for most of the game? You can spend nine innings at third base or in the outfield and field one ball. Sure, it's physically challenging to pull off a beautiful play in baseball, but as far as stressing you to the limits of your physical ability, it doesn't carry the same weight as an endurance sport like rowing. In 1920, when Jack Kelly Sr. collapsed after winning the Olympic gold medal in single sculls, he got up and dragged himself to the starting line twenty minutes later and won the gold in the double with Paul Costello. Kelly was one of the greatest athletes America has ever produced. In rowing, there is always the fear factor of collapsing before you finish. I always thought to myself on the starting line, "Will I have enough to get to the last 500 meters?" That is a fear factor that you don't have in baseball or football. You have to be an iron man in rowing and a masochist.

I have been fortunate to build strong ties with many in the U.S. rowing community since my initiation into the sport with the Vesper Boat Club. One of my closest friends is Mike Teti, who is the most successful coach in the history of the sport and now runs the rowing program at the University of California-Berkeley. Mike was the first person to be elected to the United States Rowing Hall of Fame as both a rower and a coach; I attended his induction ceremony in 2010. As a rower, Mike was a twelve-time national team member and three-time Olympian and owns twenty-four national titles. He has been a member of the U.S. coaching staff at the World Championships and Olympic Games regularly since 1996, leading U.S. crews to twenty-eight total medals — including a goal medal and world record for the eight in Athens in 2004 where the U.S. men's eight set the world record for two thousand meters. My background was similar to Teti in that he rowed both at St. Joseph's College and the Vesper Boat Club following my era at the same facilities. When he became Princeton's freshman coach in 1989, Mike gave me a locker at the boathouse on Lake Carnegie, which was not allowed. But Mike told them, "Either the Doc comes with me, or I'm not coming!" That's how close we are. My single still hangs in the boathouse in Princeton to this day because of Mike, even though he left years ago. It's a wonderful environment — like being in college again myself — that I continue to treasure. I realize it is the closest I would have ever gotten to attending an Ivy League school. Ironically two of my children both graduated from Princeton University and were members of the Princeton University crew team.

I enjoyed more success in the sport of rowing in my profession than I ever did as an athlete. My involvement as a surgeon began around 1985 when I encountered a young athlete on the United States national team in anguish in the Princeton University boathouse. He could not row because of a herniated lumbar disc causing severe pain in his leg. The world championships were two months away. He returned from seeing the surgeons on the west coast who had operated on the NFL quarterback Joe Montana for a similar disorder. They told him he could not row after surgery for at least six months. I consoled him and said there is nothing to my knowledge in the world literature that says that you could not get back into the boat the next day. Encouraged he then wanted me to do his surgery. I agreed and took out his herniated lumbar disc then put him back in the men's national eight the next day after surgery. He never had a problem maintaining his position in the boat and competed successfully in the world championships. He was named US Rowing's Athlete of The Year. That occurrence spread not only nationally, but internationally in the rowing world! I began to see rowers from all over the United States, both collegiate and national team members, not to mention an occasional athlete from Europe or Australia. To this date I have performed lumbar disc surgery on over thirty collegiate, Olympic and national team rowers and an occasional coach successfully. One Olympic rower underwent a ruptured lumbar disc removal six weeks before the Sydney Olympic Games and competed successfully. He was back in the men's eight thirty-six hours after leaving the operating room. Another athlete stroked the men's national team eight to win the world championship several months after removal of two herniated lumbar discs. The herniated lumbar disc is not an uncommon consequence of the shearing forces imposed on the low back during the rowing stroke.

Assumption remains the antithesis of the scientific method. Without evidence-based medicine, to assume continues to make an ass of you and me (ass-u-me)!

Since I moved to Princeton in 1976 I have regularly launched my single for an hour on the lake for a six-mile row. It took me a good year or so to learn to master a single. For many years I would row in the early afternoon before the university crew would be out on the water. In the summer, I could wait until later in the day, when the sun was starting to set in the early evening. These days, I love to be out on the lake in the morning with the sun coming up, hearing the sound of birds awakening to early morning fog atop the glass-like appearance of Carnegie Lake. It is paradise to a rower.

I'll continue to scull until I can't scull anymore. In the back of my head is a dream to row at Henley in my single. Of course, there are some not-so-minor obstacles in the way of realizing that dream. My carpal bones have all separated in my wrist from a radius fracture that happened when I was a medical student at Jefferson, which makes it very difficult to feather the oar, especially in rough weather. And I just can't seem to get my weight down to a competitive level because, frankly, I like to eat too much. So although I have this dream in the back of my head, the reality is, it's not going to happen, unless there's some miraculous weight loss pill that comes out and something to help my wrist. But I'm always working towards that goal, as unrealistic as it is. I think about it every time I enjoy a bowl of pasta — especially the angel hair at Rodolfo's, one my favorite restaurants just outside of Princeton. With every bite of that delicious pasta, I have to say to myself, "Well, there goes Henley."

Tony Chiurco prior to a master's regatta in the
men's open single sculls event, *circa* 1988

CHAPTER V:
THE JEFFERSON MEDICAL COLLEGE
OF PHILADELPHIA 1963-1967

"Life is a matter of luck..."
—Donald Trump

One night during the summer between my junior and senior years at St. Joe's, my Uncle Pat took me down to a nightclub in Atlantic City to unwind and celebrate my upcoming twenty-first birthday. Sitting at a table overlooking the bar, however, I found it difficult to relax. As I looked at the mostly blue-collar clientele at the bar—similar to the mainly uneducated population with whom I grew up in South Philly—I thought about my past and my future. My father was retired, living on a modest pension from Erie Railroad. There was no business to inherit. I knew that the only road for me was education, and my desire to live a better life made my feelings of urgency to get into medical school even more pronounced. As I looked over the crowd at that bar, I told myself, "I have to elevate my status. I have to rise above the masses somehow." The cocktails snaking their way through my system only served to intensify my sense of desperation.

Uncle Pat leaned over in his chair next to me and said, "Listen, I have arranged for this lovely young lady to entertain you later." He instructed me to go over to a motel a couple of blocks away to meet her at ten o'clock. At first I was totally oblivious to what was about to occur, but as I walked through the warm seaside air en route to the motel, it finally became clear to me that this was a girl Uncle Pat had hired—a prostitute. I walked up the motel's dingy, creaky steps to the room and knocked on the door. A soft voice told me to enter. I nervously stepped into the small room to encounter a girl who was actually quite good-looking and not much younger than me, probably about nineteen. She quickly got down to business and took her clothes off. I was, of course, very enthusiastic at this point and began to kiss her. After about thirty seconds, she pulled her lips away from mine and said, "Now, listen, don't make a romance out of it." We proceeded to consummate our transaction, from which I came away with two things: 1) My first sexual encounter; and 2) a line that I have used ever since, whenever someone gets too intense or overwrought on a task. Even in the operating room, I would say to my colleagues, "Hey, don't make a romance out of it."

That line also was an inspiration of sorts for me as I reflected on my thoughts from earlier in the evening. I knew that I needed to continue to work as hard as possible to get into medical school and pursue a career as a physician. During my senior year at St. Joe's, I applied to medical school at Thomas Jefferson, University of Pennsylvania, Hahnemann Medical College and Temple University. I was a good student at St. Joe's, with a B+ average and a spot on the Dean's List. It was very difficult to be an A student, especially with my brutal rowing commitments as the only pre-med student who also was a varsity athlete. I thought my prospects were solid, but when I took the MCAT (Medical College Admission Test) my results in the science section were terrible, finishing below the fiftieth percentile. My performance was poor because I had never taken an exam in that type of format which was completely foreign to me at the time — my exams at St. Joe's didn't include such pinpoint questions. It wasn't a question of intellectual ability, but rather I did not have the seasoning to fully understand the task at hand. I know this because years later during medical school my national board scores after the second year of study in the basic medical sciences were so high that the chairman of medicine at Thomas Jefferson, Robert Wise, told me I could go anywhere I wanted for my internship and residency. But at the time I was seeking entrance to medical school, my prospects were not strong, despite my decent grades, given my low MCAT science score and the competitive admissions landscape. Penn, for instance, only took one student from St. Joe's each year, while Jefferson took only six to eight students. I had one interview at Penn that did not go well. I was told at Jefferson that I would need to take the MCAT again and I would not be accepted for the coming year. I was interviewed at Temple by a Dr. Nelson, who quizzed me in extraordinary detail about my summer job managing a swim club. He wanted to know every aspect of swimming pool filtration, circulation, etc. His final question to me was, "How does chlorine kill bacteria?" It so happened I had sent away for a swimming pool management book and happened to catch a small paragraph that stated chlorine inhibited glucose metabolism in the cell wall of bacteria causing their demise. Nelson was overwhelmingly impressed.

I got on the waiting list at Temple.

I did, however, have one significant advantage unknown to me then:

Dr. Saverio F. Brunetti

my father's first cousin, Saverio (Sam) Brunetti was the chief of police and fire surgery for the city of Philadelphia. My father and Sam were very close—after my father's brother Tony (my namesake) passed away, Sam was my father's only relative of his own generation. When I was growing up, we would have Thanksgiving dinner every year at Sam's big stone house in Cheltenham, an affluent, historic community just outside of Philadelphia. Sam and his wife, Rose, who was a nurse, had two children, Camille and Jimmy, who were a generation older than me. I have many fond memories of spending Thanksgiving with their family, but what stands out for me was the recollection of entering their

Dr. Saverio F. Brunetti, *circa* 1970   home and seeing the Brunetti family coat of arms on a glass door of the vestibule at the entrance of the house. That indicated to me that the Brunettis must have come from a higher level of society in Italy, and perhaps reflected the title on my grandmother: La Donna Annetta Brunetti.

Sam was born in Philadelphia in 1901, attended Hahnemann Medical College and served his residency at Cook County Hospital in Chicago. As an Italian American seeking to excel in the medical profession in the era of the Great Depression and World War II, he faced prejudice and had difficulty getting started. He finally gained notice after a terrible train wreck in Philadelphia, in which he arrived on the scene and saved countless lives. Through that experience, he was named a police and fire surgeon for the city. Eventually he earned the highly visible and prestigious post of chief of police and fire surgery, which had a large ward at Philadelphia General and at Pennsylvania Hospital. Sam had ten surgeons working under him in this role and became very well connected throughout the city. One Thanksgiving dinner at his house, the phone kept ringing and Sam was forced to take multiple calls. I heard him giving instructions to the person on the other end: "Take a couple of aspirin." "Drink a lot of fluids." Finally, I asked whom he was talking to. He said with an annoyed tone of voice, "This guy, all he's got is a cold." It turned out the caller was Frank Rizzo, one of Philadelphia's best-known public figures, who was then the city police commissioner and eventually became mayor. Frank Rizzo enjoyed a seventh grade education. He was known by reputation as the toughest cop in the nation. His philosophy towards treating criminals was "spacco il capo" (break their heads). When Frank Rizzo successfully ran for mayor of Philadelphia one of his campaign slogans was "If elected mayor, I will make Attila the Hun look like a faggot." He successfully took on Philadelphia's gangs, its criminals, and quelled any riot activity. Frank Rizzo left no room for ambiguity.

One fall day I was Christmas shopping in center city Philadelphia thinking about my medical school prospects. The wind was blowing about fifteen knots with a significant wind chill. I decided to get warm and stop by Cousin Sam's office in City Hall. He invited me in for lunch and opened the door to a back room of his office with a long table, and I was astounded —everyone there was Italian! All of the secretaries and nurses he hired were Italian, which was his way of retaliating against the prejudice he faced as an Italian American earlier in his career. The pasta started flowing, along with plates of chicken and veal, and everyone was speaking Italian in the office of the chief police and fire surgeon of Philadelphia — it was surreal. I was impressed by Dr. Brunetti's accomplishments and his pride in our shared heritage.

After lunch, he asked what was happening with my medical school plans, so I updated him on my situation. What was about to occur would be difficult to script in a Hollywood studio. I mentioned that I had recently dined at the Warwick Hotel with my father and his friend Gerry Creskoff, a lawyer. My father wanted me to meet Mr. Creskoff because his brother was a physiologist at the University of Pennsylvania, who could have some influence at Penn. Gerry Creskoff had a different agenda. He wanted me to meet the head waiter at the Warwick Hotel restaurant because the waiter had a friendly relationship with a prominent surgeon at Jefferson, Dr. William T. Lemmon, who frequently dined at the Warwick. Dr. Lemmon was famous for developing continuous spinal anesthesia now used routinely for procedures in the abdomen and lower extremities and obstetrics. Sam, who was a portly man with very heavy eyelids, perked up. "Did you say Bill Lemmon?" he asked. When I nodded, he picked up the phone and brusquely told his secretary, "Get me Bill Lemmon on the phone." The laughter I was expressing suddenly vanished as disbelief and the significance of what was happening in front of me struck me like a lead weight. He stubbed out one of his ever-present Kent cigarettes and, after a few moments' pause, I heard him say, "Bill? Sam Brunetti here. Bill, my cousin, Anthony Chiurco, is in here saying he wants to go to Jefferson. He's my flesh and blood, Bill." Another pause. "OK," he said. "See ya, Bill." And that was it. Just forty-eight hours later, a letter from Jefferson came in the mail. It stated that the Admissions Committee had decided to rescind my rejection for the class of 1967 and offer me admission. This was *Deus Ex Machina!* Unbelievable! As it turned out, William Lemmon had a son, William Jr., who finished a surgical residency at Jefferson, Sam gave him a job as a police surgeon to get him started. His father never forgot that courtesy, and when the time came to return a favor to Sam he didn't hesitate.

Family dinner at Palumbo's restaurant in South Philadelphia, *circa* 1957

Sam's phone call was the game-change for me. Without him, I might have been drafted to fight in Vietnam, or I may have been headed toward a career of unloading trucks at the Angelo Brothers warehouse. This was an early lesson for me about the importance of relationships and connections in the professional world. While I had worked extremely hard to earn good grades at St. Joe's, my cousin's influence with Bill Lemmon ultimately provided the push I needed to gain admittance to Jefferson. It taught me a major lesson; the role of luck. When I think back to Sam making that phone call, I am reminded of a speech that Michael Lewis, the author of *Moneyball* and *Liar's Poker,* made at Princeton University in June 2012. Addressing the graduating class, Lewis said, "Life's outcomes, while not entirely random, have a huge amount of luck baked into them. Above all, recognize that if you have had success, you have also had luck." My own experience certainly attests to the truth of Lewis' message. The good fortune I experienced through my cousin's connection to Dr. Lemmon, however, came at a price. I must admit that I felt embarrassed that I had to get into Jefferson that way. I knew the school's reputation for relentless rigor— every year twenty-five students flunked out of the class of 180 in their first year — and as I began my studies there, I felt somewhat unworthy, diffident, and intimidated by the other students, lecturers, and the ambience of the hallowed halls.

My introduction to Jefferson was eventful, to say the least. One of our earliest lectures was delivered by Dr. John Gibbon, chairman of the surgery department, who invented the heart-lung machine. Prior to Gibbon's invention, cardiac surgery was nearly impossible because operating on a beating heart did not lend itself to favorable outcomes. By arresting the heart and allowing blood to pass through Gibbon's apparatus with an artificial pump and oxygenation, the age of cardiac surgery was born. John Gibbon was famous. Dr. Gibbon's lecture focused on the high risk of surgery of the neck and mediastinum, a topic we were exploring at the time in dissecting the head and neck of cadavers in our anatomy lab at the Daniel Baugh Institute of Anatomy (DBI), which was several blocks from the school and where Jefferson students spent much of their first six months. A day or two after Dr. Gibbon's lecture, as I stood at my dissecting table at DBI, the student health service called and asked me to come over immediately and that there was evidence of a deviated trachea in my chest X-ray (a chest X-ray was required for every student enrolled at Jefferson). So they ordered a barium swallow and, sure enough, the esophagus was displaced posterior. They told me I needed an operation and that they wanted me to see a surgeon, Dr. John Templeton. Dr. Templeton was allegedly the best general surgeon at Jefferson. I was asymptomatic, but this news was really worrisome because they thought I had a tumor. At the time there was no MRI or CAT scanning — all you had was an X-ray and what we now might consider primitive types of studies. So I saw Dr. Templeton, who scheduled me for surgery and told me that there was a chance they would have to split my sternum because it was up in the upper mediastinum in the upper thorax. I had sleepless nights worrying about it. I would wake up multiple times with my bed sheets soaked from the stress of what was about to happen. It was traumatic to hear this lecture by Dr. Gibbon talking about the risks of neck surgery and, at twenty-two years old, to have it performed on me days later while simultaneously dissecting that area in my cadaver was a script that could win an Academy Award for best screenplay in a horror movie. I underwent the surgery, and it turned out to be a congenital large cyst on my esophagus. Dr. Templeton told my Aunt Lucy, who came by after the surgery, that the cyst was the size of a fist. (My parents didn't come to the hospital for the surgery—I don't think they could handle it. No one was there with me before the surgery, only Aunt Lucy afterward.) I had an incision from ear to ear, and Dr. Templeton was able to go in above my sternum and get it out that way. I remember being closed with wire, which was awfully painful when they took the wire sutures out.

Three years later, when I was a senior, I was attending a monthly seminar led by Dr. Hodes, the chairman of radiology, who would gather the junior and senior class in a large auditorium at Jefferson and present unusual teaching films. During one of these "grand rounds," as they were known, Dr. Hodes put up a chest X-ray and asked if anyone can tell him the problem with the film. "This is a routine chest X-ray of a 22-year-old medical student," he said. Naturally, my antenna went right up, and I raised my hand (in fact, mine was the only hand raised). He picked me and I responded that the trachea was deviated. He said, "Excellent! Excellent! This man is a budding radiologist. Now, tell me, what tests would you order?" I told him I would order a barium swallow. "Excellent!" he said, and asked what else I saw. I said, "Well, the esophagus is displaced posteriorly." Now he was really impressed: "Wonderful! What do you think this could be?" I said, "Well, if I had my guess, I would say, that's a duplication cyst of the esophagus." He looked like he was going to shit on the floor right then and there, because this was an extremely rare condition. In fact, years later a series of nine cases of this particular entity were gleaned from the world literature and reported in the New England Journal of Medicine. Astonished, Hodes looked at me and asked, "How the hell could you possibly know that?" I said, "Because that's my X-ray." The whole auditorium went wild. People started clapping and banging— there was pandemonium for a good five minutes! Hodes couldn't control the auditorium; he was banging on the desk like a judge, calling, "Order! Order!" It was hysterical! That was the only damn good of that whole ordeal, besides getting rid of that mass in my chest, of course.

Back to freshman year, I was in the hospital for a week after the surgery and then was still not feeling well, but I had to get back to class. I had already missed ten days of anatomy, and I was terrified that I would not be able to catch up. I finally returned to my studies and, two weeks later, as I ran up to my lab partner's apartment to get his notes because I had missed so much class, my foot slipped on a candy wrapper and I fell on the stairs. I tried to break my fall with my right hand and fractured my radius in three places—a distal radius fracture known as a Colles fracture. They had to take me back to the operating room and David Hoffman, the orthopedic surgeon at Jefferson, put me in a cast from my fingers to my shoulder. He was trying to avoid opening it up to put pins in, which was primitive at that time. I already had lost almost two weeks due to the surgery with Dr. Templeton, and now I lost another four days out with the Colles fracture and surgery. And, to top it off, the break occurred in my right arm — my writing hand! I was placed in a cast from my hand to my shoulder. Everyone looked at me and thought, "This kid has had it." But I wasn't going to let not being able to take notes stop me. This was no different than the last five hundred meters of a boat race! I thought, "I have another hand, don't I?" so I learned to write left-handed. It wasn't easy but I got pretty good at it, and I was able to resume my studies (with some help from my classmate Vince Caruso, who let me borrow his notes until I mastered writing with a new hand).

With this type of start, there was nowhere for me to go but up at Jefferson. And, of course, I was no stranger to hard work. As I had done to afford the tuition at St. Joe's, I worked all summer before enrolling at Jefferson to earn tuition money. I was able to secure the manager's job at Fairways Swim Club which paid up to $100 per week, plus another $20 per week for giving private swimming lessons, so I was able to save up enough to afford the $1,300 tuition at Jefferson. I couldn't afford to board at school, unlike a lot of the other students who stayed in fraternity houses or apartments in Center City, which was not cheap (probably about $35 per month in those days). My godparents, the DiPrespis, lived at 2043 Walnut Street, right across from the old John Wanamaker home, about a block from Rittenhouse Square. So I could walk to the Jefferson campus at 10th and Walnut Streets, which was about 15 blocks. The

DiPrespis had a four-story home on Walnut Street and would rent rooms to graduate students from Drexel University. They fixed up a room on the fourth floor for me. It had a desk that I bought in a fire sale for thirty bucks. It actually smelled like burnt wood and still had soot on it. They bought me a nice red carpet for the room. My mother bought me a black leather recliner. I made my bedroom in a small side room where the bed just barely fit. In the winter, however, I couldn't stay with the DiPrespis because the heat did not make it to my room on the fourth floor — they would have had to turn the furnace way up, which would make it too hot on the lower floors, and also would be too expensive. There were nights when I was shivering so much in that room I could not sleep and I realized I needed to go back to my parents' house to have enough warmth to study. So I would take the Paoli local train back to Overbrook and walk home.

There was no social life to speak of, and I rarely had a day off. My father gave me spending money whenever he could, which amounted to about ten dollars a week, which was barely enough to feed myself. Once in a while, the medical students would go to a couple of bars around Jefferson and have a few beers, but that was rare. In this environment at Jefferson you had to study most of the night — at least four to six hours every night after a full day of classes and labs. You never knew, for example, when you might face a surprise quiz in anatomy lab, so you had to make sure you kept up with the volume of studies. You might walk in one day and the instructor announces that there is a lab practical—all of a sudden you're going from dissecting table to dissecting table where there would be parts of anatomy tagged, and you would have thirty seconds to identify the anatomical structure before a buzzer signaled that you had to move on to the next table. Sometimes they would tag the same structure three times in a row, with different cadavers, just to make you sure you really knew what it was. I remember they tagged the recurrent laryngeal nerve three times in a row, a nerve you do not want to injure when you are operating in the neck, because the patient will end up with hoarseness due to vocal cord paralysis. Years later, as a surgeon, I was performing a cervical diskectomy and fusion. I had an assistant who was told not to move the retractor he was holding. Unfortunately he inadvertently lifted the retractor and stretched the laryngeal nerve, and caused the one and only vocal chord paralysis I had in my career as a surgeon performing more than one thousand anterior cervical spine operations, because this young man did not listen. And I knew, from my rigorous training in residency, how to handle that procedure safely. I had that vocal chord injected with Teflon, and fortunately the man's voice came back. But that is a good example of how there is no room for error in neurosurgery—you cannot be inattentive. You have to apply the standard of perfection in the operating room or disasters can happen in high-risk surgical interventions. To this day, I curse that assistant because I am intense in avoiding complications, and he didn't listen.

In the early afternoon of November 22, 1963, while standing at my dissecting table we received the word that President John F. Kennedy had been shot while in a motorcade through Dealy Plaza in downtown Dallas, Texas. Details were not as yet revealed by the press. In subsequent days as the story unfolded the assassination was apparently committed by a lone gunman, Lee Harvey Oswald, from the tower of the Texas School Book Depository, which overlooked the motorcar parade. In subsequent years the lone gunman theory became disputed and a source of national controversy. Theories ranged widely from implication of the CIA to participation by a second gunman in what was known as the "Grassy Knoll theory," as well as implication of the mafia employing Cuban sharpshooters in the sewer on the side of the road that the motorcade passed. The issue has never been laid to rest for many Americans, despite the Warren Commission's conclusion that a lone gunman was responsible. A videotape of the assassination known as the Zapruder tape again lent credence to the two gunmen theory. By the next day, Lyndon Johnson had been sworn in as the thirty-sixth President of the United States.

As my first year progressed and I saw that I could compete favorably against my classmates, I regained my confidence. I finished my first year ranked thirty-first in a class of 180 students with an average of 84.5. In the school's tradition twenty-five students failed out. If I had not missed the time early in the fall due to the surgeries, there is no question in my mind I would have finished in the top ten. My average in my second year climbed to 90.0 and, eventually, I wound up with extremely high national board scores. I came alive at Jefferson. I was studying something I wanted to learn. I was in the Honors Society, which reflected my high grades, but I didn't get into the Alpha Omega Alpha (AOA) honor fraternity even though I had the grades, because I wasn't political enough. It actually made me wonder how I had so much trouble getting into medical school when many students there were, quite frankly, poorly prepared. I mean, either they didn't study or they just didn't care. I realized there was a system that allowed some people to gain access based on money, family or other connections, with myself as a prime example. Granted, I owed my admission to Jefferson to Sam Brunetti's phone call to William Lemmon, but at the same time I worked hard to excel.

I remember before matriculation walking into a surgeon's office from Temple that my father asked me to visit. He was obese but well dressed, who was clearly impressed with himself—arrogance is a not uncommon trait especially among surgeons-- who questioned my ability to achieve in professional school. I said to him, "If you don't think that I have the intelligence to go through medical school, then you are mistaken, Sir." I essentially told him he was full of shit, though in more polite terms. I guess I had a way about me that was a typical surgical personality even back at age twenty-two—I did not accept his demeanor and condescension. That was my attitude. No matter how high the wall that was put in front of me, I would get over it. That was my approach to life back then—and still is. And I think that goes back to my experience with rowing—knowing that when you're in last 500 meters of the boat race, when you feel like you're going to die, you just can't quit.

E Pluribus Unum... American dollar bill.

This attitude facilitated my selection of the most difficult, high-risk specialty. Certainly, neurosurgery is not for everybody. The proof is that of the Thomas Jefferson graduating class of 1967, I am the only neurosurgeon. In my third year at Jefferson, when surgery rotation began, we spent one week on anesthesia, watching induction techniques and procedures such as putting in an endotracheal tube. The very first day I was on anesthesia, they let me go into this room to watch a craniotomy, or a brain operation. I had never seen, nor heard of, a craniotomy. The surgeon was John Whiteley, who was one of only two neurosurgeons at Jefferson at the time. He came in, the patient was put to sleep and was put in what looked like a barber chair that was tilted back. Dr. Whiteley did a bicoronal incision, ear to ear, and peeled the frontal scalp down over the eyes, then opened the frontal bone, opened the dura, the covering of the brain, and lifted the brain up. I could see this right over the drape; I read the chart and saw that the patient had a pituitary tumor. The patient made binoculars for a living, and he noticed while looking in his binoculars that he couldn't see on either side, in the periphery, which is called a bitemporal hemianopsia. That's a classic sign of a compression of the optic chiasm, where the optic nerves cross over at the floor of the skull and go to each hemisphere. When you compress the chiasm, you lose vision in the temporal fields. I watched the surgeon lift the frontal lobe up and take this pituitary tumor out. I was instantly spellbound! I said to myself, "That is the greatest thing I've ever seen. That's for me!" I knew it spontaneously, and combined with my love of neurology I have pursued it ever since.

Today the subfrontal approach to the pituitary and optic chiasm has largely been replaced by the transeptal (through the nose), transsphenoidal approach to the sella turcica (Turkish saddle which is the resemblance of this anatomical structure in which the pituitary lies) pioneered by Jules Hardy of Canada, an operation I have performed numerous times in my practice.

When I was a senior medical student, they farmed us out to different hospitals. I was farmed out in a surgical rotation to Misericordia Hospital in West Philadelphia. During that rotation, on Thanksgiving Day, a family of eight African Americans came in—every one of them had been stabbed. They had gotten into an argument over the seating arrangement at their Thanksgiving dinner, so they all grabbed knives and stabbed each other. And we were in the operating room all day and night. I assisted a surgeon named Joe Dombroski, who worked so hard exploring all those bellies and chests. It was a memorable taste of emergency room medicine in the inner city.

The chief of surgery at Misericordia was John Gowan. Dr. Gowan took an interest in me, as I was a surgical extern, meaning I was a medical student on the surgery rotation at Misericordia. He asked me what my interest was and when I told him I was interested in neurosurgery he let me know of a good friend of his, Don Cooper, who had a group practice of neurosurgery in New London, Conn. Dr. Gowan arranged for me to go to New London on elective. Dr. Gowan was trying to encourage me to pursue my internship at Misericordia, but I had my sights set on Pennsylvania Hospital, which at the time was the most prestigious internship in the United States. But in any case, the opportunity to student with Dr. Cooper was too valuable to pass up.

I received a ten-week vacation block from Jefferson prior to graduation, so I went to Connecticut to learn from Dr. Cooper and The Neurological Group, which included Dave Cavicke, Henry Brown, John German and Dan Moale, a neurologist. I spent a month with them, stayed in the nurses' dorm, scrubbed in the operating room, made rounds with them, and enjoyed an excellent exposure to neurosurgery. This was an eccentric choice to make, as this was my vacation time, but I needed to find out if this specialty was really for me and I wanted to learn as much as I could — plus, there was no money to while away the time in the south of France. I enjoyed my time with Dr. Cooper, who was known as "Coop" and was a Clint Eastwood type in terms of projecting a cool authority and presence. And, of course, you know, I was having a great time with the nurses there. They were looking at me as a new partner coming on in neurosurgery, when I really was a medical student. Three weeks prior to the completion of my stay in New London, a phone call from the Angelo brothers asking me to accompany Uncle Rocky to Japan was a bombshell.

The Japan excursion was another valuable experience aside from touring. While Uncle Rocky was conducting business for Angelo Brothers, I went to the University of Tokyo and watched neurosurgery. I saw the Japanese surgeons removing a third ventricle tumor. I also watched them do a gastrectomy, because cancer of the stomach was so very common in Japan. These Japanese surgeons could remove a stomach in fifteen minutes because they did so many of them. And at the time, the doctors were on strike because they were making the equivalent of twenty-five dollars a week in American money. I took the operating room team out to lunch after I observed them in surgery, and we talked about my interest in neurosurgery. I recall watching how they inhaled rice with their chopsticks—they made a swooshing sound, almost like they were slurping soup. I was amazed at how skilled they were with using chopsticks. And they were always bowing. It was an eye-opening experience with a different culture, in my first trip overseas.

Uncle Rocky was a wonderful tour guide in Japan, as the locals loved him! There was a whole entourage that met us at the airport. His business associates took us to geisha houses and Japanese inns. Prostitution was legal. The Japanese men would go to a bathhouse after work, or a geisha house or a nightclub. And girls would come and sit at your table, and keep rotating until you found one you liked, and then you would go to a Japanese inn. At the Japanese inn, sex was a ritual. The American counterpart would be to go to a motel, jump in bed, have sex, pay the girl and move on. In Japan, the ritual was the girl would first feed you with chopsticks, then draw you a bath, then lay you on a table and give you a total massage. Then would come the sex. All the time the customer was living in anticipation. It was reminiscent of a line from *Ode to a Grecian Urn* by Keats: "Heard music is sweet, but that unheard is sweeter." Just like with music as you live in anticipation of hearing the part you love, with these Japanese girls you would live in the anticipation of the ultimate release.

One night, Uncle Rocky had two female associates take me out on the town. Unknown to me beforehand, they took me to a Japanese gay bar, where the men were dressed up as women in kimonos. I was with these two women, having a lot of fun, and then came the bill. In terms of today's money, they probably charged $100 a drink. I said, "This is crazy —I'm not paying that!" They bolted the door and it looked like there was going to be a problem, so I paid it. I was really angry with the girls for taking me to get ripped off, and Uncle Rocky didn't appreciate my response because they were his business associates. He told me, "If you're getting crowned, get crowned. Just shut your mouth and chalk it up to experience." I was very naïve to the ways of the world—I had been a student all my life. So Uncle Rocky helped start my learning process as to how the world works.

While in Japan, I rode the high-speed trains. I visited Hiroshima and went to the harrowing A-bomb exhibit hall. I was aghast at the incomprehensible level of destruction of a city and it's people from a weapon conceived for the destruction of one's fellow man. I looked for a place to hide as I was the only American among multiple Japanese tourists. There were remnants from the blast on display, such as bicycles twisted. A photograph of a trolley car to this day remains vivid in memory with the passengers still holding the straps above with their hand only they were black from having been instantly incinerated where they stood and somehow the trolley car was preserved. The town of Hiroshima was completely rubble except for occasional foci of building foundations and construction skeletons. I was uncomfortable to be an American. I thought about my Catholic programming with particular attention to divine providence — a concept that a God is looking out for us. The religious programming in which I was raised suddenly struck me as delusional. I visited the A-bomb hospital and made rounds with the Japanese physicians and saw patients still in there from the blast more than twenty years later. They suffered from radiation sickness, thyroid cancers, and other sequelae of the radioactive fallout. I even rowed on a river in Hiroshima and raced two Japanese in another boat. All of this had major impact on me and inspired my desire to continue to travel and experience other cultures, which I have been fortunate to do.

Upon my return to the States, I graduated from Jefferson with my medical degree and took the next step in my journey, which brought me to The Pennsylvania Hospital as an intern, responsible for the lives of others.

79

Anthony Chiurco upon graduation from The Jefferson
Medical College of Philadelphia, 1967

Emidio Angelo and Anthony Chiurco, M.D., June 1967

CHAPTER VI:
THE PENNSYLVANIA
HOSPITAL 1967-1968

"Listen to the patient, he is telling you the diagnosis…"
— *Sir William Osler*

I was one of eighteen rotating interns arriving at the Pennsylvania Hospital on June 18, 1967. Having arrived from Japan one week earlier, I was refreshed and ready to start another apprehensive adventure because I would be responsible on my own for human life. The Pennsylvania Hospital was probably the top internship in the United States at that time. The hospital was founded in 1751 by Benjamin Franklin and Dr. Thomas Bond "to care for the sick, poor, and insane, who were wandering the streets of Philadelphia."

At that time, Philadelphia was the fastest growing city in the thirteen colonies. In 1730, the population numbered 11,500 and by 1776, its 40,000 residents made Philadelphia the second largest English-speaking city in the British Empire. The docks and the wharves along with Delaware river teemed with activity as ships bound for foreign ports loaded up with their wares. The Philadelphia region was "a melting pot for diseases where Europeans, Africans, and Indians engaged in free exchange of their respective infections." The civic-minded leaders sought a partial solution to the problem by founding a hospital.

The year prior to my arrival, the Pennsylvania Hospital interns earned $1,200 a year. After a revolt by the house staff, the stipend was increased to $2,200 the year of my arrival. Internship required work every day and every other night with every other Sunday off and no vacation. You paid for every cup of coffee. You wore a white jacket, white pants, and a white shirt with a tie. At that time, there were large twenty-bed wards, ten hospital beds on each side of a large room, which beds were separated by curtains. When the curtains were not drawn, one could look out and see twenty patients with a glance — unheard of today. Soon, however, Medicare rules would state there can only be two people per room — wonder why Medicare is going broke? The rotating internship is also unheard of today and does not exist. At the time, to be a doctor you had to be experienced with not only medical problems but surgery; pediatrics; obstetrics; gynecology; ear, nose, and throat surgery; urology; and orthopedics as well as emergency medicine. When you finished your internship at the Pennsylvania Hospital, you could readily open an office and care for a general population as a family practitioner with an excellent fund of knowledge and experience. You served twelve weeks on medicine and twelve weeks caring for the surgical ward and assisting

The Pennsylvania Hospital rotating interns 1967 (Top left Tony Chiurco)

on operations. The remainder of the time you rotated on emergency medicine and the rest of the specialties as listed above. Exposure to pediatrics was at the Children's Hospital of Philadelphia at 17th and Bainbridge Streets, which hospital has now been replaced by a modern facility adjacent to the University of Pennsylvania at 34th & Spruce Streets. I began my internship on the Medical Service. I shared on-call as alternating nights with another intern, Lenny Shapiro, assigned to my ward. We had a resident over us, Jeff Hartzell, ex CIA, who answered to the chief resident. Life at that time as an intern was extraordinary. You had complete control in management of the patient with access to your resident when you thought you needed help. An attending would round once a week. A resident would round daily with the interns in the morning. Lenny Shapiro and I divided the patients between us. Since we took call every other night, any patient that came in while you are on-call fell under your management. It was inner city medicine at its finest. There was a significant African American clientele as Pennsylvania Hospital was located in the heart of the inner city. In general, African Americans had poor outpatient care leading to ill health and the sequelae of disease which could have been aborted had they had regular doctor visits and regular outpatient care. For the most part, they were too poor and came to the emergency room when their health had so deteriorated in many instances that they realized that death could be imminent. On the surgery service frequently, these indigent patients would be operated upon by the residents or junior residents without supervision. This was prior to Medicare rules that an attending surgeon had to be present during operative interventions. There were no rules for the indigent, however and interns and residents did whatever they thought necessary for patient care. For the most part, the patients received adequate care, but there were times when the patients could have received better care. Interns were eager to learn and tried to do the best they could with the best knowledge they had from their education. The medical and surgical services were so busy that the interns were usually up all night. During the early afternoon, it was common to take a two-hour nap to be able to function because you knew that it was highly likely you would be up all night or most of the night. Our quarters were localized around the old surgical amphitheater, which was the first surgical operating room in the United States. I can honestly recall one night pleading for a critically ill patient to please die, so I could get to sleep. This type of life pushing the house staff to the extremes, did endanger patients' lives in my opinion because exhaustion can frequently lend itself to unclear thought processes and incorrect management especially at three o'clock in the morning in the operating room or on the medical floor. This situation for interns and residents (house staff) would change in later years after a landmark suit occurred at New York Hospital in 1984. This became known as the Libby Zion law, which is a regulation that limits the amount of resident physician's work in New York State hospitals to roughly eighty hours per week. The law was named after Libby Zion who died at the age of eighteen under the care of what her father believed to be overworked resident physicians and interns. In *The New York Times*, her father, a journalist, in an Op-Ed piece wrote, "You don't need kindergarten to know that a resident working a 36-hour shift is in no condition to make any kind of judgment call — forget about life and death." In July 2003, the Accreditation Council for graduate medical education adopted similar regulations limiting the number of hours that residents and nonresident physicians work. This legislation changed the landscape for work hours for medical house staff in the United States. By the year 2000, however, the pendulum swung clearly in the opposite direction where house staff on one occasion told me at the University Medical Center at Princeton that they had already had their three-patient admission criteria for the day and cannot accept any more patients on the Medical Service. In many instances, house staff today take call one night a week at best and do not experience the continuity of care for a critically ill patient. So, which is better, the extreme exposure to the point of physical exhaustion or inadequate exposure in patient care in the form of poor continuity with multiple doctors managing a patient on different nights in the hospital? I think that a compromise is always best, but what I have seen currently based on my training, is not what I would respect at this time.

An episode occurred during my internship, which helped in the long run to further my career in the contemplated field of neurological surgery. One evening a middle-aged woman presented on the medical service with severe back pain, which occurred suddenly associated with some headache but her main complaint was inability to walk because the back pain was so severe. She was evaluated by the medical service resident and attending without positive results. Because of the headache, the neurology service was consulted and they did not feel there was anything to do but treat the headache and back pain symptomatically. They could not determine the cause for the back pain. The residents had x-rayed her back and did not determine abnormality. She subsequently was evaluated by Dr. Frank Elliot, the Chairman of the Neurology Department at Pennsylvania Hospital, who did not have much to offer. That afternoon I thought about her and remembered a case of similar nature that I had seen with Dr. Henry Brown in the emergency room at Lawrence and Memorial Hospital in New London, Connecticut. That patient also presented with severe back pain and headache. Dr. Brown explained to me that rarely blood from an intracranial aneurysm rupture will travel down the spinal fluid pathways and irritate the lumbar meninges (the covering of the sac around the spinal fluid and nerve roots) causing severe back pain. Admittedly in my career in neurosurgery I can attest to the fact that this presentation of a brain aneurysm rupture is relatively rare. When an aneurysm ruptures sudden severe headache is the norm often described as "the worst headache of my life" by the unsuspecting patients, half of whom would die from the initial leak of an intracranial aneurysm.

That being said, I took it upon myself to perform a lumbar puncture (spinal tap) on this woman, much to the discouragement of my resident. When the needle entered the subarachnoid space bloody spinal fluid came out under elevated pressure which I sent to the laboratory. I then called the neurology service and explained that I believed this woman sustained a subarachnoid hemorrhage from a brain aneurysm and should undergo cerebral angiography. The neurologists accused me of performing a traumatic tap (the needle that was inserted caused the bleeding). Not discouraged, I took it upon myself to call Dr. Thomas Langfitt who was the neurosurgeon at The Pennsylvania Hospital to please listen to my thoughts and please consider cerebral angiography to see if an aneurysm was present. The reader should remember that in 1967 CAT and MRI scanning did not exist. Dr. Langfitt agreed and did a cerebral angiogram and found a large aneurysm on the Circle of Willis with spasm of the surrounding vessels. Spasm indicated that the aneurysm had recently bled. Langfitt was going to prepare the patient for surgery. Frank Elliot, Head of Neurology, who had missed the diagnosis came back to the bedside and lectured to the residents about the patient having "the lumbar variety of subarachnoid hemorrhage" in his eloquent British accent. While Elliott was standing at the bedside the patient screamed in pain from headache and died. In that era acute aneurysm surgery was not performed because of the high mortality prior to the development of microsurgical technique and the operating microscope. I do not believe anything different could have been done. However the only light at the end of the tunnel was Frank Elliot offered me a residency in neurology after my internship. More importantly Dr. Langfitt was impressed at my out-scooping the neurologists and I believe it all added up to Dr. Langfitt offering me residency and subsequent fellowship in later years at the University of Pennsylvania after he became Chairman of Neurological Surgery.

Other issues which occurred in the 1960s during my era in medical school and internship took place in many American cities in the form of numerous riots despite the fact that victories were achieved against legal segregation and disfranchisement in the south. The civil rights movement had raised hopes for further progress toward racial equality, but as blacks in northern cities saw their hopes frustrated, a setting was established for large scale disorder in cities such as Newark, New Jersey, Rochester, New York, Cleveland, Ohio, Cincinnati, Chicago, and Detroit. Most significant were the Harlem Riots of 1964, the Watts Riot of 1965 in Los Angeles, and the Detroit Riot of 1967. The government used force to contain the disorders. Rioting did not occur in Philadelphia, a city with a major black population because Frank Rizzo was so feared. Although rioting tended to quell after the 1960s era, in 1992 there was a major riot in Los Angeles after the police beating of Rodney King, an African-American motorist. Police brutality and social injustice voiced by African-Americans was largely ignored by government authorities, which led other nations to be dismissive about American claims for leadership against abolishing human rights abuses.

At the time of this writing, medical school graduating classes are more than fifty percent female. The number of medical school graduates is probably three times in quantity from the time I graduated from Jefferson in 1967. There were between seven and eight thousand graduates of medical school in the mid-1960s. At Jefferson, I believe we graduated four women in our class compared with today's volume of female students.

The important thing about being an intern was that for the first time you are a doctor and responsible for human life. You are not yet licensed, however, until you pass Part Three of the National Board of Medical Examiners towards the end of your internship. Part One and Part Two of the National Board were taken prior to graduation. After passing Part Three, one could apply for license in any state in the United States with some restrictions in Florida. So, by the completion of our internships, we were licensed physicians able to open up a practice anywhere in a state where one applied for the license of that particular state. Almost all states honored the National Board of Medical Examiners. Your options after internship would be to open a general practice in the community or go into specialty training as a resident. If you do not obtain a residency with a deferment such as the Berry Plan, you would be drafted more likely than not into the armed services because the Vietnam War was intense in 1967-1968. I had worked extremely hard as an intern. I was physically exhausted towards the end of spring of 1968. The internship ended in mid-June, but I could not face a residency. The year had taken such a toll on me mentally and physically that I decided to enter the armed services. I applied for a commission in the Navy since my father served in the Navy in World War I. I subsequently received a commission.

Life continued to be exciting in its uncertainty.

CHAPTER VII:
ON THE RESERVATION

"Look at all those fucking Indians…"
— *Possible last words of General George Custer*

Exhausted from my time as an intern at Pennsylvania Hospital, I decided that before going into a residency I would instead get my military service obligation out of the way. I applied for and received a commission in the Navy. At this point, in the spring of 1968, the United States had more than 460,000 troops in Vietnam and unrest was growing in America about the country's commitment to this war. Thousands of Americans were participating in public protests — including 100,000 demonstrators marching on Washington a few months later — against U.S. involvement in the Vietnam War. "Hell no, we won't go!" was heard resonating by the youth of America being drafted out of college and high schools. Many who were called to the draft escaped to Canada rather than engage in military service. The idea of being sent into war was unsettling to me, as it was for many young men of my generation. During my internship we had every other Sunday off, so during one of those off days I attended a family cocktail party at my parents' house. My cousin Joya — the oldest daughter of my Uncle Emidio, the artist — was at the party with a friend named Bob Diorio, a physician in the U.S. Public Health Service who was stationed in Philadelphia. Bob had a nice apartment in Society Hill and treated servicemen from the Merchant Marines and Coast Guard. As I related my plans to Bob, he counseled me, "You know, if you take that Navy commission, I can guarantee you — you're going right to Vietnam. That's fine if that's what you want, but if you go into the U.S. Public Health Service, you can get stationed like me in a major city, which is far better."

I had not previously considered this option, not knowing much about the U.S. Public Health Service. Bob explained the procedure for applying, which involved scoring in the top echelon on a four-hour entrance exam that you had to take in Silver Spring, Md., just outside of Washington, D.C. I applied, scored well on the exam and was offered a commission. I was told they could use my services in Phoenix. So I called the Navy to ask if I was obliged to take the Navy commission, but I wasn't. I also was told by the Naval officer that if I accepted their commission, I would be assigned as a medic to the Marine Corps in Vietnam. So I thought, "I hear it's hot in Phoenix, but probably not as hot as Vietnam." And that's how I found myself heading west.

The U.S. Public Health Service Commissioned Corps is the world's largest public health service and was founded more than 200 years ago, when President John Adams in 1789 signed into law the Act for the Relief of Sick and Disabled Seamen. The mission of the service is to improve public health on numerous fronts: providing health care to military personnel, immigrants and other communities; and engaging in disease control and prevention and biomedical research. As I prepared for my two-year stint in the U.S. Public Health Service corps, with my parents sobbing in the background, I packed up my car in Philly to drive across the country to Phoenix. I was driving a British racing green E-Type Jaguar with four thousand miles on it, which I bought with $1,000 that I saved from my internship. En route to Phoenix, I called home and my father told me that the Public Health Service was looking for me. When I called the office, I was told to reroute my trip because they needed someone at the Indian Health Service outpost on the reservation in Winnebago, Nebraska.

The Indian Health Service, which is now an agency within the Department of Health and Human Services, provides federal health services to American Indians to 566 federally recognized tribes across the country. The reservation where I was assigned was about 20 minutes south of Sioux City, Iowa, and an hour from Omaha in the Missouri River Valley. We handled medical care for members of the Winnebago, Sioux and Omaha tribes in the tri-state area of Nebraska, Iowa and South

Dakota. The Winnebago operation is overseen by the Aberdeen Area Office in South Dakota, which includes 19 Indian Health Service units that provide care to one hundred and twenty-two thousand American Indians in the Dakotas, Nebraska and Iowa.

As I traveled across Interstate 80 en route to begin my stint in Nebraska, I had a true feeling of freedom. I was finally a licensed physician and had my professional future in front of me. Cruising through the flat countryside of Iowa and Nebraska, I put the top down on the Jaguar and pushed the pedal to ninety and one hundred miles per hour. Looking out the window and seeing corn and cows on the side of the road — this was an eye-opening experience for a guy from South Philly who lived in and around the city his whole life. I even blew my horn at the cows, but they didn't move.

When I arrived at the Winnebago Indian reservation, which was relatively isolated in the Missouri River Valley, I was a bit shell-shocked. The Winnebago reservation was established by an act of Congress in 1863 and is one of about three hundred and ten Indian reservations across the United States. Reservations were established by peace treaties between the U.S. government and Indian tribes, who in exchange for surrendering large tracts of land to the federal government would receive parcels designated as sovereign (or "reserved") lands for the tribes. The Winnebago tribe, whose name means "People of the Big Voice," had been known to white settlers for more than two hundred years prior to the establishment of the reservation, with the first interactions between Winnebagos and whites coming in Wisconsin, near Green Bay. As epidemics of smallpox and measles decreased the size of the tribe population, the Winnebagos moved from Wisconsin to Iowa to Minnesota to South Dakota and, finally, to Nebraska.

Upon my arrival at the reservation, I learned that all of the Public Health Service doctors were supposed to be provided a small two-bedroom house to live in, but my house was occupied by an Indian family. All of my belongings had already been delivered by a moving van, so it was put into a shed and I was put up in the nurses' dorm before everything got straightened out and I moved into my new residence at the top of a hill about five hundred yards from the hospital where I would work. Almost immediately, I hooked up with a graduate student in social work from the University of California at Berkeley who was studying Indian populations and helped me (among other interactions) gain understanding of this unfamiliar new community in which I found myself.

It was actually quite a revelation to see how the Indians lived, and how the health care policies of the administration at that time, in my opinion, damaged an entire people. It was handout after handout. They got housing and free health care, and still they were not achieving. This experience helped me conclude that the more the government gives to people, the less incentive they have to achieve. It was evidence to me that the welfare state simply doesn't work, in any form. It's degrading to a people. What I saw in my experience on the reservation was Indians being programmed with, or growing up with, the notion that the white man took everything they have and that they were owed everything because of that. The people there were miserable, because they had been given no incentive to pursue success. I saw a lot of depression and suicide. Alcoholism and diabetes were both prevalent, and the combination was lethal. We saw premature death from cardiac disease. We were very, very careful not to give out sleeping pills, because I saw several deaths, often suicides, due to overdoses. We saw patients come in with lethal doses of chloral hydrate and alcohol, which was known as a Mickey Finn — Indian women, more often than men, would mix the two and commit suicide.

In the middle of my tenure on the reservation, I was flown up to the area headquarters in Aberdeen to be reprimanded for, among other things, wearing Italian shoes with my uniform. Honestly, I was never quite with the program there. I thought it was outrageous how the government just handed the Indians everything. For example, Indians would regularly lose their medicine, because they could easily just get a free refill. And I would have to go down to the clinic at night and refill it! To me, a guy who came up paying for everything, this was absolute horseshit — and that's what I said to the officers in Aberdeen. Liberal bullshit! This is what happens to people when they are given handouts in a welfare state — this is how the liberals destroyed the Indians and how they destroyed incentive among many of the black population in this country. This was the consequence of entitlement. Henry Ford accurately described my perception of life on the reservation in his comment "Any man who thinks he can be happy and prosperous by letting the government take care of him better take a closer look at the American Indian." I was not shy about expressing my opinion that 100 years after these reservations were established, we were still oppressing the Indians by enabling the attitude that the white man had to pay for what he did to them generations earlier. My upbringing, having to pay for everything myself, was the antithesis of what I was seeing on the reservation.

I was working with three other doctors at a seventy-bed hospital on the reservation. I must say, I found that the medical knowledge and experience of my colleagues there was far inferior to my own education and experience. I had graduated from the best medical school — and completed the best internship — in the United States at that time. The quality of my own education was demonstrated to me when I compared myself to the other young doctors there. And we did everything, in terms of medical services, which maybe wasn't fair to the Indians given our level of experience and expertise. The Winnebago reservation was a referral center for all the Indian hospitals in the Public Health Service north of us, mainly in the Dakotas, Minnesota, and Wisconsin. They would refer their diagnostic problems down to the University of Nebraska in Omaha, and they would come through us. They had a plane that would land in Sioux City, and then our ambulance would pick them up and bring them to our hospital. We would do a work up on them, and then send them down to specialty clinics at the University of Nebraska where they would be evaluated, treated or admitted. So here I was getting to see all these diagnostic problems from a huge area because they would filter through us.

While working at the reservation I started to see an epidemic of infectious hepatitis on the Macy Indian reservation in Macy, Nebraska, which was right next to Winnebago and was where we had a clinic. Years earlier, Dr. Baruch (Barry) Blumberg, a physician and anthropologist at the University of Pennsylvania had found a peculiar antigen in an Australian aborigine, which he named the "Australia antigen." This antigen eventually showed up in patients with Down's syndrome, who have a high prevalence of infectious hepatitis. He made the correlation that this antigen could be the virus of hepatitis, and he was right. I wanted to see if I could detect this antigen in the Indians who were coming to the clinic jaundiced, so I took their blood. I called Jim Cerda, who was my mentor in gastroenterology at The Pennsylvania Hospital, but he was going out of town for his annual U.S.Naval cruise as he served in the Naval Reserve, so he told me to call Al Sutnick at Women's Medical College (which is now the Medical College of Pennsylvania) to run these blood tests for me. Al worked with Barry Blumberg at the Philadelphia Cancer Institute, and they were more than willing to run the blood tests. So for four weeks, I took the blood of every patient who came in jaundiced or was suspected of having hepatitis, in addition to anybody who lived in the same house with the jaundiced person. I took their blood also every week for four weeks, hoping to catch the virus as it infected them. We found antibody to Australian antigen, but we did not find the antigen.

After talking over the findings with Blumberg, Sutnick, Cerda and a serologist from Finland named Raunio, we decided to have a meeting in Philadelphia. They felt I was doing something wrong because they couldn't believe that there was no Australia antigen. It was clearly hepatitis because the serum bilirubin levels were quite high, and all the symptoms were all clearly infectious hepatitis. No one had ever shown up to that point in time in the world medical literature that whenever there was hepatitis, there was an absence of the Australia antigen. So I flew to Philadelphia and we met at Sutnick's home on St. James Place in Center City. We sat in the living room and I explained to them exactly how I took the samples, and after clotting/centrifuge put the serum in dry ice and shipped it. I asked them if it ever occurred to anybody there that perhaps it was truly an antigen-negative epidemic and that there were unknown factors like cross antigenicity if we were finding antibody.

They delayed my paper and, lo and behold, we finally decided to publish and just after we submitted the paper for publication, the New England Journal of Medicine featured a lead article about an Australia antigen-negative outbreak of infectious hepatitis in the Holy Cross football team. They scooped me because of the delay by the scientists at the Philadelphia Cancer institute who didn't believe that this could happen. Here I was, the lead author on this paper and, about four years later, Blumberg won the Nobel Prize for his discovery of the Australian antigen, which had opened up so many vistas in medicine. And that's how I, as a young doctor just out of an internship, found myself arguing with a future Nobel Prize winner and other leading figures in their field. Dr. Al Sutnick subsequently became Dean of The Medical College of Pennsylvania.

This period represented a crossroads in my intellectual pursuits because I truly did love gastroenterology. Jim Cerda was my mentor and a close friend when I was an intern at the Pennsylvania Hospital, where he was the head of gastroenterology. Jim was an accomplished individual — he eventually became chair of medicine at the University of Florida at Gainesville, and he also was an accomplished musician who at one time played with Woody Herman. When he visited me on the Indian reservation for a long weekend we went to the bars in Sioux City, and Jim took to the piano and jammed with the musicians. He was terrific fun. Although I finished medical school planning to pursue neurosurgery, because of Jim's influence on me, I was now at a relative conflict over pursuing gastroenterology as a specialty, especially after being exposed to major players in the field like Jim and Barry Blumberg.

But, as it happened, a path leading me to decide on neurosurgery emerged. After months of the day-to-day drudgery of seeing Indians in the clinic and making rounds in the morning, I needed some diversion so I joined the Sioux City Ski Club. At the club I met a neurosurgeon named Horst Blume, a German immigrant who had been in the German army. He claims he fought on the Russian front as a teenager. Horst had trained in neurosurgery under Bert Selverstone at Tufts in Boston. He was not however, a diplomate of the American Board of Neurological Surgery. I mentioned to him how I had an interest in neurosurgery and how I had spent six weeks with The Neurological Group in New London, Connecticut. He took an interest in me, and said he would call if he had any cases for which I could provide assistance.

I was dating a girl named Mary Beth, with whom I was infatuated, and we were lying in bed one night when Horst Blume called. "Can you help me with zee craniotomy?" he asked in his thick German accent. "I'm about to do zee craniotomy on zee woman. She has zee tumor." I quickly agreed, threw Mary Beth in the Jaguar and drove over one hundred miles per hour to get to Sioux City, drop her off at her parents and get to the hospital to join Blume in the operating room. The young woman on the operating table was pregnant — she had been suffering terrible headaches and then a seizure. She came in with what looked like a mass in the frontal lobe, so Blume was going to perform an emergency craniotomy. Again, at this time I was just out of my internship and not trained in neurosurgery. But having had a surgical rotation as an intern, I could at least assist with a sucker and a sponge. Blume performed the craniotomy and sent down specimens to the pathologist, but they were all coming back without showing a tumor. Blume felt he missed the tumor and closed up the patient, but he did not know for sure because frozen sections of brain are unreliable for showing tumor — you need to examine the permanent sections.

I left the hospital around one a.m., picked up Mary Beth, and went back home to the Indian reservation. A couple of days later, Blume called me and I asked what happened with the patient from the other night. He said she was not doing well, that he missed the tumor and needed to go back into surgery. Because of the increased levels of estrogen that are present in pregnant women, a thought popped into my mind about a condition that was quite rare. Maybe she didn't have a tumor at all, I told Blume, perhaps she had a spontaneous thrombosis of the superior sagittal sinus. The superior sagittal sinus is the major draining vein that drains both hemispheres of the brain. If it clotted, there would be inability to drain the hemispheres of the brain causing massive bilateral (both sides) edema (swelling) which this patient demonstrated. CT and MRI scanning had not yet been invented and diagnoses depended on the results of the examination, angiography and pneumoencephalography (injecting air into spinal fluid pathways). At that time, I had never really seen a thrombosis of this type — I wasn't even trained in neurology to come up with a diagnosis like this. Blume then considered my diagnosis but wasn't sure it was correct. The next thing I know, he called me an hour later, saying, "My god!" He looked at her angiogram and saw that the superior sagittal sinus did not fill — my diagnosis was in fact correct! He thought I was a genius!

From then on, Blume started calling me to ask my opinion on cases, which was flattering but unrealistic in view of the fact that I was not trained in either neurology or neurosurgery. He even took me to the 1969 World Congress of Neurosurgery in the New York Hilton — and paid for my airfare and hotel. The field was small enough then that the conference could be held in the New York Hilton because there were a few hundred attendees. When I went to the same conference forty years later, it was at the Heinz Convention Center in Boston, because the number of neurosurgeons attending from around the world grew to several thousand. At the conference in New York, Blume introduced me to George Perret of the University of Iowa, whom he knew from Europe. George was from Neuchâtel, Switzerland. As soon as I met Perret, I realized he was the individual I needed to train me. He was a difficult personality — actually, he reminded me of my father. And I knew my own personality. In fact, Perret told Blume that I was *luftikus.* I said, "What the hell does that mean?" Blume told me, "It's German and means somebody whose head is in the clouds." Perret could see that at that time my interest was in women and having a good time. I could see that Perret was the one that I needed to mold me into what I wanted to become, because I knew that Dr. George Perret was spot on about my persona. After I had applied to Iowa, Perret offered me a residency based on Blume's recommendation, my academic record and National Board scores.

Blume was a great influence on my life. He was a good technician in the operating room. I assisted him ligating an anterior communicating artery aneurysm, one of the toughest cases in neurosurgery, and saving the patient's life. I'll never forget being in that surgery with Blume when a nurse handed him the wrong instrument. Because of the intense pressure of the operation, he got on his knees and starting yelling, "Lord, she is trying to kill zee patient! She is trying to kill zee patient!" He was not unique, however, and like many in the field of neurosurgery, he expressed his way of dealing with the stress of the specialty albeit in a histrionic fashion. He had this beautiful home he built on a large tract of land just outside Sioux City. The driveway to the house was about a half a mile. And he had hills in the back of the house, so he put in a rope tow, and created his own ski resort — he even sold memberships. One day when everybody was on the hill skiing, I went in his bedroom because he had his telescope on a tripod to watch the skiers. I was in there looking through the telescope, and his son's babysitter came in. She sat on the bed next to me and, as I was looking through the telescope, all of a sudden I felt her tongue in my ear. I said, "What are you doing?" And she responded, "I know what I like." Ah, the days of being young!

At the Indian reservation, I continued to see many interesting cases. Very few things got by me. I would diagnose chronic active hepatitis, acute lupus, and subdural hematomas, I would deliver breach babies — things an intern would never do today. Anything from the waist down was fair game surgically by doing a spinal tap and putting in hypobaric anesthesia in the form of Xylocaine. A girl would fall on her bike and get a hematoma on her labia, and I would put that in and incise it. With broken femurs, I would set up what was called Buck's traction. We did everything. Really, the Indians deserved better than having a group of relatively inexperienced physicians performing all of these procedures. But I did have excellent training as an intern at Pennsylvania Hospital —I knew pediatrics, ob/gyn, surgical principles, and internal medicine. I even helped open up a diabetic clinic for the Indians. One snowy night, I got called for a woman in labor. I had just bought a new pair of bright red Fisher skis and, since my house was up the hill, I decided to try out my new skis and get down to the hospital right away. So I skied down — as I did a turn to stop, the snow sprayed across the family, the patient and the door to the hospital. They complained about the incident for years and probably still talking about it today!

97

While on the reservation I communicated frequently with Steve Byrne, a classmate from Jefferson. Steve was serving as a physician in Vietnam and became suicidal. He would send me tapes to play in which he had his M-16 in his mouth and was saying he was going to kill himself. He couldn't tolerate pronouncing innumerable eighteen-year-old kids dead as a routine. I would send him back tapes with my thoughts. I listened to the daily body counts on television, which were underestimated to the public for political purposes.

Steve received a Bronze Star for his service to his country.

I was thankful for my decision to join the Public Health Service not only for avoiding the experience of Dr. Byrne but also for meeting Mary Beth. Mary Beth was nineteen when we met, and had her own apartment in Sioux City. I used to go to the Sioux City Hilton to eat dinner once in a while and I ran into her in the parking lot. I wore a Naval Lieutenant Commander's uniform and this beautiful girl was impressed. The only difference between a naval officer's uniform and an officer in the U.S. Public Health Service was in the insignia on the gold buttons on the jacket, an item not really visible). It turned out she worked at the hotel, so the next time I went in for dinner I saw her and spoke with her again, and we agreed to go out to a nightclub. Subsequently we became intensely intimate for the next six months. She moved in with me. When we split up, I took it really hard. She became involved with a drug dealer for whom she dumped me. He fed her a hallucinogen LSD (lysergic acid diethylamide), which became popularized at the time by Dr. Timothy Leary, a Harvard psychologist. Mary Beth ended up on a psych ward in a Sioux City hospital. She eventually recovered to abandon such activity and went on to lead a productive life. This type of behavior is relatively common in contemporary adolescence and young adults. To be honest, I think that the tragedy of that affair made me fearful of intimacy, in the sense that I never wanted to spend my emotion on someone and then lose it. I think that may have influenced my choice for my first marriage, as my wife was more or less aloof, cerebral, WASP. The breakup with Mary Beth was so hard on me, I must have smoked three packs of cigarettes a day after it happened. If I die of lung cancer, I blame her!

An amusing episode occurred when I received a phone call from Uncle Rocky while rounding in the Winnebago hospital one morning. He wanted me to meet him in LA and accompany him to Las Vegas for a long weekend on his return from Japan later that month. I arranged for time off and flew to LA. He rented a large black Cadillac and we drove through the Mojave Desert to Vegas. As we entered Vegas there were abundant banners and signs representing a celebration. The signs stated "Welcome Pueblo Crew." The Pueblo was a United States Navy gunboat, which was boarded and captured by North Korean forces on January 23, 1968, in what was known as the Pueblo incident. The Koreans claimed we strayed into their sovereign waters. They captured the crew and imprisoned them where they were severely beaten. After intense international negotiations over the incident the crew was finally released. Incidentally the North Koreans realized that crewmen were secretly giving them "the finger" in staged propaganda photos. They were released in December 1968 shortly before my Las Vegas excursion.

Whenever traveling I always wore my uniform as the airlines offered a discount to active duty servicemen. The USPHS wore Navy uniforms and I had lieutenant commander stripes. Coincidentally I had fractured my left tibia in a ski mishap three weeks prior and my left leg was in a cast from my ankle to my upper thigh. It slowly dawned on me after being picked up by a third Las Vegas beauty that people assumed that I was part of the Pueblo crew, who had been beaten by the North Koreans with particular attention to my left casted leg I then understood these girls were just showing me their appreciation for my assumed heroics. No one asked me and I never told. I spent the first night in a spectacular penthouse apartment in the Sands Hotel with an African-American dancer who lavished me with her patriotic duty.

In late September 1968, three months after I arrived on the reservation, my parents came to visit. They took the train, as my father had free passes to go wherever he wanted because he worked for Erie Railroad. As I had a two-bedroom house, they stayed through the month of October. I took them to dinner in Sioux City, and I bought a television so we could watch the Summer Olympics from Mexico City. I never saw my father have such a good time because he saw that I was an M.D., that I really had accomplished something. I last saw my dad alive at the Sioux City train station where my parents departed en route to Philadelphia. While riding through the Nebraska terrain with my father next to me I noticed how similar the architecture of his hand was to my own and I realized that I was his immortality. I can still remember the night I had my last conversation with my father on the telephone, and I told him that I was going to pursue neurosurgery as a career. What was really tragic was that I was in bed with an Indian girl who worked at the hospital in the laboratory and I didn't want to talk to my father too long because I was about to entertain her. So I told him I would call him tomorrow, but we did talk for at least ten minutes. He died the next day. My mother found him next to the closet on the floor. He was seventy three years old when he died in November 1968, three months shy of his seventy fourth birthday. My father had suffered from angina from the time he was fifty; I would see him walk a block, and he would have to stop and rest. I flew back from the Omaha airport to Philly for his funeral, which I paid for. When I returned, I thought often of my dad as I sat in my house and watched tumbleweeds roll across the Nebraska plains.

I was able to make spending money during my time on the reservation by covering for a family doctor named Max Coe in Wakefield, Nebraska, which was about a forty-five minute ride from Winnebago. Max had a sign on his door that said, "Bones Set, Bullets Removed." When you used the bathroom and lifted up the toilet seat, it said "Go Big Red" — Max and everyone else there was mad for the University of Nebraska Cornhuskers football team. Max loved to gamble. He would take off for a few days to Las Vegas and he would pay me and my colleagues $100 a day to cover his practice, which was great money back in 1968. If we stayed overnight, it was $120. While we took turns covering Max's practice, I did see some harrowing cases. One time I was called out in the field to find that a tractor had overturned on a farmer. He had a crushed pelvis and I knew he was in shock because one likely hemorrhaged retroperitoneal with a crushed pelvis. An ambulance arrived with IVs and I put a big bore needle in his vein where I could find one, but he arrested right in the middle of the cornfield, and I couldn't save him. I had to go up to the house and call for his wife. She came down the steps, and I told her I had very bad news for her. Before I could say anything, she was screaming. The shrieking and screaming was unforgettable, resonating throughout the two-story framed farmhouse. It was horrible to have to tell someone that their loved one died — a very, very difficult experience, especially for a young doctor who wasn't yet hardened.

Another common injury in this area of the country occurred when cars would be going at a fast pace over the top of a hill, but the driver did not know there was a tractor right on the other side of the hill, going in the same direction in the same lane, but traveling five miles an hour. That's why you would see signs saying "Danger: Tractor" on the roads because it was a common cause of death to slam into the back of a tractor that you couldn't see and that was going one-tenth of the speed you were traveling. For a Philly guy like me, another oddity of living in the Midwest was tornadoes. You would see a descending finger-like dark funnel while riding across Nebraska or Iowa, and you didn't know which way the damn thing was going! One time I was in Sioux City, I saw the funnel cloud coming so I ran into a bank building. As I was lying on the floor of the bank, I saw the tornado lift a police car and deposit it down the street. Years later, after I began sailing, I would see something similar while racing to Bermuda — it was called a waterspout. It looked just like a tornado, but it was over the ocean. You had to worry it was coming in your direction because in a sailboat, you are only going seven or eight knots and certainly not going to outrun it.

One of the most significant cases I encountered on the reservation was an Indian boy who came in with a spinal cord compression at the junction of where the skull meets the spine, at the foramen magnum, from osteochondroma. This child had multiple *exostoses* of bone, which are little outpouchings from cartilage abnormalities. He had one that compressed his spinal cord at the foramen magnum and caused his demise. I transferred him to neurosurgery at the University of Nebraska where patients with diagnostic problems would go. He expired during his hospital stay. I went to the Nebraska hospital and did a postmortem myelogram, putting dye in his spine and running it to the base of the skull. This was highly unusual, but I felt it was necessary to learn more about the case. I was able to demonstrate how the osteochondroma pushed on his cord, right where the cord met the brainstem. I published this with a review of the literature of multiple exostoses. Tom Langfitt, chair of neurosurgery at the University of Pennsylvania reviewed the paper, and it was published in the journal *Neurology*. This was noteworthy for someone just out of his internship to have two major papers published in respected academic journals (also counting my paper with Blumberg and others).

Things were looking good for my academic career. After meeting George Perret at the World Congress of Neurosurgery, I ran into Tom Langfitt, the neurosurgeon at the Pennsylvania Hospital where I had interned. Langfitt recently became the Chair of Neurosurgery at the University of Pennsylvania. I had not done my elective with Langfitt because I preferred to work with Jim Cerda in gastroenterology. Langfitt may have resented my choice. When I saw Langfitt at this meeting, I had also applied to Penn but had not yet been accepted. I told him I was interested in coming to Penn, and that I had been accepted to Georgetown and Iowa. He said, "Well, a bird in the hand is worth two in the bush." Ultimately I was accepted for residencies at Georgetown, Iowa and Penn. Langfitt, after dragging his feet, finally came through with a spot for me but I felt more comfortable with George Perret and declined. I had been waiting to hear from Yale, but I went there for an interview and the chairman of the department, Dr. Collins, did not show up for the interview, so I wrote Yale a letter saying I decided not to go there. I was offended that I traveled halfway across the country for the interview and he couldn't be bothered to show up. En route to New Haven, however, I was able to visit my cousin Romolo, the Italian diplomate. We enjoyed dinner at his Greenwich, Connecticut home on Deerfield Drive. There was a mural of a pastoral Japanese scene in the dining room. He spoke fluent French with his Haitian maids. He also took me on tour through the Greenwich hospital. He died not long thereafter in Florida at age ninety. As for Georgetown, I liked the idea of being in Washington, D.C., but I saw a lot of foreign medical graduates in the program and on the staff, which at the time was frowned upon. Today, more than half the residents in New Jersey and New York are foreign medical graduates, but that was not the case in the '60s. There were only about seven to eight thousand graduates of medical schools in the United States in 1970 — that number tripled by the early 2000s. Also there were only 90 first year positions in neurosurgery. In the mid-1960s, if you had a lot of residents from, say, India, Korea or the Philippines, the program was not looked upon as academically pure. So, Georgetown and Yale were out, leaving me to choose between Iowa and Penn. So I wrote Langfitt that I had decided to train at the University of Iowa, thanked him for his advice on my recent paper, and spent the night before I left the reservation in the Sioux City Hilton with a beautiful lifeguard from the Sioux City Country Club who was a student at the University of Kansas. And then I got in my Jaguar and rode across the State of Iowa to Iowa City.

The time spent on the reservation was invaluable for taking what I learned in medical school and during my internship and putting it into practice. I was relatively isolated and I could not turn to a resident or attending physician for help. It gave me enormous confidence. Frankly, my colleagues were not helpful because they were not as well trained as I was. For the most part, they did not have a rotating internship (exposure to all services including medicine, surgery, peds, ob/gyn, emergency medicine, otolaryngology and urology) as I had but rather "straight" internships meaning they were exposed to only medicine or surgery for that year as the rotating type internships were being phased out. I learned another very crucial lesson through observation during these years. Of the four doctors there, the one whom I judged to have the least knowledge, but who was a fine person, was the most popular with patients. Everyone who came in that hospital asked for him because he was kind, compassionate, sympathetic to their needs — a hand-holding doctor who would take the time to listen to patients and commiserate with them. His medical knowledge was the antithesis of his personality. And it taught me a great lesson. Later in life, I realized that a surgeon who had mediocre or less knowledge was apt to get sued. If he had good bedside manner, however, he was going to get sued far less than the surgeon who had excellent knowledge and lousy bedside manner. Because patients don't know what you know. They are not able to determine if you are doing the job correctly. Some of the worst and least knowledgeable physicians—even dangerous in their incompetence—sometimes had large practices. Another important issue warrants discussion as well. If you are a surgeon, you can't hide your results in a community, but you sure can in a university setting. If you are hurting people in the community, everybody knows it — word gets out among referring doctors and patients. But that's not the case in the university. Someone may be a total hack, but patients figure he is better than a doctor in the community because he is at the university. Both the community surgeon and the university surgeon finished equivalent training programs, yet there is a spurious perception that if one stays at a university hospital he is immediately "smarter" and better. Nothing could be further from the truth. Moreover, if a surgeon has difficulty with his technical ability the place to hide is in the university. Patients will keep coming because of the reputation of that institution. Surgical ability is not germane to the individual who is world-famous for his research papers. One, of course, has nothing to do with the other. He might be world renowned, but a disaster with a scalpel. I have witnessed as much incompetence in the university setting as in the community hospital. This is why I say your SAT scores don't reflect your ability to bring people together, to make crucial judgments in business or in life and certainly have nothing to do with abilities required in an operating room!! They are just not related.

These lessons would be reinforced in the strictest, most intense period of training in my medical career under George Perret at the University of Iowa, where I was headed next after saying goodbye to the reservation.

CHAPTER VIII:
IOWA

"University politics are vicious precisely
because the stakes are so small..."
— *Henry Kissinger*

When I left the Indian reservation in Winnebago, Nebraska, on June 30, 1970, I put the top down on my XKE and headed for Iowa City. As I pulled into the city, I listened to a new recording, *Teach Your Children*, by Crosby, Stills, Nash & Young on the radio, and wondered, "What am I getting myself into?" Iowa took in two new residents each year in neurosurgery, and I was looking at this five-year residency as an adventure. I didn't know if I was going to like it, or if I was even cut out for it. But that fear of the unknown also was a motivating force. Every time in my life I was confronted with a challenge, I would always reach inside and find that part of me that would say, "Bring it on!" I think it goes back to the competition I experienced in rowing. When it comes to the last five hundred meters, you have to reach inside — and that's what I always did, no matter what the challenge was.

I chose to take my residency under George Perret, the chairman of neurosurgery at the University of Iowa, because I felt he was the one who could teach me the most. My instinct was correct, as he became a seminal figure in my life and career. You did not simply learn from Perret — you had to survive him. He struck an almost unassuming figure, with his medium height and build, crooked teeth, male-pattern baldness, French accent, and brown buckskin shoes. And within the field, he was a relative unknown — not a high-powered researcher producing academic papers like the chair of neurosurgery at Penn, just a solid physician who was a no-nonsense, strict taskmaster with the residents he trained. But make no mistake, Perret was a force whose training developed me into the neurosurgeon I became.

At the time, the University of Iowa was the largest teaching hospital in the United States with a resident house staff of over one thousand physicians and over one thousand hospital beds. It offered some of the top, number-one-rated residencies especially in the surgical subspecialties in America. Patients arrived from all over the country and the world for care.

In neurosurgery major university hospitals on the east coast could not begin to approach the volume of brain tumors treated at Iowa City. It was also the only tertiary center in the state and attracted patients from surrounding states as well. There was a university ambulance system

The Division of Neurosurgery University of Iowa *circa* 1973 (George Perret bottom center, Carl Graf to the left of Perret, Tony Chiurco top row third from right)

that provided transportation from the small farming communities bringing patients for specialty opinion, surgery or inpatient medical care then transported back. There were hotel facilities for families as well to facilitate the support patients need in times of health crises.

In some ways, Perret reminded me of my father. The reason I survived Perret, when many others left or were dismissed from their residency, was because my father shared a similar approach to discipline. My father did not hit me, but he was very verbally abusive — and so was Perret. He spoke fluently or frequently in French and would scream at me in French in the operating room. To me, the yelling was familiar — it was just like home. I'm sure for some of the residents it was disheartening to deal with this behavior if they had never been exposed to verbal abuse. If you are sensitive, it can really knock the wind out of you. Perret was a no-nonsense, ruthless perfectionist. He once threw out a surgeon who was a professor of neurosurgery from Egypt who wanted to get his American boards, because during his operations he would get blood on the drapes. With Perret, you had to be neat and careful — and God forbid you hurt a patient. He would rip you a new asshole and you were not going to operate until he decided that you learned your lesson. This is why the results at Iowa were excellent. To tell the truth, this type of training doesn't exist anymore. But in my view, that is what is needed in a field like neurosurgery, which is so dangerous. Now what I see coming out of residencies often is mediocrity, i.e. inattention to detail, lack of concern and dependency on MRI scanning rather than a painstaking neurological assessment.

Perret made me paranoid, to which I attribute my strong surgical results and negligible litigation in my career. When confronted in practice with any situation, I looked at studies and planned my approach. Let's take a patient with an anterior communicating artery aneurysm, an extremely delicate and difficult case. I would plan the best way to get at the neck to avoid the dome and an intraoperative rupture, the timing of the diuretic agents such as mannitol, the timing of induced hypotension — everything detail was carefully planned to prevent complications. I would call continuously to talk to the nurse taking care of the patient even after I had left the hospital. You have to be right on top of post-operative assessment and management. You have to be concerned and paranoid about something happening in order to get ahead of it. The difference is in attention to detail. This is what Perret hammered into his residents, time and time again. Complications are avoidable most of the time or minimized if meticulous attention to detail in patient care is followed. Any success I've enjoyed in my career, I attribute to Perret, for training me his way, making me paranoid about getting complications, making me think critically, and making me look for reasons not to operate because surgery was dangerous, especially in the era in which I trained.

Before I began my training in neurosurgery, I had to do a one-year residency in general surgery at Iowa. In my first year, we had a thirty-five-year-old male patient who came in with significant weight loss and an eczematoid rash. Everyone in the University who was connected with gastroenterology had seen him, including the head of gastroenterology, Jim Christianson, and all of the surgeons and professors. No one could understand why this man had lost this weight. One night I was sitting at the desk in the lounge and noticed a copy of Howard Spiro's seminal text, *Clinical Gastroenterology*, which one of the senior residents had gotten as a present from a pharmaceutical company. I was attracted to the book because it had a bright red cover (my favorite color) and I started to page through the text, looking for information that might pertain to this puzzling patient whose problem no one could solve. I came across a footnote of a case reported by McGavren, one case in the world literature where the patient had weight loss, diabetes and an eczematoid rash. One case. It wasn't even in the print – it was at the bottom of a page as a footnote.

So I looked up the case, because our patient had diabetes also. It said this fellow had an extremely rare tumor of the pancreas that secreted glucagon, a hormone secreted by the pancreas that raises blood glucose levels. I reached out to Jim Cerda, my mentor at Pennsylvania Hospital, and asked how I could get a glucagon level for this patient. He pointed me to Anne Lawrence at the University of Chicago, who told me how to send the specimen. I took his blood and sent it to Chicago. A week later, my name was called over the paging system at the hospital in Iowa City, and I took the call from Anne Lawrence asking, "My god, where did you get this blood?" She told me the glucagon levels were sky high and that if I had suspected this man had a glucagon-secreting tumor, that diagnosis was surely right. Well, to make a diagnosis like this as a first-year resident was extraordinary, and Jim Christianson offered me a fellowship in gastroenterology without having to do an internal medicine residency. The surgeons and faculty were so impressed by this. I also impressed them by giving a "grand rounds" presentation on my findings from the hepatitis study at the Indian reservation, which showed that Australia antigen was not the only virus of hepatitis. These two factors combined gave me a reputation as an extraordinary young doctor. But the truth was I just happened to be sniffing through a book and found the case that led to the glucagon-secreting tumor diagnosis. If anything, I was an opportunist. I told Christianson that, as much as I loved gastroenterology, I really wanted to pursue neurosurgery. But I was heartened that my first year in general surgery turned out to be a success.

During my initial month of residency in general surgery having just arrived at Iowa City, I would park my car quite early in the morning, usually around 6:30 am when the garage was relatively empty. Some mornings I would accompany other house staff at five am with a thermos of coffee and a bag of donuts. We would shoot pheasant from an automobile with shotguns from the car windows on country roads outside of Iowa City. We never got out of the car and it was a fun activity before rounds. After one of these excursions I drove to the hospital. I liked to park against the wall on the first level so that the car would be protected from inclement weather. One morning after parking I was walking briskly towards the University hospital when an elderly gentleman yelled to me to get my car out of there. I said, "Excuse me sir?" He said, "Get that car the hell out of there, that's for us. That is not for you, move it!" And I said, "Fuck off, pal. If you don't like it move it yourself!" And I continued walking toward the University. About four days later one of my attendings approached me, Dr. Hrair

Gulesserian, who was the cancer surgeon at the University Hospital and whose service I was assigned to. We were friends. He came to me and said, "Oh, Chiurco, you are in such trouble. Flocks wants you fired, he wants you out of this university immediately." I said, "Who the fuck is Flocks?" He said, "Ruben Flocks? He is the Head of Urology and is very, very powerful." Gulesserian then went on to explain how Flocks wanted me to move my car and I told him to go fuck himself. I said, "Well, I'll worry about it another day," not being that concerned. The next thing I knew about an hour later, George Perret, the Chairman of Neurosurgery, whose residency I was about to enter the following year called me over when he saw me walking in the hall and said, "Chiurco, come here." And it was then I knew that I was in deep shit and more likely than not would be fired. I was imagining packing up my room and leaving Iowa City. As Perret approached his mustache was twitching to either side, a habit I grew accustomed to in later years. As he said with his characteristic French accent, "Chiurco, do you own a green Jaguar convertible?" I said to myself, "Shit, here it comes." I answered in the affirmative. Perret just looked at me and smiled and said, "Good, very, very good!" and just walked off. Then it dawned on me that Perret appeared to be pleased that one of his residents told Ruben Flocks to go fuck himself because as I gradually learned Flocks pretty much had his way in the University hospital and pushed people around. Moreover, as I learned throughout the residency, my attitude and reaction to Ruben Flocks was compatible with Perret's concept of what a neurosurgeon should be—a no-nonsense, aggressive, son of a bitch and the antithesis of the mild-mannered, benevolent physician stereotype. Ruben Flocks, who by rumor had operated on the prostate of the Shah of Iran, was world famous and had the number one urology residency in the United States at the time. An example of Flocks power occurred when the University hired a new Chairman of Surgery, Dr. Robert Condon, who decided to bring in a plastic surgeon to the hospital. Flocks was the driving force along with Brian McCabe, the Chairman of ENT, that got Condon fired. Neither Flocks nor McCabe were willing to give up any plastic surgery that their urology residents or the ENT residents were performing. Years later as Chief Resident in neurosurgery I again got into trouble when I was called in an emergency to the otolaryngology operating rooms. Brian McCabe was doing an acoustic tumor through the posterior fossa that is, the suboccipital approach, a standard and strictly neurosurgical approach. He got into significant life threatening hemorrhage that he could not control and I was called to bail him out. I got in there and stopped the bleeding and turned to McCabe and said, "You are out of your territory, pal," not knowing that McCabe was as powerful as he was, nor did I give a shit. Once again, McCabe made a lot of noise and wanted me kicked out but was unsuccessful. Egomania it appears has its boundaries.

Carl Graf's accusations that I was abusive had some validity.

During my year in general surgery, I was assigned for three months to Ed Mason and the "fat team." Mason was the pioneer of surgery for obesity, as the inventor of the gastric bypass operation. He originally started with clamping the stomach a third of the way down, allowing just a passageway to fit two fingers from the upper one third of the stomach to the lower two thirds of the stomach, so that as people ate they would feel full immediately — and if they overate, they would have to throw up. This was a very clever innovation. On the fat team, we would get patients between four hundred and eight hundred pounds. We routinely would have to push two operating tables together to tend to one of these morbidly obese patients. The mortality of operations to address morbid obesity — called barometric surgery — was ten percent, but for these patients the odds of surviving the surgery were better than their odds of continuing to live in their current state. I was called upon to work with the fat team because these patients were so huge the surgeons needed extra hands in the bodies to expose the anatomy. Three decades after my residency, barometric surgery became very popular in America, but it started at Iowa in the 1970s under Ed Mason.

In addition to my time on the fat team, I was exposed to a wide range of cases and procedures on the general surgery service. I learned how to handle patients, fluids, blood loss, shock, wound healing and other key facets of the surgical experience. I was permitted to do less risky surgical procedures, such as removing gallbladders and appendices.

On the general surgery service, we evaluated patients in the surgical clinic twice a week. The highlight of going to clinic for me was ogling Elke, a beautiful former Pan Am stewardess from Bavaria who worked as the clinic secretary. I would always stop and talk to Elke, admiring her beautiful face and figure and hoping that I would eventually find my way to her boudoir. One morning in June with a particularly busy clinic as usual I stopped to hit on Elke. Although she was busy she suggested that I come to visit her and have lunch with her that Saturday. I was now pleased with myself because this was real progress. So, Saturday morning looking my best I drove out to Solon, Iowa, which was twenty minutes from Iowa City. Elke told me where she lived and that it would be very pleasant having lunch overlooking Lake McBride. I found what I thought was the correct address, walked up to the house and knocked on the door. A tall blonde haired man answered and I assumed I knocked on the wrong house. I said, "Excuse me I must be at the wrong address. I am looking for Elke." He responded to my astonishment, "You must be Tony. We were expecting you." And I said, "What?" I had no idea who this man might be. He then volunteered, "I am Elke's husband." And I said to myself, "Oh no" as my blood pressure dropped in severe disappointment along with my pulsatile erectile tissue as I realized that Elke was just being nice asking me to lunch because she liked me "as a friend." I tried to hurry through lunch because I was not interested in being "friends" and had to get out of there and move on. What was about to happen, however, was a game change in my life. Elke's husband, Chase Hunter, an ophthalmology resident and an ex-Vietnam chopper pilot, said to me, "Tony, would you like to go sailing? I keep a boat at the dock here behind our home." Thinking I needed to get out of this situation I said, "Yeah, sure I would like to go sailing although I don't know how to sail and have never been sailing." Chase then took me onto this sixteen-foot sailboat on a day with high pressure and blue skies, gentle breeze with the wind at ten to twelve knots. We sailed hard to windward up Lake McBride. The boat heeled over gently about twenty degrees and we put our weight on the windward rail. This moment struck me with the same intensity as when I saw Dr. John Whitely lift the frontal lobe of a patient in the operating room with the very first craniotomy I ever witnessed. As I knew instantly that neurosurgery was for me I knew that sailing would be a lifelong pursuit. Getting from point A to point B by tacking was pure geometry. The sensation of apparent wind in my face and the physical challenge of a heeling boat were of enormous appeal and persists to this day. Since a sailboat cannot sail directly into the wind the tactics of sailing to a destination as well as the various positions of the sails with respect to the apparent wind angle were of great intellectual curiosity and appeal. The failed attempt to seduce Elke Hunter because of a miscalculation of her marital status turned out ultimately to be a silver lining in my life. Many years later, having participated in many of the world's great ocean races and world cups, I went on to win numerous regattas as a member of the New York Yacht Club and won several North American championships with particular attention to the International Twelve Meter Class, the yachts used in America's Cup competition following World War II.

Whenever the opportunity arose I went out to visit Chase and Elke to continue my sailing lessons. We became great friends. Elke and Chase ultimately moved to South Carolina after he finished his residency where he entered the private practice of ophthalmology.

After twelve months on the general surgery service, I moved on to neurosurgery, where I spent my first six months in radiology. We learned to master cerebral angiography, in which you would either stick the carotid artery directly in the neck and inject dye to see the blood vessels in the brain, or pneumoencephalography, in which you would sit the patient in a chair that rotated upside down and sideways and you would inject air into the spinal fluid via a lumbar puncture. The air would rise to fill the ventricular system in the brain providing a contrast i.e. density differential so an observer could see the outline of the ventricles and determine if they were shifted or displaced by an underlying tumor. It was a barbaric procedure. We had several deaths doing pneumoencephalography. Patients screamed with headache during the procedure, which was not performed with anesthesia except on children. Now if a patient had on examination papilledema (blurred optic discs) looking in their eye grounds, which suggested increased intracranial pressure, you would have a mortality if you did a spinal tap to inject the air because the brain would herniate down, compress the midbrain at the incisura (where the brainstem passes through the opening of the dura shelf on which the cerebral hemispheres sit). So we would drill a hole in the cranium and put a cannula into that ventricle itself and inject air and pantopaque, which was an oil-based dye, and watch it flow down to see if there was any shift of the normal anatomy. That was called ventriculography.

Pneumoencephalography, incidentally, was found to be a great diagnostic tool by serendipity at Johns Hopkins by Walter Dandy, one of the giants who helped establish our specialty. One day a patient came in with a skull fracture that caused air to get into the head. The air filled the ventricular system and demonstrated beautifully its anatomy. Dandy realized the potential of his observation as a diagnostic tool since neuroradiology was primitive in the 1930s.There was also great difficulty when he was trying to diagnosis patients with a tumor or hydrocephalus. That became the start of neuroradiology. For patients with a focal deficit, like weakness on one side, they would get an angiogram, in which the carotid artery would be punctured and dye injected up under pressure into the vessels of the brain, and then the x-ray machine would rapidly sequence as the dye went through. You would have multiple films per second and see the arterial phase, the capillary phase and the venous phase. If you were doing more than one vessel, both carotids, or the vertebral artery, the catheter would be put in from below, through the femoral artery, and you would thread it into the carotids or vertebral inside. Of course that's still done today, but in 1971 this was accomplished without CAT scanning or MRI scanning. They were not yet available and under development. Cerebral angiography was discovered and developed by Egas Moniz, a neurosurgeon in Portugal who also served as an ambassador in the Portuguese diplomatic core. He received the Nobel Prize in medicine not for angiography, a valuable diagnostic test still very much in use today, but for the invention of the frontal lobotomy, an operation no longer performed.

The other procedure we had to master was myelography — looking for spinal cord or nerve root compression either in the cervical or lumbar spine. You would inject pantopaque into the spinal fluid in the lumbar region and look at the lumbar spinal canal, or tilt the table down and look at the cervical canal or the thoracic region. For six months that's all I did — angiography, pneumoencephalography, ventriculography and myelography. For the most part, all of these procedures have been superseded by MRI and CAT scanning today. Myelography is still done presently but not often. In conjunction with CAT scanning however, it remains the definitive gold standard for evaluation of neural compression within the spinal canal. The newer dyes for a myelogram are water soluble, and they are excreted in the urine, but when I was learning these procedures you would have to reinsert the needle and suck the dye out when the procedure was over. This was painful because the nerve roots would get sucked to the side of the needle. At the time, forty-plus years ago, these were state-of-the-art techniques.

The deaths involving pneumoencephalography typically involved children, which was very tragic. We would do the procedure in adults, too, especially people with severe headaches as we didn't know if the cause might be a tumor or hydrocephalus, which is an enlargement of the ventricles inside the brain caused by obstruction in the spinal fluid pathway (non-communicating) or impairment in the absorptive pathways (communicating) where production of spinal fluid in the ventricles exceeds absorption causing the ventricles to enlarge. In radiology in the early 1970s, the initial work-up was a skull series. You looked to see if the pineal gland was calcified, because that structure was in the midline. And then you would look to see if it was shifted to one side or the other on a frontal view of the skull. You would look for radiographic characteristics of increased pressure in the skull films, such as in the sella turcica, which is a transverse depression crossing the midline on the superior surface of the body of the sphenoid bone and containing the pituitary gland. All of this intense radiology knowledge is obsolete these days, because you can see the brain much better through MRI scanning than at autopsy! But it was critical for me to learn how to perform thorough examinations and master these procedures because we did not have the benefit of technology like doctors do today.

After the six-month radiology rotation, I moved on to taking care of the neurosurgery patients on the neurosurgery floor and serving as a second assistant in the operating room. Patients with tumors, aneurysms and other neurosurgical issues would go from the neurology service to the operating room, and then to the neurosurgery floor. In between the neurosurgery floor and the operating rooms were the intensive care unit and the post-operative unit. Severe head injuries would go to the ICU, and less severe cases would go to the post-op unit for closer observation. On our daily rounds on the neurosurgery floor, it was necessary to perform a detailed neurological assessment because we did not have CAT or MRI scanning. You had to rely on examining the patient and understanding the subtle changes that could occur as a harbinger of developing hemorrhage or increased intracranial pressure. Change in the mental status, change in the pupillary dilatation or reaction, change in the motor findings — these were the signs we were trained to detect. Neurosurgeons being trained these days don't know any of these things with skill because they trained with machines. It's a different world today. This is not to say that these technologies do not significantly improve patient care, because today you can see in two minutes what was hotly debated for an hour fifty years ago. So if you're not so smart and not so skilled or not so well trained, you'll get by today.

During the first year, we would get up at six a.m., make rounds between 6:30 and 7:30, and then work in the operating room all day until about three or four p.m. Then you got out of the O.R. and saw consults or new admissions. You were usually done for the day around 7:30 or 8:00 p.m., so it was a long day. I devised a reading program for myself and I owned just about every available book on neurosurgery, neuroanatomy, neurophysiology and neurology. Every night, I would read and read in this big leather chair that my mom bought me for $90. After one year, I knew neuroanatomy cold. My dedication to neuroanatomy and neurophysiology studies enabled me to pass the written board of neurosurgery after one year of residency, which had never been done at Iowa. The only problem was that I was not eligible to take the exam for credit in the second year of training, which was March 1972 in the middle of my six-month stint in neuropathology. We were supposed to take the written board for practice just to impress upon us how much we didn't know. When I passed it everyone was pretty much in shock. The funny thing was I continued to maintain a playboy image — and I certainly did enjoy spending time with women — but nobody really knew that I was studying most of the time. I knew that there was going to be no free lunch as far as gaining the knowledge necessary to succeed and that the boards were not going to be easy. So I started from day one. I even used to read neuroanatomy while I was in general surgery, memorizing everything because you really had to know it cold. In fact Perret called me into his office and said, "How could the chief resident flunk? Does he drink?" I said with a laugh as I could not resist reinforcing my playboy image; "I don't know. I'm in the bars every night and I never see him." Perret just shook his head and waved me out of his office.

I subsequently took it the following year when I was eligible and again passed.

In the start of my second year, I moved up to first assistant in surgery and took care of the post-op unit and the ICU patients. We saw a plethora of brain tumors, severe head trauma, cervical spine trauma, quadriplegia, intracranial hemorrhage and aneurysm rupture cases. You name it, it came in there every four hours. It was not for the light of heart, because it was human tragedy after human tragedy. Young mothers with malignant tumors, fathers with sudden death from aneurysm rupture. Quadriplegic teenagers asking, "When will I walk again?" We would put them on circle electric beds, so that they wouldn't break down their skin, which they almost always did, from pressure sores. One memorable tragedy occurred to a beautiful twelve-year-old girl who fell on an escalator while shopping with her mother. Her hair was caught in the moving steps as the escalator arrived at the next floor ripping her entire scalp off the skull and breaking her neck. She arrived with permanent quadriplegia. We spent weeks putting skin grafts on her bare skull after drilling holes through the outer table to create bleeding bone which might accept the graft by providing a blood supply.

After six months as first assistant, I went onto neuropathology. We would look at autopsies of intracranial deaths and what was called brain cutting. We took the brain out of a cadaver or corpse, and you'd have to fix it for three weeks in a formaldehyde solution before you could cut it to determine the cause of death. You couldn't cut a fresh brain, because it would be in a gel form and fall apart with cutting. You have to fix it to make it firm and then cut it, then dissect the vessels and look for aneurysms or other causes of death. We had brain cutting once a week, and the brain and brain stem would be cut vertically about every inch so as not to miss a small tumor or other pathology. The rest of the time I would study.

Every day I would show up with a towel that I had my bathing suit in, and after brain cutting or looking at slides of tumors under the microscope, I would go over to the swimming pool at the university and swim a mile. One day, one of the neurologists who was rotating on neuropathology with me asked where I was going. He and I both called each other "Doc." I told him I was going over to the pool, so he asked to join me. I was swimming laps in a 50-meter pool, and I was not a bad swimmer. He showed up, we got in the water, and I thought I would leave him behind in no time. But before I got to the other end of the pool, he had already made the turn and was on the way back. After the workout, I got out of the pool and said, "OK, Doc, where the hell did you swim?" He said, "Oh, I swam for Doc Counsilman at Indiana" (who happened to the best known collegiate swimming coach in the country). I said, "So, how well did you do, Doc?" He said, "Well, I did swim in the freestyle in the Rome Olympics." I looked it up and, sure enough, my colleague, whose name was Al Somers, was a U.S. Olympic swimmer! He broke the 400 meter freestyle Olympic record at the Rome games.

I always kept myself physically fit, which I recognized early on would be an important factor in succeeding in neurosurgery. You can't be in the operating room for ten or twelve hours and then go out and start seeing head injuries and making rounds without being physically fit. So during my neuropathology rotation I made sure that every day I either swam a mile or ran three miles. Even now, I try to maintain my physical fitness by rowing. The only thing I didn't do during my years in Iowa was stop smoking. I didn't quit smoking until the late 1990s, even though in the

1970s and 80s I watched my uncles — who were all Lucky Strikes or Winston smokers — die of carcinoma of the lung.

Moving into my third year in neurosurgery, I was sent to the VA hospital so I could be on my own before becoming chief resident at the university. At the VA, you got to be independent but you were always with a staff person whenever you went into the operating room so he could instruct you while you performed surgery on the brain, spine, and peripheral nerves. After six months at the VA, I moved over to become chief resident at the university for nine months. In this role I had the ultimate responsibility, and the workload was tremendous. I had to have a history and a physical and neurological assessment on every patient that came in. I had to teach the younger residents coming up. Not everybody survived to be chief resident. In my five years there, including general surgery, I saw six people either leave or get fired in neurosurgery. We were always shorthanded on the service. There was one resident from Harvard who was on call one night and simply disappeared. They found his beeper on the desk and never heard from him again.

Perret was very difficult and could be eccentric at times. Once at 3:00 a.m. he called me because he was making rounds at an unusual hour and looked over my progress note on a head injured patient who had been on the neurosurgery floor for over a month. He stated, "You did not record the reflexes in your examination." To perform a detailed neurological assessment on a patient lying around for over a month was quite frankly absurd. I had to get out of bed, travel through the ten-below-zero Iowa night, and honor his request. Perret could be extreme. When he fired you, he would leave a note on your door. He didn't talk to you or call you in his office. He just left a note that read: "Your services are no longer needed." But he was right. You were either going to do what he expected or you were out. And if he did not think you were neurosurgery material, you were out. He once fired a resident for being nice — he said there was no place for nice in neurosurgery. And I can understand where Perret was coming from in those days, because I learned in my career that there isn't a place for nice in neurosurgery. The stakes are too high.

Another example of George Perret extending a teaching moment to extremes occurred at the time of my very first craniotomy. I was completing my second year of training when Perret admitted a patient who was forty years of age and presented with a headache and seizure disorder. A pertechnetate brain scan, a primitive study, compared to today›s MRI and CT scans, demonstrated a mass in the right frontal lobe, most certainly meningioma because of the dense uptake. A large frontal lobe tumor with swelling will cause personality changes in the form of apathy, disorientation, indifference, lack of spontaneity, and render a patient rather dull. As we entered the operating room, Perret questioned me as to what incision I would make for this particular tumor and how I would remove the bone flap. I answered his questions to his satisfaction when he said, "I want you to do this case." In retrospect, the right frontal lobe of the brain in a right-handed patient is in the non-dominant hemisphere and is an ideal location for an inexperienced surgeon. Surgery in this region potentially would have the least or minimal harmful effects. Naturally, I was as excited as I was fearful, since this was the first time I would ever open someone's head. After the cranial flap was made and I lifted the bone overlying the tumor, there was significant bleeding from the dura, which is the covering over the brain, which was somewhat difficult to control. Perret was excited and started yelling for blood to be brought to the room. I was able to get the bleeding under control with gentle pressure, a fundamental surgical principal, which most often will stop excessive bleeding. Gradually and slowly, meticulously, the larger tumor was removed after the dura was opened. I was able to roll the tumor out of its bed in the white matter of the brain where it was submerged like a peach. Because the incision was cosmetic, i.e. behind the hairline, it extended from the front of the left ear to the front of the right ear and the scalp flap reflected down over the eyes. It took a long time for an inexperienced surgeon like myself to close the wound-- to wire the bone back, close the dura, close the galea and then subsequently the scalp. It took at least an hour and a half. When I finished the closure, Perret came back into the room and said, "You left a cottonoid in the tumor bed." And I said, "Sir, I do not believe I did so." He insisted that I did. Perret made me reopen the entire craniotomy and find the cottonoid, which he knew was there the whole time, but he let me close anyway. He then stated, "If you do that in private practice, you will be sued for over a million dollars." If there had been strings on the cottonoid as there are today, the hidden cottonoid would have been readily recognized because the string would be coming out of the wound. In that era, however, cottonoids did not have strings and when filled with blood you could not tell them from blood stained white matter of brain. This was Perret's method of teaching me to be meticulous and always be sure the sponge count is correct. The surgeon must be paranoid. More than forty years later, I have yet to leave anything in an operative site, which I had to reopen to remove. It may not have been fair to the patient, but the only rationale was that the patient was asleep and it did no surgical harm. Was Perret's lesson worthwhile? I will leave it up to the reader to decide. This patient was separated from his wife and undergoing a divorce, and the reason his wife gave for wanting the divorce was that the man had changed from the man she had married. The reason his personality had changed, however, was because he had a tumor in the frontal lobe. His condition caused him to become apathetic and indifferent and to lack spontaneity. Once he had a seizure, the tumor was found. After I took it out, Dr. Perret made me carry the tumor down in a jar to show the wife because he had seen similar situations. He wanted me to impress upon her the cause of this man's personality change. So I took the tumor down to the postoperative waiting area and showed the wife his tumor in a jar. I explained to her how big it was and what it had done, and that he had a very good chance, over a year, to regain his original personality. But I think that the damage may have already been done as far as emotional toll on the relationship. This was nature at work.

The patient and his wife eventually divorced despite his complete recovery. Life is cruel to many people — and if you want to know how cruel, do a neurosurgery residency.

After my tenure as chief resident, I spent time on neurology seeing patients in the clinic. During these years, I learned how to handle my emotions. As a neurosurgeon, you have to put your feelings in a freezer and detach yourself from the drama around you. But of course you are still human. I can even recall Perret being affected after operating on a beautiful, seventeen-year-old red-haired girl. He went through the back of her head to take an ependymoma out of the fourth ventricle, which is sitting right on the brainstem. She was awake for a while, but then became unresponsive in the recovery room. She bled in the operative bed. As chief resident, I tapped her ventricle because she developed acute hydrocephalus, and we took her back to the operating room. Perret re-operated on her and took out the clot that was sitting right on the medulla, but she died. It was a very difficult experience. But as a neurosurgeon, you have to be able to face it. You have to accept that maybe something could have been done better. You have to explain it to the family. You have to confront the family's grief. And you have to be able to understand that this has happened and will not uncommonly happen to every neurosurgeon. He will question whether he did the optimal thing, whether he could have done it better, whether his judgment was the best at that time. Is he obfuscating the result through a delusion that he really did what was called for? Is he in denial as to what he failed to do, or failed to realize, or didn't know, or didn't pay attention to? As a resident under Perret, I learned to address these painful questions and still come back the next day, ready to do the same procedure again.

The first time I saw a death on the operating table was when Carl Graf, a veteran neurosurgeon at Iowa, was operating on an aneurysm. Graf, in my opinion, should not have been operating aneurysms. He was dissecting a middle cerebral aneurysm with a sucker and the aneurysm exploded. I actually got nauseous and felt like vomiting for the first and only time in my long career as a neurosurgeon. I lost a patient in the same way twenty-five years later. And I keep asking myself, even now fifteen years after I performed that particular surgery, if I could have put the clip on differently or used a different clip. It still haunts me. I have had four aneurysm fatalities in my career, and I remember everyone in detail. In fact, I operated on aneurysms for seventeen years before my first aneurysm fatality. Three of those fatalities were women on whom in my opinion I performed technically flawless surgery, but they never woke up. Now, for these four cases, there are well over one hundred postoperative aneurysm patients that walked out of the hospital fine. But every surgeon suffers through patient mortality, and it may affect some surgeons more than others. I look back and ask how I might have done these cases differently, but I don't know if I could have. Sometimes there are no right answers. If you are doing high-risk surgery, you are going to have mortality. American Board scores, academic achievement, and publications have very little relationship to technical skill and surgical success.

An amusing incident occurred during my chief residency in neurosurgery. One night a gentleman came in on the urology service through the emergency room with his penis hanging off and held to his body by a small piece of skin. What occurred while the gentleman was enjoying a bout of fellatio from his girlfriend, was that she inadvertently had a grand mal seizure. When people seizure, they typically clench their teeth and as she clenched her teeth she bit off his Johnson. The story went around the entire university hospital by morning. The urology residents were up all night sewing this patient's penis back on. Ultimately they were successful with microsurgical technique. The next morning en route to Horsley, which was the name of our operating theatre in neurosurgery I stopped and banged on the door of the head nurse who ran the operating room. She said to me, "What do you want, Chiurco?" and I said, "I'm requesting that every nurse that works in the operating room be placed on Dilantin immediately." She looked at me and slammed the door in my face. The reader must understand that Dilantin is an anti-convulsant and my implications were not amusing to her. The story caused enormous laughter among the staff as my antic spread beyond the operating room floor.

When I was chief resident, I was performing an emergency shunt on a three-year-old boy, and Perret insisted that the distal end of the shunt —which went from the brain ventricle to the right atrium of the heart — be put in the right atrium, rather than the peritoneal cavity in the abdomen. The boy had been operated on before, and the venous pathway was scarred down. When I tried to advance the tubing into the heart it would not go. It was standard procedure to use a dilator to break through the scar. Unbeknownst to me, it opened up a hole in the vena cava as it entered the atrium. Post-operatively the child died from an undetected cardiac tamponade — the blood got between the heart and its covering, the pericardium. This was my first operative mortality. Even though it was not recognized as such, try to live with that — killing a three-year-old boy. I was so disturbed that, for the first time, I wanted out. I did not want to do this. I could not face having that complication. And if you think that's difficult, try getting up the next day and putting another shunt in another child. To this day, it's as fresh in my mind as if it happened yesterday. It's a haunting memory. Maybe I am super sensitive, but parents who trusted me lost their child's life. That's what a surgeon has to live with. I learned as a resident that this profession is not for the light-hearted, and it takes a certain amount of courage to go on after these things happen to a surgeon. A sociopath might have an easier and less stressful life.

Professor Carl Graf was a significant figure in my time at Iowa, but for the opposite reason as Perret. Graf looked — and acted — like a hawk. He had thick grey hair and was tall, with a hawkish nose and a protuberant belly, and walked around with his Phi Beta Kappa key hanging from his vest and quoting literature. Graf had a very prominent upper bridge — almost a little bit more prominent than Humphrey Bogart — so he would speak through his teeth. He and I did not get along. That's being kind — actually, he disliked me. In my opinion, Graf was a misanthrope and the antithesis of what I considered a professor of neurological surgery.

One night Perret gave a dinner party at his home for the residents and staff. Graf made some comments about seeing me fooling around with one of the scrub nurses in neurosurgery, who was a very sexy-looking girl. And he commented that she never gave him the time of day. And I said, "Well, maybe she has graphesthesia," which is a term in neurology but was, of course, a play on words with his last name. (If you write a number or a letter on a patient's hand with their eyes closed, they should be able to detect what number you wrote or what letter you wrote. But if there is a parietal lobe lesion, then they can't tell what you wrote — that's called graphesthesia.) Well, Graf didn't take kindly to my joke, but everyone else was beside themselves with laughter — Perret almost choked! I think Graf, being paranoid as he was, felt that I was derisive toward him and after that was on a quest to have me fired.

Graf actually was a skilled surgeon but a lousy aneurysm surgeon because he never re-educated himself as to conventional techniques for aneurysms. He was dismissive of the five percent mortality rate reported from Zurich by Professor Yasargil. In public conference he called those results "bullshit." One of my most vivid memories of Graf took place during my chief residency. A young man in his mid-twenties came in on the neurology service with a ruptured A-V malformation, which is something you're born with where the arteries go directly into the veins. There are no capillaries —it looks like a bag of worms, all blood vessels, and they can rupture. This young man had ruptured into his dominant temporal lobe, and Graf refused to operate on him, saying it was a waste of time because such patients don't do well in surgery. The neurologists led by Maurice Van Allen were furious with Graf for not operating. Van Allen was the brother of the famous physicist who discovered the Earth's radiation belt, which bears his name. I felt that this was a mistake in judgment. And sure enough, this young man was left severely impaired then expired.

About two weeks later, a pregnant woman in her third trimester was brought in after rupturing an intracranial carotid aneurysm. She had a large hematoma in the temporal lobe, and Graf told me not to operate, that it was not going to help. I went behind his back, since he wasn't the on-call attending that day, and I asked Shige Okawara, another veteran and associate professor of neurosurgery to help me. He agreed. I told him I really wanted to operate on this woman. First of all, I thought it was possible to save her life. Second of all, she was pregnant. Third of all, I needed the experience. If they were going to let her die, at least let me get the experience of operating on her. So I took her to the operating room with Okawara and performed a craniotomy. Graf came up into the operating room. My goal was to just take the blood clot out and stay away from the aneurysm — to operate on a freshly ruptured aneurysm in that era of neurosurgery carried about a ninety-five percent mortality risk. My goal was to take the clot out and hope that she didn't re-bleed, and to worry about the aneurysm another day. At the same time the obstetricians were doing a cesarean section on her to extract the baby. This type of high drama is not only seen in movies! As I was taking the clot out, Graf started moving the operating room lights all around and yelling, "Get in there. Get in there with your sucker." Okawara whispered to me with his Japanese accent, "Don't go with sucker. Trying to get you to kill patient." Graf wanted nothing better than to rupture this aneurysm, because he knew I was a completely inexperienced aneurysm surgeon. And that would have been a disaster for the patient, a mortality for me, and proof of point for Graf to show the neurologists that he was correct in not performing surgery on severely impaired patients with intracranial hemorrhage such as the young man with the malformation.

Heeding Okawara's advice, I just took the clot out and didn't touch the aneurysm. As soon as I took the clot out, the obstetricians prepped the belly and took the baby out, because we didn't know if the mother would survive. I opened up the mother's neck and put a Selverstone clamp on her carotid artery, which would lower the head of pressure on the aneurysm, which arose from the distal, intracranial portion of the carotid. I would then on a daily basis turn the clamp down gradually and hope the artery occluded. If the patient developed any neurological Impairment from gradual clamp occlusion the clamp would be reopened and attempts made another day. Sometimes the clamp was left with the carotid partially occluded if complete occlusion was not tolerated. This type of treatment is obsolete today after the advent of microsurgical techniques and instrumentation for aneurysms especially with the use of the operating microscope. Six weeks later, I saw this woman walk out of the hospital with her husband, holding his hand and carrying her baby. Thankfully, Okawara kept me from killing this patient. As for Graf, I used to dream about knocking on his door and parting his hair with a 12-gauge shotgun. As far as I was concerned, Carl was a misguided misanthrope, and a terrible aneurysm surgeon who couldn't face the fact that he was obsolete. Graf's mortality rate was at least thirty-three percent. He may have been good in his day before technical advances, such as the operating microscope and micro technique with micro instruments, but he was oblivious to the advances.

Years later, Graf blackballed me from getting a job. He disliked me so intensely. It had nothing to do with my knowledge — he felt I was abusive. Well, I was abusive because that's the way I was treated as a child and as a resident. And if my father hadn't been verbally abusive, I would have left Iowa just as half a dozen others did. But it was just like home to me. And Perret protected me. No matter how much Graf was opposed to me, Perret protected me because he respected the fact that I was knowledgeable enough after one year of neurosurgery to pass the written board and I had excellent surgical results.

Perret was the opposite of Graf in every respect. Perret may have yelled a lot, and even smacked residents and staff on the knuckles with surgical instruments when he was mad, but he was a good person who was very concerned about residents doing the right thing. He was a very good teacher who ran an excellent program. He made sure there was always a staff member scrubbing with a resident and made sure the patients got the best care possible. The great thing about Perret as a teacher was that he would instill in his residents that they should look for reasons not to operate. In my career I have seen so many surgeons that trained at institutions where they were taught to always look for any reason to operate. And this is a great issue in the private practice of surgery, where a decision to operate or not to operate, has direct remuneration to the surgeon based on his decision. Patients need to be protected from surgeons who operate in the gray zone, where it's really not definite that surgery is going to be beneficial.

One trait that Perret shared with Graf, however, was a reluctance to think progressively about advances in neurosurgical technology and techniques. By the time I studied under him at Iowa, Perret was in his mid-sixties and would be dismissive of anything new because he felt that most innovations, sooner than later, would be found to have problems and not really worth much. This was one area where I disagreed with Perret, because that's what a university was for!

When I was a second-year resident, I realized from my own reading that the management of closed head injury was obsolete at Iowa. And I took it upon myself to pay for a flight to Richmond, Virginia, to see Don Becker, who was chair of neurosurgery at the University of Virginia. Becker had come up with a bolt that you screw into the skull to measure intracranial pressure, which was the proper way to manage these severe closed head injuries. Becker and his team showed me how to put the bolt in and I took it back to Iowa, but Perret wouldn't let me use it because he thought there was a risk of infection. I actually thought about leaving the program over this issue, but to leave a program to go elsewhere was very difficult. One night a severe head injury came in the emergency room, and I had to call the attending, who happened to be Perret. I thought, "OK, here it goes. If he says no, I'm out of here." And I told Perret I would like to monitor this patient's intracranial pressure. "Fine," he said and hung up. I was shocked! I put the bolt in, and it turned out the patient had normal intracranial pressure. Typically a patient in this scenario would be given dehydrating agents and minimal fluid, which is actually harmful in someone who has normal intracranial pressure, because it was assumed that was the best treatment: keep the patient relatively dehydrated to prevent the brain getting too much volume because it was assumed that the intracranial pressure after severe head injury was always elevated. Through this experience, I created an awakening that changed the entire management of closed head injury at Iowa. I presented my findings in a large series of head injured patients with monitored intracranial pressure to the Congress of Neurological Surgery in Vancouver, Canada in 1974.

Another interesting occurrence was the sudden decrease in emergency room admissions for severe head trauma toward the end of my residency. I was typically up every four hours during the night but suddenly for some unexplained reason we were getting sufficient sleep. It took several weeks to realize that a gasoline shortage prompted lowering the highway speed limit to fifty-five miles an hour for the first time in our history. The impact on death and disability from head and spine injuries, most of which happened from road accidents was so dramatic that fifty-five miles an hour became a national standard to this day, another discovery by serendipity which should have been common sense which I realize the longer I live, is not so common.

Though Perret did relent in the instance of placing intracranial pressure monitors in severely head injured patients, I did realize that ultimately I would need to do a fellowship at a different university to learn techniques that were not offered at Iowa. Neurosurgery is practiced differently at different institutions. This recognition ultimately led me back to my hometown of Philadelphia and a fellowship at the University of Pennsylvania with my laboratory at The Pennsylvania Hospital where I had interned several years earlier. Neither Langfitt nor anyone else at Penn ever bothered to call Iowa for a recommendation. They remembered me, my academic ability, my work ethic, and my personality.

I went back home where I came from.

CHAPTER IX:
THE PRACTICE OF
NEUROLOGICAL SURGERY

"If I got upset I would not be very good at my job, now would I?"
— James Bond, Agent 007 responds to Vesper Lynd
after killing two people in the film Casino Royale

My embattled relationship with Carl Graf created a significant problem as I moved toward the end of my residency at the University of Iowa. Graf undermined me with the goal of making it impossible for me to find a job, as payback for what he considered my abuse toward him. However, I had the benefit of forging good working relationships with other respected figures in the neurosurgery community, and Tom Langfitt from the University of Pennsylvania stepped in to provide the opportunity for a fellowship in the fall of 1975 that would help take my career into its next phase.

Langfitt was a world-renowned neurosurgeon, who was trained under Earl Walker at John's Hopkins. Langfitt focused his research on head injury. He eventually served as vice president of health affairs at Penn before leaving health care administration to become president of the Pew Charitable Trusts and the Glenmede Trust. I knew Langfitt very well from my time as an intern at Pennsylvania Hospital, and had remained in touch with him during my residency at Iowa. After our encounter at the World Congress of Neurosurgery, when he cryptically told me that "a bird in the hand is worth two in the bush," Langfitt ultimately did accept me for a residency at Penn. By that time, however, I already had made up my mind to train at Iowa under George Perret. When my residency was completed, Langfitt agreed to take me on as a fellow at Penn followed by an Assistant Professorship, without so much as asking for a recommendation. He knew me well enough to know that Graf's efforts to undermine me were rubbish and had nothing to do with my skill and potential as a neurosurgeon. He told me that he didn't have any lab space to assign to me, so I would have to put my lab at Pennsylvania Hospital with Fred Simeone, a noted neurosurgeon.

I was very thankful for Langfitt's faith in me, and I liked him very much. Langfitt was the archetype of a successful surgeon — tall and handsome, always sharply dressed in pinstripe suits and horn-rimmed glasses. His distinguished, square-jawed features bore a resemblance to a young Jack Lemmon. He was a Princeton graduate (and later served on its Board of Trustees) who spoke with a little Virginia twang and carried himself in a very cerebral, aloof manner. While he was a well-respected and world-famous neurosurgeon, I don't think his hands-on expertise in the operating room was his greatest strength. But as a researcher and administrator, he was brilliant.

After my years of training at Iowa, when I landed at Penn as a fellow I thought I landed on a different planet in terms of the difference in approach to neurosurgery. At Iowa, our training was focused on patient care, whereas at Penn it was all about the next research paper. Langfitt was, as I said, a gifted researcher — his work on intracranial pressure and cerebral blood flow was legendary around the world. But he was not as talented in the operating room as in the research lab, nor was he primarily interested in patient care. I saw more complications at Penn in a month than I saw at Iowa in a year. Patient care just wasn't what was stressed. This helped reinforce for me that I made the right decision to train under Perret at Iowa.

As a fellow at Penn, I lived on the sixteenth floor of Hopkinson House, a high-rise condominium community in Center City Philadelphia. I practiced with Fred Simeone, conducted research in my lab at Pennsylvania Hospital, and attended meetings and conferences at Penn.

Simeone had an enormous practice at Pennsylvania Hospital, covering all of South Philadelphia. Simeone and I would alternate nights, covering hospitals such as St. Agnes, Daroff (Einstein Southern), Metropolitan and St. Luke's, in addition to Pennsylvania Hospital. Fred, who is now retired, is a very intelligent man and a good surgeon. I learned a lot from him during that stage of my development and evolution as a surgeon.

Fred also was great fun — we used to laugh a lot during my fellowship. Fred is well known for his collection of rare racing sports cars. He has one of the top collections in the world and is on display at the Simeone Automotive Museum in Philly, which has attracted visitors such as Jay Leno and Mario Andretti. Many nights while working together, Fred and I would eat at Villa di Roma and Cous' Little Italy in South Philly, which were run by a guy named Cous Pilla and were among the city's best-known restaurants. Cous was a local legend and allegedly the best southern Italian chef on the east coast. His restaurant was frequented by actors, politicians and mob bosses, as well as regular families from all around South Philly. Cous would often come out and visit with his customers, sitting at the table telling stories and jokes. One night, Fred and I were having a dish of chicken Sicilian with linguini and talking with Cous, when he took a phone call. He listened for a moment and then barked into the receiver, "Look, lady, I'm closing at 10:30. You're not here by 10:30, I can't feed you. I don't care who you're a friend of — 10:30, that's it!" He hung up the phone and I asked, "Who was that?" He said, "Some broad who says she's a friend of Billie Jean King. Some Evert broad." I said, "Chris Evert? Cous! She's the greatest tennis player alive!" He said, "I don't give a shit — she ain't here by 10:30, she ain't getting fed." That was Cous.

I knew Cous very well from frequenting his restaurant. One night, I remember examining him right on the butcher table in the kitchen of his restaurant after he developed acute back pain. Years later, when I was in practice in Mercer County, I used to take people down to Cous' for special dinners, because no one cooked as well as him. One night I brought a group in for dinner and he told us we had to stay in the main dining room because Angelo Bruno — one of Philly's most infamous mob bosses — was in the back room with his bodyguard.

Well, one of my dinner party guests, Joy Backes, whose husband Bill was a well-known attorney in Trenton, got up and marched toward the back room. Cous and the rest of us were shocked. "What's with her?" Cous yelled. "Get this crazy broad back here!" We all rushed to follow Joy as she walked into the room. Angelo Bruno saw Joy, rose from his chair, and proceeded to open his arms to give her a big hug! It turns out they were cousins. Cous didn't know what to make of it. An interesting observation was Judge Pelletieri, a prominent figure in Mercer County dining with Bruno. (As a Philly historical footnote, Bruno was shot and killed after eating at Cous' restaurant, as was another mob boss, Phil Testa, and others.) In my own experience, Cous was a wonderful guy and a terrific cook who always sent me gifts when my children were born and always made me feel welcome — and full!

During my fellowship at Penn, I was able to firmly establish that my interest was in surgery, rather than in academic research. During that time, while practicing alongside Fred Simeone, I was in my lab at Pennsylvania Hospital doing investigation with electrical responses called evoked responses, which no one was doing in 1975. I would clip the middle cerebral artery in cats through the transorbital approach, inducing an infarction in the ectosylvian gyrus of the cat brain. Then I would put an electrode on the gyrus and put auditory clicks in the animal's ear, which would cause evoked responses in the gyrus. As the gyrus infarcted after applying the clip on the middle cerebral artery, the electrical potentials would come down, and I would try to bring them back with various protocols for stroke. In other words, I was investigating what a surgeon could do to keep the brain viable as determined by electrical response rather than metabolism. Part of the problem I had was a terrible allergy to cats. I would weep with rhinorrhea (runny nose). I had a lab technician who assisted with the investigation, but I had to conduct the surgical parts of the work. Ultimately, as I gained more experience, I realized that I did not want a career where I tried to combine surgical practice with academic investigation.

During my fellowship, I met Frank Pizzi, who was chief resident at Penn and, like me, an Italian American neurosurgeon. I think 90 percent of the Italian American neurosurgeons in the country were at Penn in 1975 — myself, Fred Simeone, Frank Pizzi and Lenny Bruno, my resident. When I met Frank, we immediately got along well, with a great camaraderie and shared sense of humor. By the time I concluded my fellowship in July 1976, Frank had launched a practice in Mercer County, New Jersey, and he invited me to join him. With $30 in the bank (no, that's not a typo — $30), I decided to take him up on the offer. Simeone wanted me to stay and made me a reasonable offer, but I was not fond of our professional relationship and knew that departure would be in my best interest. I realized I was Fred's "fall guy" i.e. high risk cases, such as tumors in the calcarine cortex or on the motor strip where in the process of removal, the occurrence of complications such as blindness or paralysis could be significant were delegated to me. The decision maker occurred one morning when Simeone asked me to close an operative case he had finished because he had to be at a meeting. I was free and went to the operating room, closed the dura, wired back the bone, and closed the scalp. Simeone had been operating in this patient's third ventricle in the form of biopsy. Post-operatively the patient was vegetative. I heard, "I let Tony do the case and look what happened."

I declined the appointment of assistant professor but did remain on the staff at The Pennsylvania Hospital. In subsequent years Simeone was fired as Chairman of the Department of Neurological Surgery at Jefferson. Rumor surfaced of injudicious behavior not dissimilar to what I experienced. It was unfortunate and unnecessary because Simeone was a very good surgeon with an excellent fund of knowledge.

I packed my bag and moved to Mercer County, New Jersey, to join Frank Pizzi in the practice of neurological surgery.

At that time I had been married to my first wife for about two years. She wanted to live in Princeton because Princeton University's Gothic architecture resembled that of Duke University, where she went to college. I borrowed the money to make a down payment on a house on Brookstone Drive, and we settled in Princeton. Frank and I established our practice as NeuroGroup, P.A. Our first office was a small space at

Five Points on Quakerbridge Road where five streets came together. Our office building had been the previous site of a church, which had exploded. It was easy to direct patients to our office, we would just comment, "It's where the church blew up."

When he first set up in Mercer County, Frank would bring his aneurysm cases down to Pennsylvania Hospital because the hospitals in Mercer County were not equipped for these types of high-risk procedures. I would assist him at Pennsylvania Hospital. Once we went into practice together, we had to develop the capacity for handling high-risk cases in Mercer County. We upgraded the hospital operating rooms, especially at St. Francis Hospital in Trenton. We acquired operating microscopes and developed the operating room to do high-risk intracranial surgery. The first CAT scanner in Mercer County was acquired at Mercer Hospital around 1978, not long after the first scanner was acquired in Philadelphia at Episcopal Hospital. Henry Shenkin, the neurosurgeon at Episcopal, demanded the scanner but the hospital refused because of the expense, so Shenkin arranged to acquire the scanner and own it personally. He made quite a bit of money through this arrangement because no one else really understood the amazing impact that this technology would have on patients with neurological impairment. Computerized Axial Tomography (CAT Scanning) was invented by Hounsfeld of the UK and revolutionized the practice of neurological surgery. Henry Shenkin, incidentally, was the person who informed me that my last name means "surgeon." In the Greek roots, "chi" means "hand," and "urgon" means work. The surgical societies in Europe are known as "chirurgical" (chi + urgon) societies.

When Frank and I came to Mercer County, Walter Scheuerman and William Segan were the local neurosurgeons in practice. Scheuerman, who had trained at Penn, was covering hospitals from New Brunswick and the Jersey Shore to Cape May because there were very few neurosurgeons in the 1950s and the 1960s when he developed his practice. The field was very, very young and very stressful for neurosurgical specialists. You know, there's probably a good reason why the earlier generations of neurosurgeons were borderline crazy — they dealt with tremendous morbidity and mortality and human tragedy, with primitive techniques, primitive instrumentation and primitive diagnostic ability.

The far-flung nature of early neurosurgeons' coverage areas did not lend itself to the best patient care. Obviously there should have been a way to centralize neurosurgical patients such as occurred in later years in trauma with development of trauma centers, but that's not how the field developed. In our era, we realized that it was not prudent to do high-risk intracranial surgery in every hospital. So we centralized initially at Mercer Hospital, where there was a CAT scanner. But then when St. Francis acquired a CAT scanner, we moved all the high-risk intracranial work from Hunterdon and Mercer County to St. Francis Medical Center. Around 1981, our group of three neurosurgeons (we had added a colleague named Fred McEliece) performed more than 100 craniotomies at St. Francis Medical Center. We subsequently added a fourth surgeon to our group, Frank Schinco, who trained at Northwestern University in Chicago and whose parents owned a famous northern Italian restaurant on Washington Square in Philadelphia named Gaetano's.

It has been shown that high-volume centers have lower morbidity and mortality than community hospitals where risky procedures would be occasionally performed. The higher-risk cases should be centralized, and that's what we did with base skull tumors and aneurysms in particular.

Starting in private practice, I was a bit nervous and apprehensive. You are on your own and there is no one looking over your shoulder anymore in a high-risk, high-pressure field. It was do or die, literally. At a university you can be shielded if you encounter a lot of complications, but that's not the case in private practice. You cannot kill or maim. NeuroGroup covered eight hospitals: Lower Bucks, St. Mary's in Pennsylvania, Hunterdon in Flemington and the five hospitals in Mercer County. In our early years, we had to reverse the trend of the local family doctors sending their neurosurgical cases down to Penn and Richard Davis, who was the king of bedside manner and had a huge practice of cases coming down from Mercer County. Frank started the practice in Mercer County because during his time at Penn he saw how many cases from our area were being referred to Davis and realized there was an opportunity to gain a hold in the market by establishing a practice here.

When I arrived at Penn, Richard Davis was Professor of Neurosurgery. He was an intelligent man and a relatively slow surgeon. When I left Iowa City, George Perret made a comment, "You're going to meet one of the worst I have ever seen." I did not know who he was talking about nor did I ask. However, I did recall Perret's association with Loyal Davis when Richard Davis, his son, served his residency. Most of Richard Davis' practice were patients with lumbar spine disorders referred to him by Eric Simon, a neurologist at Mercer Hospital in Trenton, New Jersey, who once told me he pronounced his name "Sim-own" so that he would not be "mistaken for a Jew." Simon had served in the Hitler Youth Corp as a teenager. He was enamored with the German Army, especially the Panzer Division. Richard Davis was a kind gentleman who also had interest in the Third Reich. He once published in a surgical journal the results of his interviews with families of the Nazi hierarchy as to the manner they met their demise. Rumor has it he was given twenty-four hours to get out of Czechoslovakia or be arrested. The key factor enhancing his practice was an outstanding bedside manner. Apparently Richard suffered under his father, Loyal Davis, who was extremely prominent as Chairman of Neurosurgery at Northwestern University in Chicago. He was a founder of the American College of Surgeons. One famous story explained how hundreds of inner-city predominantly African Americans would be seen in emergency rooms long after Loyal Davis' retirement with gunshot wounds, stab wounds, and other criminal injuries with the name "Loyal Davis" in front of their surname. It was traditional even in my era as an intern for house staff to name babies they delivered, which again were predominantly among the inner-city black population. Loyal Davis was allegedly a bigot and disliked ethnic groups as much as the house staff disliked him. Their retribution was giving all these babies his name and legacy. Many stories about the Davis family were told to me by George Perret after my fellowship which again surfaced in Kitty Kelly's book, *Nancy Reagan*. Loyal Davis had Richard with his first wife and Nancy with his second wife. Nancy Davis married Ronald Reagan, a Hollywood actor who subsequently became the thirty-ninth President of the United States and Nancy Reagan became the First Lady. I spoke with her at some length at a cocktail party at Richard's home when Reagan announced his candidacy for the Republican nomination. She was ambitious for her husband and a driving force in his candidacy.

It is noteworthy that there was no love lost between Richard Davis and Thomas Langfitt, the Chair of Neurosurgery at Penn. They intensely disliked each other. Langfitt was unable to get rid of Davis because Davis had a large practice and was allied with the right people. It is noteworthy that they were both graduates of Princeton University, where Langfitt served as a Trustee. I recall when Richard's daughter was denied admission to his alma mater he angrily declared that Ronald Reagan will never give a commencement address at Princeton University.

Once we established NeuroGroup, we ran into a problem with Eric Simon at Mercer Hospital. He made his living performing myelograms and angiograms on patients, which was more lucrative than consultation work. He did not want competition. Therefore he continued to send surgical patients to Davis at Penn, instead of keeping the patients in the community. Patients told me that Dr. Simon said that they could not have their operations — even simple cases like disc ruptures in the neck and back — in Trenton because there was no one who was capable to do the work. One year, I went to the medical record room and saw that he had discharged fifty-one patients with a diagnosis of herniated lumbar disc and sent them down to Penn. So I had to take it to the hospital board because the hospital was losing tremendous income through these actions. He denied the accusations. We ran into a similar problem at Princeton Hospital, where a neurosurgeon, James Beggs, was successful in keeping us out on technicalities for a good year or more, until they could not keep us off the staff forever. It was a rude awakening to the realities of medical practice. Here I came out of a residency and fellowship, eight years after medical school, and I could not get onto hospital staffs because of people protecting their pocketbooks. Roger Baisis delayed my application at Hamilton Hospital. Walter Sherman delayed my application at Lower Bucks Hospital for more than a year.

The early days of our practice were very, very difficult. Every hospital would have severe head injuries coming in with patients on ventilators and hysterical families, and we were taking care of these patients in three counties. We got on the staff at Hunterdon in 1978 after an orthopedic surgeon, Connie Stover, called me and said, "I have a child here with a broken neck. We need a neurosurgeon." I said, "Well, I don't have staff privileges at Hunterdon." He begged me, "Please come up." So even though I wasn't on the staff, I drove up there in a new Chevy Impala that I had just purchased. En route I listened to a Fleetwood Mac song "Dreams" on the radio. When I got to Hunterdon, I put the child in tongs and reduced the fracture. Then I operated on him and fused him later on. Every time I hear that song, I think of that child.

Another night around that time, I was eating a steak in Lorenzo's in Trenton across from the train station after working late. It was about nine o'clock and the staff brought a phone to the table so I could take a call from the Hunterdon emergency room. Two surgeons from Philadelphia were severely injured in a glider crash. I rushed up to Hunterdon and saw the patients. I saw the first surgeon but I couldn't do anything for him. He appeared to have consumption coagulopathy and brain death. The second one lived. The wife of the surgeon who expired was an internist and sued Hunterdon Medical Center and all of the doctors on call. She did not sue me. Thereafter, Hunterdon refused to accept trauma patients. Trauma cases in Hunterdon County were thereafter sent to Sacred Heart Hospital in Allentown, Pennsylvania. We did not have our first trauma center in Mercer County until 1993 at Helene Fuld Medical Center in Trenton.

Covering all these hospitals was not easy. We would have patients on respirators in five different hospitals, driving around to make rounds and trying to care for all of them. If I was on call at night, I might get calls from three or four different emergency rooms, about patients with severe head injuries, spine injuries, cervical fracture dislocations and quadriplegia, and I would have to get out of bed and race to the hospitals to tend to the patients. I remember one night getting out of bed going down to Lower Bucks Hospital, putting a cervical fracture dislocation in tongs and then doing a craniotomy for an acute subdural hematoma. At two a.m. I left Lower Bucks and drove up to Hunterdon, where I had another acute subdural hematoma. I opened that head up at 3:30 a.m. and got back home at six a.m. This is an example of the life we led as community neurosurgeons trying to provide excellent service to patients in need in three counties.

Life was not easy.

There are so many tales of human tragedy that I witnessed in my years of practice. I remember a young mother, thirty-eight years old, coming into the emergency room. I examined her, and she was brain dead. She had hemorrhaged into the brain stem and forth ventricle. The husband thought she had just passed out. He was out there in the waiting room with his three of four kids, and I had to go out and tell this poor man, with his kids still on his lap, that she was dead. That is neurosurgery. It can be devastating. I just destroyed somebody's entire existence. And there were the children, asking "Where's Mommy?" If you want to see something awful, see children crying for their mother, see a grown man go to pieces, crying for somebody he really loves.

I saw countless patients come in after accidents. In the Princeton Hospital, there was a little waiting room nearby the intensive care unit where we talked to families. There were so many times I had to inform families about their teenager, their husband, their wife, their mother — to be the bearer of terrible news. It was devastating. What's even worse is a complication with surgery. I remember a case removing a tumor that was going well until all of a sudden, toward the end of the case, the brain started swelling uncontrollably and herniating out of the craniotomy. I had to do a lobectomy, meaning I had to take off the frontal lobe. I ended up with a patient who was hemiplegic (paralyzed) on one side. The tumor was malignant, but I still had to go out and talk to the family. Of course they're going to think it's my fault, and of course I knew it was not. In those situations you go through the protocol prior to the procedure to make sure the brain swelling doesn't happen. Then you have to stand your ground and explain to the patients' family what happened, why it happened, and what the consequences are, which obviously is a very difficult thing to do.

Neurosurgery is not for everyone.

When I was on the Indian reservation I learned of an unfortunate incident in Sioux City, Iowa where a neurosurgeon, Carroll Brown, had to operate as an emergency on his son after a motor vehicle accident, since Dr. Blume, the other neurosurgeon, was out of town. His son died. In my mind this had to be the most awful occurrence in the life of a surgeon to be forced to operate on a loved one, especially a family member. In 1995 on a Sunday afternoon I was called to the emergency room at Princeton Hospital where an elderly woman was having seizures due to an acute subdural hematoma after a fall in Merwick, a nearby retirement facility. I arrived to learn it was my mother. All the neurosurgeons in Mercer County were away for the weekend. I was confronted with the probability of having to do a craniotomy, my worst nightmare. I was fortunate to find Ira Kasoff at home in New Brunswick watching a ball game. He did not have staff privileges. He came down immediately and after we stopped the seizures we observed her for several days, delaying surgery as long as she remained conscious. Subsequently, the hematoma liquefied and Frank Pizzi drained it through burr holes. She recovered only to expire in the ensuing weeks sustaining a stroke from an embolus due to atrial fibrillation after discontinuing anti-coagulation.

Frank and I remained associated until 2011 — we enjoyed a long, fruitful association. We had an amicable separation because Frank developed a practice at Hunterdon and was not active in Mercer County. I was busy in Mercer County at Princeton Medical Center, so it was not cost-effective to continue the association. Over the years, we had several associates in NeuroGroup, but Frank and I were the core. In 1978, we took on Fred McEliece, whom Frank knew from Children's Hospital. Fred trained at Hahnemann under Axel Olsen and was a good surgeon and an intelligent man. Fred stayed with us for about ten years and then split off because he thought our overhead was too high. It was a compliment to me when Fred McEliece had enough confidence to request that I operate on his mother with a dominant middle cerebral artery aneurysm from which surgery she made an excellent recovery with a normal neurological examination. Sadly, Fred passed away in 2011.

As part of our practice, before MRI scanning became more prevalent, we used to do myelograms (injecting dye into the spinal fluid) to tell whether or not a patient had nerve compression. I insisted on putting an imaging center in our office at Quakerbridge Plaza because we were traveling to multiple hospitals in the afternoon doing studies, and I thought we could more efficiently do them in our own office. I felt particularly strongly about that after the introduction of water-soluble dye to be put in the spinal fluid, where it was excreted in the urine. Before that, we had to use an oil-based dye that would have to be sucked out in a very painful procedure. With the initial water-soluble dyes half the patients got very ill, with vomiting and terrible headaches. When improved dyes were introduced and we didn't see these types of adverse reactions, that is when I decided we had to do our own imaging center. So we put in a CAT scanner and a myelogram suite, and it was a real home run. It was one-stop shopping for patients. They would come in, get their myelogram and then get a CAT scan, which was the most sensitive test for nerve compression. When MRI scanning became prominent, we knew that putting in an MRI scanner was the next logical step, but we didn't have half a million dollars to lead shield the room which was necessary to protect the outside world from the magnetic force.

Then I had a great idea. On a Tuesday morning while seeing patients I received a phone call from Teddy Turner, the oldest son of Ted Turner, Founder of CNN. Teddy had acquired a Maxi yacht, eighty feet overall length, to compete in the next Whitbread Round the World Race (now called the Volvo) sponsored by the Whitbread Brewery of the UK. Teddy wanted me to come to Charleston to crew in a match race against a Russian yacht, the *Fazisi*. While staying in Charleston I had a bright idea. While I was lying in my hotel bed I was thinking about how to put together the money for the MRI scanner. We had previously established Quakerbridge Plaza Scanning when we installed the CAT scanner, which had a reasonable annual profit. My idea was to have QPS as a corporate entity approach the bank to borrow the money. This would pull a group of doctors who had invested in our CAT scanner into a further investment in an MRI scanner, which they could also utilize for their patients as well as share in the liability. With that arrangement the bank agreed on the loan and we established Quakerbridge Plaza Imaging, which included x-ray, a myelogram suite, a CAT scan suite, and MRI imaging, as well as our offices comprising eight thousand square feet. Ultimately, we were forced to sell Quakerbridge Plaza Imaging because of the Stark Amendment of 1989 (named for California Rep. Fortney Stark), which banned doctors from referring patients to clinical entities in which the physician had a financial interest.

In the 1990s, this amendment was altered to scale back restrictions on doctors, but by that point we already had been forced to sell our interest in the imaging center. This was classic government interference where it did not belong. In a surgical practice like ours, we could not see a patient without a scan — it would be very difficult to be abusive and refer patients unnecessarily to the scanner. So here is a good example of the government getting involved unnecessarily. Now patients would have to come to our office, we tell them they need a myelogram or a scan, and they have to take a second day off from work and go get the scan somewhere else. Then they need to take a third day off from work and come back to our office with the scan. Before this ridiculous government interference, patients could just go in the next room at the time of the initial visit, get their scan, and have their answer within the same hour. It turned what was a very efficient operation, with the patient only taking a morning off from work, into a loss of three days of work and terrible inefficiency for the patient and the doctor.

Government does not need to be interjected into the private practice of medicine.

The truth is, eighty-five percent of doctors practice ethically and honestly — but there will always ten to fifteen percent of physicians who practice dishonestly. Really, that same percentage applies everywhere you look, in every profession. There will always be a bad apple or two, but it doesn't mean you ruin it for everybody. If you let the government come in, they can never do anything efficiently. This is part of the reason for the outcry over government intervention in health care. Private interest will always do it better and more efficiently, whether it's the Postal Service or healthcare — and in a more cost-effective way for the patient. The heavy-handed role of government is one of many changes that I have witnessed and endured in my forty-plus years in neurosurgery. I think it's important to reflect upon how the specialty has evolved in that time — in both good and bad ways for the patient.

CHAPTER X:
MEDICAL ECONOMICS

"Because that's where the money is..."
— Willie Sutton, when asked by the sentencing judge why he robbed banks

Looking in the rearview mirror of my years in the medical profession, it is my opinion that the overall standards in medicine have declined. I observed mass production of specialists with less hands-on tutoring by professors during their training, all of which is leading to diminished quality of patient care. When I completed my medical degree at Jefferson in 1967, there were roughly eight thousand medical school graduates per year in the United States. Today, that number has more than doubled to seventeen thousand per year. In New Jersey and New York states alone, the influx of foreign medical graduates produced over fifty percent of the residents in training in the various specialties. Whereas nationally foreign medical graduates compose twenty-five percent of the resident house staff. Over that same period, medicine gradually evolved into a big business. Hospitals that train residents began to receive a stipend from Medicare for every resident in training, so a lot of institutions adopted goals to expand their residencies and get more of the federal money. The medical profession has become much like the legal profession. There are more than 1.2 million lawyers in the United States, which in my opinion is excessive. What we are seeing is that there is money to be made in running an institution that produces professionals, whether they are needed or not.

I witnessed the evolution of HMOs — health maintenance organizations. Then came "managed care" a term adopted by major insurance companies to control the costs of medicine or in other words, to increase their profits. A highly trained physician must now utilize his valuable time calling these managed care companies to obtain "permission" to order MRI scans or other valuable diagnostic tools. If the insurance company denies the test, then the patient would be responsible for the cost out of pocket. Frequently, the physician or his office staff are discussing the case and requesting sanction from a nurse or a physician's assistant or physician who has no knowledge or expertise in the particular specialty where the patient's concerns lie. Moreover these certifiers have not seen the patient, talked to the patient, or examined the patient let alone have any knowledge of the difficult specialty of neurological surgery. Often they will request a letter from the physician stating all the reasons why this test is indicated. More time wasted, more utilization of office staff requiring the physician in private practice who is in reality running a small business, to increase his overhead costs. Insurance companies not uncommonly have been guilty of criminal behavior. One major insurer in New Jersey held on to premiums without reimbursing physicians for their services for more than a year, causing the physicians to file a class action suit and win in court. Deceptive practices and fraud are common in the insurance industry, which caused me to conclude that in many instances these institutions were run by criminals. United Healthcare was recently fined over one hundred million dollars for fraudulently adjusting their computers so that patients would be unjustly responsible for more of their balance bill. But yet, look the profits of the top insurance companies, they are in the billions. They entice families to join for the first year at a low premium and then after the first year jack the premiums up. "These companies continue to press for higher premiums, even though their reserve coffers are flushed with profits and shareholders have been rewarded with new dividends. They defend their proposed double digit increase in the rates they charge, citing a need for protection against any sudden uptake in demand once people have more money to spend on their health as well as the rising price of care." (*The New York Times, Business Day Section*)

An excellent summary of the truth about health insurance company profits is contained in the following article from The Huffington Post Business Section of April 4, 2013:

"The health insurance industry's mouthpiece doesn't want the rest of us to know what Wall Street knows well -- the record-breaking profits of the health insurance companies are, in fact, excessive.

In response to astonishingly high first-quarter profit reports from health insurance companies, the industry trade group America's Health Insurance Plans (AHIP), claims it is among the least profitable health care industries. AHIP says the health insurance industry profit margin is only 4.4%, and that this "low margin" represents less than one penny out of every dollar spent on all health care in the U.S. These are simplistic and misleading statistics. Last week *The New York Times* reported that the health insurance industry is enjoying record earnings while millions of Americans get less medical care. Wall Street investors are delighted with the industry's profits, and to health insurance executives, that's all that counts. Insurance CEOs want investors to buy their stock and keep share prices marching higher, and that's exactly what has happened. To achieve excessive profits, insurers are happy to gouge consumers and small businesses, do little to rein in medical costs and spend billions of our premium dollars on lobbying, secret political activities, bloated executive pay and stock buybacks. AHIP's focus on profit margins is misleading and designed to protect their massive income by shifting attention away from their return on equity — a key measure of profits as a percentage of the amount invested. That return is a phenomenal 16.1% as of today. By that measure, health insurers are ranked fourth highest of the 16 industries in the health care sector. They also deliver a higher return for investors than cellphone companies, beer companies, mortgage companies, life insurance companies, TV broadcasters, drug store companies or grocery stores. AHIP likes to talk about how insurance profits are a small share of national health spending — less then one penny of every dollar spent on health care in the U.S. — but that is an absurd, deceptive and self-serving statistic. Yet even their own chart of this data shows that the share of the health care economy sucked up by health insurance profits has more than tripled over the past decade. One penny of the health care dollar is worth $347 billion over 10 years ending in 2019. That one penny would pay for more than one-third of the entire cost of the health reform program."

The health insurance industry opposed the Affordable Care Act by bank rolling the Republican appeal effort because this act in part attempts to end the worst insurance company abuses which have pervaded the health insurance industry since the passage of the McCarran-Ferguson Act of 1945 exempting them from federal regulation and our anti-trust laws. ObamaCare has rewarded health insurance companies with enormous financial benefit. Whereas the S&P 500 has gained seventy percent since 2009, the stock in health insurance companies has more than doubled. Meanwhile, those who can afford insurance without subsidy have seen premiums rise, deductibles increase and responsibility for more of the balance of their medical bill. Many who struggle to pay for insurance have diminished their working hours to qualify for subsidy. In similar fashion, many employers have diminished available working hours to avoid paying the mandatory premiums for full time employees. Obama indeed has fulfilled his campaign promise of "redistribution of wealth"—into the coffers of the health insurance industry.

American business in many instances is pervaded by fraud and the health insurance industry is no exception and is right up there in a leadership role. The lowly physician, however, is in a quandary. He or she graduates from medical school with an average debt for education being about $200,000. This highly trained individual is now subject to control by hospitals, insurance companies and the government. When he or she graduates, they are faced with the prospect of trying to build a practice, which is now becoming obsolete. That is because the insurance industry now controls the patient population and unless the doctor signs up with different insurance companies and agrees to care for their patients for a fixed price, he will not be allowed to treat those patients i.e. he will not get paid. The physician then is faced with a dilemma; either have a large patient population automatically by signing up with insurance companies for reimbursement that is the professional equivalent of "minimum wage" or abandon insurance companies and be "out of network." The insurance industry sells out-of-network policies, which costs the patient a higher premium. That allows a patient to go to any specialist and the insurance company will cover eighty percent of the physician's fee. The patient is responsible for the balance. These types of policies are seen primarily in the suburbs, and more affluent areas rather than the inner city. Remarkably, the insurance industry recurrently attempts to abort the fees charged by out of network physicians through legislative means. In New Jersey they unsuccessfully attempted to have the Commissioner of Health sign into law that out of network surgeons would be reimbursed the Medicare rate plus twenty-five percent while they continued to enjoy the income from the high premiums of patients buying out of network policies. Even more offensive was the attempt to induce legislation in New Jersey that would force surgeons to mandatory collection of the balance of their out of network fee, which many surgeons "forgive" because often the entire balance was a formidable cost to the patient. Not to forgive a substantial part of the balance would discourage patients from seeking out of network providers. The penalty they wished to impose for failing to collect this balance was six months in jail, loss of your medical license, plus a substantial fine.

A steaming turd is a euphemism for a health insurance company.

Look at the salaries of the executives and their bonuses in the health insurance industry. I know of one founder of Aetna who allegedly walked off with over a billion dollars and the corporate jet. Likewise the individual who began United Health, also walked off with several billion dollars. Meanwhile, in our community, a general surgeon who gets called at night to the emergency room to evaluate a patient with an acute abdomen due to appendicitis and then takes the patient to the operating room for surgery with all the postoperative care included is reimbursed by Aetna about $300. Now, I ask the reader, is that a fair reimbursement for the expertise required to correct a potentially life-threatening bodily dysfunction since a burst appendix can have mortality? Likewise, the same insurance company would reimburse a neurosurgeon or orthopedic spine surgeon about $900 for removing a lumbar disk rupture. If the average spine surgeon is paying over $100,000 per year and most often far more for malpractice insurance, that means that a spine surgeon would have to perform more than one hundred laminectomies in a year just to pay his malpractice insurance premiums. This situation engenders a disposition for doing more surgery than is necessary for the average spinal disorder by many surgeons in order to boost income to survive. The reimbursement for cervical spine and brain surgery is not much better.

How does an individual surgeon possibly maintain his overhead including malpractice insurance, employees' salaries, rent, cost of education, etc. with such meager reimbursement? I was performing more than two hundred and twenty major intracranial and spinal procedures a year and yet my spouse who manages real estate with her sister was making far more income. The catastrophic consequences to physicians in general and surgeons in particular of the emergence of "managed care" were substantial. Both my associate and myself were forced to sell our homes when our incomes plummeted seventy percent due to the meager reimbursements despite our significant high volume including many high-risk cases. When this happened to us I would frequently retire to bed at night angry that I was controlled and taken advantage of and financially raped. To do a high-risk intracranial or spinal operation and be paid barely enough to meet your overhead was starting to force us out of business. The only option was to bail out and take a risk on having enough of a practice out of network, not participating with insurance companies, and be able to provide for our families with enough income. The deciding factor for me personally arrived one day with a reimbursement from an insurance company for $700.00 for removing a spinal cord tumor on a woman who became paraplegic and subsequently recovered which case took six hours under the operating microscope using a laser to get an excellent result. This was so outrageous a reimbursement which included all the post-operative care that I decided I would rather go out of business and work at Burger King than be raped one more day by these whores in the insurance industry. I sold the dream house I wanted to build my entire life to a five-foot perfidious dwarf from Wall Street who at thirty years of age was making millions. It was hard to control my inner rage. I began to intensely dislike a country that would allow this type of abuse. I moved to a townhouse where I lived for the next ten years, however dropping out of network was the best move my associate and I made because we were able to recapture our previous income and then some. Moreover it is illegal for physicians to unionize on setting fees. It is illegal for surgeons to get together and try to determine prices. It would not do any good anyway because the insurance industry will only pay a fixed amount and the only recourse for a surgeon is to drop all policies and go out of network. Having done so several years ago quite often I am sitting at home doing *The New York Times* crossword puzzle, reading novels, or painting in my studio instead of performing operative neurosurgery which I am trained to do and in which I have achieved a high level of expertise. What a waste! There are hundreds of patients who could benefit from this expertise while I sit at home doing hobbies. I have a diminished workload because I am out of network in my refusal to be raped financially by the insurance industry.

After ten years I built another home.

In any business successful risk taking usually comes with substantial reward. To take substantial risks in the operating room where patients lives are at stake and they may live or die, be maimed or vegetative depending on your judgment as to how best to take that tumor out attached to the brain stem or place a clip on the neck of an aneurysm where you can see the blood swirling through the thinned out dome where a wrong move is literally life or death must be rewarded commensurate with the risk and result. Not to do so will result in inferior and less able individuals seeking and achieving these positions.

In my own experience, I acquired seven postgraduate years of education after receiving my MD degree. It took another two years thereafter before I was qualified to take the Oral Board of Neurological Surgery, which after passing would declare me commensurate in knowledge and skill with my peers. One then enters practice in a high-risk speciality where adverse outcomes can render litigation of millions of dollars. Performing a cervical disk removal where an inadvertent complication can occur such as injury to the spinal cord and quadriplegia, could cost the surgeon millions of dollars covered, hopefully, by malpractice insurance, however, not every case can be settled to the limits of the policy. I have witnessed this happening to colleagues. Fortunately settling outside policy limits is the exception. You take high risks on Wall Street and get an excellent result, there is high reward, but not in neurosurgery.

Then, there is the influence of the Joint Commission on Accreditation of Hospitals meddling in an area which is specialized and in which they have no knowledge. An example of their meddling is the rule that hospitals can no longer provide razors or allow razors into the operating room for shaving because it can lead to an increased incidence of infection. I have been shaving the patient's head in the operating room after induction of anesthesia for almost forty years and have experienced two infections. Operative infections whether deep or superficial almost always occur from suboptimal surgical technique. Meticulous attention to the preparation and draping of the operative site and the handling of tissue should result in negligible infection in conjunction with prophylactic antibiotics. Let us consider the consequences of the JCAHO Rule: A patient comes in from an automobile accident after going through the windshield. That patient has a comminuted depressed skull fracture with brain and hair matted down in blood in the depths of the wound. I would love to see one of the JCAHO rule makers come into the operating room and use a clipper and try to get the hair removed for a clean operative site in order to repair the brain, dura, skull and scalp. It is impossible without shaving with a razor. This represents typical interference from the rule makers who don't do this type of work but feel they can use statistics to interfere with the art of surgery. They would rather a surgeon perform an incompetent operation risking contamination of the brain due to matted hair in the field and follow their stupidity. I can only speak for my specialty, but I am sure that other surgeons can voice the same outrage in their specialty.

One positive aspect of JCAHO rules was the identification of patients coming into the operating room and a confirmation made of the side and site of the surgery as well as the planned surgical procedure. Any competent surgeon would think this is absurd that a surgeon does not know who his patient is and what side he is operating on, but guess what? Operating on the wrong side of the body happens not uncommonly throughout America, and operating on the wrong patient as well, I have seen these instances occurring in my own community. An excellent reference book was written by Dr. Gawande, a Harvard surgeon, entitled *Checklist Manifesto*. The reason that such a rule had to be implemented was the vast potential incompetence as well as overt incompetence in the medical and surgical field. Where is the mind while the hand is pulling the lever? There was even a surgeon who left the patient's abdomen open while he went to the bank to cash a check. Doctors are humans and as such they engage in unbelievable folly with the patient's life dangling in the outcome.

The future of surgical practice may be in jeopardy. With low reimbursements a new business model must evolve that is financially acceptable to well trained, intelligent individuals in order to enter not only the general practice of surgery but the high-risk specialties as well. At this time half of the medical school graduating classes in America are composed of women. Men in general, but women in particular, do not wish to engage four to eight year subspecialty training in high risk fields such as neurosurgery or cardiac surgery. They tend to gravitate to specialties where they have opportunity to practice and raise a family, which becomes near impossible in a high-risk long-term residency where call is frequently every second or third night. Consequently there is a significant waiting list to enter residency training in specialties such as dermatology, radiology, physical medicine, and rehabilitation, and even ophthalmology to provide this advantage. If one anticipates finishing long years of training and receive average income it will discourage and has discouraged the best and the brightest from seeking these opportunities. In support of my comment, it was published in JAMA that the Jewish application to medical school plummeted by fifteen percent when managed care gained control. Ergo, enter the foreign medical graduate. Your chance of a foreign medical graduate doing your operation in the state of New Jersey is about fifty percent.

It is my opinion that in America we have the most dysfunctional health care delivery system in the world. At the time of this writing the consequences of Obamacare are unknown, but already we are seeing insurance premiums rising and the continuation of profiteering by the insurance industry.

I cannot abandon this discussion on healthcare costs without bringing in the legal profession and the cost of defensive medicine. In the United States thus far it has been impossible to have tort reform so that the "pain and suffering" element of litigation can be capped at a reasonable amount, such as $250,000. The state of Texas achieved tort reform and dramatically reduced healthcare costs, especially with malpractice insurance premiums reduced for surgeons practicing in that state. The cost of defensive medicine in the United States is astronomical in the billions of dollars. Building off a new study put out by Jackson Healthcare says "defensive medicine is leading to between $650-$750 billion in wasteful spending in the United States. Researchers in Oregon have found that that state could have saved almost $100 million in healthcare spending with a modernized medical liability system, aka tort reform. Defensive medicine has been estimated to cost between twenty-six and thirty-four percent of annual healthcare cost in the United States. Physicians practice "rule-out medicine" rather than "diagnostic medicine" out of fear that they will miss a diagnosis and be sued." Every headache gets an MRI scan for fear of missing the one in a thousand patient that may be harboring a brain tumor. Every concussion in an emergency room gets a CT scan of the brain and a neurosurgery consultation after admission all of which is unnecessary in ninety-nine percent of mild head injury.

Today the graduating physician cannot evaluate and treat a concussion. Today it requires subspecialty evaluation and recommendations, driven by insecurity, fear of litigation, and in my opinion inadequate medical education. This holds true for many other clinical entities as well—poorly educated doctors running up the bill because of lack of knowledge. In this milieu, now enter and combine the diagnostic ability of the average physician's assistant, who in many hospital settings has taken over managing patient care without a medical degree. The lack of education in a subspecialty in particular leads to unnecessary ordering of MRI scans and CAT scans further running up the cost of healthcare, not to mention unnecessary radiation which can be harmful to patients. Our national organizations and neurosurgery in particular at the time of this writing have failed to establish proposed guidelines for the use of the physician assistant in our high-risk specialty. I recently reviewed two cases of potential litigation where neurosurgeons sent a physician assistant to the emergency room to evaluate and treat a cervical fracture dislocation and in another instance an acute subdural hematoma. Both patients died because neurosurgical expertise was not provided. This outrageous situation prompted me to write a letter to the President of the American Association of Neurological Surgeons demanding a statement of position on utilizing physician assistants in the high-risk specialty of neurosurgery. At the time of this writing I await their response.

The reader might be interested in my own malpractice history and of the litigation I experienced during my career. I have settled three lawsuits in almost forty years. The first occurred around 1977 at a hospital in Bucks County where an obese patient underwent lumbar laminectomy and experienced a dural tear. The dura is a thick membrane around the nerve roots and spinal fluid, which occurrence is like nicking yourself shaving and has been reported in the literature to be in the range of fifteen percent during a laminectomy. Personally, I think this figure is quite high, but has more credibility with a re-exploration where the dura is scarred down from previous surgery, lending itself more apt to be violated in the course of a laminectomy. At that time, there was a field that was so bloody with nerve roots exposed that I feared their injury and decided the best option was to cover them over and keep the patient down for a week until the wound healed. If a pseudomeningocele developed (fluid under the skin from dura leakage), I would then reoperate and repair it electively. The next day, I found him out of bed in the bathroom sitting on the toilet, which violated my order of absolute bed rest flat. I chastised him and told him the risk and consequences of his action. He continued to disobey and was out of bed on a second occasion on the third postoperative day. On day six, he developed a low-grade fever and confusion due to E-coli meningitis. I over sewed the wound and he survived the infection. I then repaired the dura after a pseudomeningocele developed. He was discharged home. He instituted litigation because he claimed that he could not work for six months. There were witnesses that stated that he was building his house during that time and riding horses. He pocketed the money from the surgeries. I received no reimbursement. None of this was admissible in court. I fought it in court, but the jury awarded him $50,000. My barber told me the judge disagreed with the decision since the judge went to the same barbershop. When the judge complained to the barber, the barber had no idea that I was the defendant.

Years later in the mid-1980s, I was operating upon a very obese woman with an L4-L5 disk herniation. She had a washboard spine, meaning that there were multiple disks bulging at every level, but the L4-L5 was more pronounced. We took six x-rays in the operating room to try to identify the correct level. Since she weighed three hundred pounds, the x-rays were unable to penetrate her. I therefore extended the incision to identify the sacrum and counted up to be sure I was decompressing the correct level. Unfortunately the sacrum was anomalous on that side. There was no palpable interspace between the L5 lamina and the sacrum. As I counted, I ended up at L3-L4 instead of L4-L5 level and took the L3-L4 disk out. Postoperatively, when I realized the error, I took her back a week later and took out the L4-L5 disk. She instituted litigation and although my lawyer felt we could fight this in court because of the anomaly, it was cheaper to settle. She received $40,000.

The last case was around 1991, performing a lumbar diskectomy in a woman with a massive lumbar disc rupture and foot drop, I felt my pituitary forceps penetrate the anterior longitudinal ligament on the other side of the disk space. Not knowing whether there was vascular injury to the iliac artery, I asked the anesthesiologist to call me after I closed if there was any drop in the blood pressure, since I had seen a slight amount of red blood through the disk space. Sure enough, she told me the pressure dropped. In the meantime, I had found a vascular surgeon and brought him in the operating room prior to waking her up from anesthesia and removal of the endotracheal tube. He agreed the belly demonstrated potential vascular injury and he explored the iliac artery. He put two stitches in that vessel where my instrument had penetrated. She made a complete recovery, although she woke up with an incision in her back and an incision in her belly, which no one planned for. I felt this was a technical error and the patient should be compensated. She received $70,000. The patient told me that she did not want to do this, but her friends and relatives felt that she really should institute litigation. She was grateful that her foot recovered and that she no longer had pain in her leg.

It has been reported that the average neurological surgeon in the United States in sued every eighteen months. In my forty-year career of over six thousand operations on the brain and spine, I cost the insurance company $160,000. Meanwhile, I have paid millions in malpractice premiums and continue to do so. With a substantially excellent malpractice history were my premiums lowered? Of course not.

In my opinion, my surgical expertise is due to the rigid training at Iowa under George Perret, a perfectionist who would destroy a resident if he or she ever hurt a patient—the sole reason my litigation history is relatively negligible by most accounts.

CHAPTER XI:
REFLECTIONS ON NEUROSURGERY

**"He who thinks he has graduated from the school
of experience becomes a public menace."**
— *John Chalmers da Costa*

Today doctors are being produced in record numbers, but the quality of training they are receiving is lacking in comparison to my generation. When I was a resident at Iowa, for example, no resident did an operation without an attending — a board-certified staff member — scrubbing with him, unless it was a very minor procedure. When I was a fellow at Penn, however, I saw residents taking care of cases with no one looking over their shoulder. That is more of the norm these days, which is disheartening and dangerous. In the field of neurosurgery, there is a steep learning curve. Young surgeons are going to have morbidity and mortality that an older surgeon would not. Historically, surgeons would acquire that skill and experience by working on indigent patients in the hospital ward. But hospital wards died off in the late 1960s. The key, then, is to ensure that young neurosurgeons are closely supervised by experienced, seasoned surgeons, which is not happening today as much as it should be.

Any neurosurgeon reflects the professor and chairman of the department in which he trained. In my own case, my training and judgment reflect the teaching of George Perret, who was a difficult taskmaster and perfectionist who put patient care above all else. We learned every facet of patient care by rotating through each phase of surgical development. Today, residents have a much easier patient management because of technological innovations such as CAT scanning and MRI scanning — they often do not have to do much of an examination of the patient because the answer is right there from a referring doctor. I can recall not long ago a patient with a meningioma on the tentorium, near the area where the midbrain passes through the incisura en route to the cerebral hemispheres, referred to me by a chiropractor. This condition historically would be very difficult to diagnose. Now, even a chiropractor — who is not a physician — can order an MRI because it is not x-ray (radiation) and uncover such a condition. After all, if someone has a severe headache and double vision even the plumber can deduce the problem is intracranial. A lot of diagnostic challenges are eliminated through technology, which of course is better for patients. But what is the impact on medical training? It means that many young physicians are not learning the nuances of the neurological examination that can be critical in so many situations. Technology undoubtedly has given doctors better tools to assess patients' physical conditions, but it cannot take the place of training, practice and good judgment nor a thorough history and neurological examination.

It is also crucial for young physicians to read and study! There is no substitute for knowledge. All physicians must know anatomy because even though we have machines for diagnosis now, they can be misleading. For example, a patient can come in with terrible pain in the leg, neurological impairment and an MRI scan in the lumbar spine with nerve compression, and yet that's not the cause. If you know how to examine in detail, you can deduce that the problem may not be from nerve compression. If a good examiner picks up motor weakness in muscles innervated by more than one nerve root he can conclude that despite the abnormality noted on the scan the problem may be an inflammatory plexitis not amenable to surgical correction.

Recently a well-known Mercer County judge presented for a second opinion several days prior to undergoing a cervical disk removal and fusion at a major medical school in Philadelphia. He had weakness in the shoulder girdle muscles and a moderate disk herniation at the C5-6 level. On examination he had weakness in muscles innervated by nerve roots that did not come from just the C5-6 level and I advised him not to have the surgery. He heeded my advice and went back to his neurologist. His Lyme titer was one of the highest I have seen in practice. The cause of this gentleman's brachial plexopathy was Lyme's disease. The operating surgeon in Philadelphia failed to do a detailed examination despite the fact he was a full professor and author of several texts on spine surgery. Fifteen percent of patients with no complaints will have a herniated disk in the neck or back as an incidental finding on MRI scanning and may not be germane to their problem. Only a careful examination and knowledge of neuroanatomy is definitive.

What I see today is that doctors do not conduct careful examinations and do not take careful patient histories. Recently a surgical colleague asked me to evaluate his mother who was wheelchair bound and unable to walk. She was incontinent of urine. Her gait was so impaired she could not ambulate without someone holding her. She failed to improve despite two operative procedures on her cervical spine, the first from the anterior approach and the other from the posterior approach performed by a professor and chairman of an orthopedic department of a major medical school in Philadelphia. Her cervical spine x-ray looked like the second shelf at Ace Hardware. Her examination also demonstrated increased reflexes in the legs and extensor plantar responses (positive Babinski reflexes). Her symptoms and signs suggested spinal cord compression. One way to differentiate however, whether the cause is due to spinal cord insult or intracranial causes is the Romberg test. If the patient stands with her eyes closed and feet together and doesn't fall over the problem is unlikely due to spinal cord compression. The brain would not know where the legs are in space with the eyes closed if the cord was compressed to the point of inability to ambulate. A CAT scan demonstrated marked hydrocephalus due to aqueduct stenosis, which can cause increased reflexes in the legs and a positive Babinski sign because the white matter fibers from the motor area representing the legs are stretched over the dilated ventricles and cause the gait impairment. Failure to do a complete neurological assessment or ignorance of the pathophysiology of the nervous system caused this patient unnecessary surgery. Three weeks after placement of a ventriculo peritoneal shunt for hydrocephalus she was ambulating normally and the incontinence stopped.

It is my opinion that orthopedists who wish to perform spinal surgery should be educated in neurology for six months during the course of their fellowship.

Headaches are another example. If a patient comes in with a sudden-onset headache that is the worst in his or her life, a physician must presume it is an aneurysm leak until proven otherwise. You must err on the side of patient safety. If you do not — and it does turn out to be an aneurysm leak — you have just given your patient a death sentence. This is why a careful examination and history is crucial. I have reviewed dozens of malpractice litigation claims against family doctors and emergency room physicians who failed to comply with this standard of care. My advice to doctors in training is not to rely on machines — they are a supplement, but not the most important aspect of evaluation of the patient.

Another example from my own experience that illustrates my point. On Thanksgiving Day of 2010, I was driving with my wife and kids to meet her father and sister for dinner, when I received an urgent call from a colleague who told me that a friend — a very prominent Philadelphia businessman — was just admitted to the hospital after suffering a brain hemorrhage. I was asked to come to the hospital and offer my opinion because they were already setting up the operating room and the on-call neurosurgeon was getting prepared to do the craniotomy. Minutes later I got a call from my friend's son, who pleaded with me to come immediately to evaluate his father. So I dropped the family off and headed to the hospital. When I arrived, I found the patient unconscious in bed. I examined him and then looked at his films. There was a sizeable hemorrhage in the right temporal lobe, but the thing that impressed me was there was no brain stem compression. You could see the cerebral spinal fluid pathways around the midbrain, and I felt that there was no reason why he should be unconscious based on the films and based on my examination. I noticed his pupils were pinpoint and I realized this had to be a drug effect. I asked, "Did this man receive any narcotics?" and was told that, yes, he received Dilaudid, a narcotic painkiller, and then he was given a reversing agent. I proposed that the amount of reversing agent he received may not have been sufficient, so I told the nurse to bring another five cc's of the reversing agent and I pushed it in myself at the bedside. Within one minute, he was awake and talking to his family, and I said, "Cancel the surgery." This man was twenty minutes away from getting an unnecessary craniotomy! The surgeon who was going to perform the procedure came in the room and was astounded when he saw that the patient was awake and talking. I took him aside and said, "Where I trained, if you gave any patient with an intracranial lesion a narcotic, you would lose your position in your residency. There's no way you ever, ever give a narcotic because you can't follow a patient's state of alertness, pupillary size and reaction, not to mention the narcotic effect on depressing respiration thereby increasing the pCo2 causing cerebral vasodilatation, increased cerebral blood volume, and subsequently increased intracranial pressure." Now, again, I trained in an era when there was no CAT scanning, but in this instance the doctor had the benefit of CAT scanning and saw a sizeable hemorrhage, so why did he fail to diagnose the problem? Because you have to understand neurology, neurophysiology, pathophysiology, and be able to examine the patient and apply reason to your conclusion. Today, most physicians depend on the machine. Few know how to deduce from a clinical assessment. Here was a doctor who trained with machines, who saw a patient with an intracerebral hematoma and immediately reacted by thinking, "Well, you take it out." But the hemorrhage had nothing to do with the patient's state of consciousness.

In the recent past a lead article in *The New England Journal of Medicine* was entitled, "The Demise of the Physical Examination." Nothing could be closer to the truth. I recall a statement that twenty percent of the graduating fellows in cardiology could not detect the cardiac murmur of mitral regurgitation with a stethoscope in that article. A detailed neurological examination is even further on the backburner.

I recall another case in Mercer County in which a very experienced neurosurgeon saw a patient in the emergency room and diagnosed him as brain dead — he even spoke to the family about organ donation. In fact, he failed to take a competent history and obtain the information from the emergency room that the patient had been given a paralytic agent like neurcuronium. About a half-hour after the doctor left, the patient started moving around under the sheets. The family was hysterical. They said, "Get us out of here!" and they flew the patient down to a Philadelphia medical center. Whenever I got called for a head injury, the staff would often want to use paralytic agents to insert the endotracheal tube, but I would tell them, "Don't give the patient anything until I assess him." If you are trying to make a decision whether to operate or not, it's based on the neurological assessment. Does the patient have brain stem compression to the point where it is irreversible? Or is it reversible? You have to do a detailed neurological examination and see the brain stem reflexes accurately which cannot be done in the presence of a paralytic agent. Remember, you have people managing the emergency room who do not know anything about neurosurgery or neurology, and they will do what they think is prudent when in fact it may be harmful. But the surgeon has to glean accurate information.

The worst combination in a neurosurgeon is mediocre knowledge and an indifference to the outcome. You will see that reflected in a doctor's litigation history. If you know what you are doing and you care about your patients, your litigation history should be anecdotal. It has been published that the average neurosurgeon is sued every eighteen months in the United States. But many deficient surgeons are able to compensate for their inadequacies with bedside manner. Likewise with an adverse surgical outcome, if family members detect or sense indifference in that surgeon they will more likely than not institute litigation. I have seen doctors who really should not be doing high-risk procedures but they can often get by because they romance the patients and their families. I even knew of a surgeon in Waterloo, Iowa who prayed with the family before an operation, which is absolutely frightening. Now, with eighty-five percent of cases, even the worst surgeons can get by. But it is that other fifteen percent that show the difference between really skilled surgeons and those who are mediocre or even less than mediocre. The latter leave wounds on the patient that look like Rin Tin Tin had lunch.

They have high infection rates, and postoperative complications with wound healing and hematomas because they are sloppy, not technically skilled, and they are often in a hurry. They do not care. But all these complications can be "solved" with modern antibiotics and reoperation. There are some surgeons who actually make better livings than their more skilled counterparts, because they have so many complications that they have to take the patient back to the operating room several times. And they bill accordingly. I saw one patient have four operations on the same level of his lower back because the surgeon didn't do it right the first, second or third time. A lot of these criticisms are based on observation, but also I have reviewed an enormous number of cases for lawyers who sought an opinion regarding whether or not negligence or substandard care existed.

For young neurosurgeons, I think the most important thing is to pay careful attention to the best surgeons that they assist as they progress in the residency. Watch their small motions and approaches and keep a notebook of how every procedure is done, because there are a lot of nuances in a surgical procedure that one develops over years of experience. Surgery is not some type of rote procedure or exercise — it must be approached with strict attention to detail and care. It is an art form. It is highly improbable that two surgeons would perform a procedure in exactly the same fashion. Every hospital, which I attended in practice, had at least two surgeons who would take eight to ten hours to perform an operation that a good skilled surgeon would do in an hour. Fifty years ago they would have had such a mortality they would be out of business in no time because anesthetic agents such as ether were volatile and inaccurate and dangerous to keep patients under their effect for a prolonged period of time. That is why historically the great surgeons fifty years ago were the fast surgeons because they were able to get the patient off the operating table before the anesthetic killed them. Today, however, with modern anesthetic agents such as propofol, whose injudicious use killed Michael Jackson, you can keep a patient asleep for a week. These unskilled surgeons unsure of anatomy, timid in their approach exist not only in the community but equally if not more so in the university hospitals. I assisted one surgeon who was so slow in a university hospital on a case that he eventually found his way into the Guinness World Book of Records for the longest operation in history.

One case that stands out involved a group of three neurosurgeons in the Mid-Atlantic states and a patient with a routine middle cerebral artery aneurysm. The first surgeon operated and thought he clipped the aneurysm. But the clip actually was nowhere near it — I read his operative note and looked at the films, and his negligence was ignorance. Then he went away to attend a meeting out of town, and in his delusion ordered the patient up and out of bed with an aneurysm that could rupture at any time — sure enough, it did! So his associate took the patient back to the operating room and, just like the first surgeon, failed to clip the aneurysm even though he thought he did. Then the patient ruptured again for the third time when the original surgeon returned from his meeting. He took the patient back to the operating room and put the clip across the entire Circle of Willis, which is the blood supply to the whole brain. The conduct of these surgeons was incomprehensible, and the patient, of course, was absolutely vegetative after their incompetent management. Does this represent all of neurosurgery in America? Of course not. But I have seen this in cases that I have reviewed, and it is discouraging. I long for the day that the professors and chairmen of neurosurgery departments who released these individuals in their inadequacy on society are present in the courtroom as co-defendants because they share the irresponsibility.

We have a surgeon in our community who took almost fifteen hours to do a routine brain aneurysm. As section chief I called him to my office and stated, "You know, not everyone should be doing aneurysms." His answer was, "Well I passed my boards, I am doing aneurysms." And I reiterated, "Just because you are board certified does not mean that you are an aneurysm surgeon." The words of Clint Eastwood resonated from a *Dirty Harry* film, "A man has got to know his limitations." I explained that we are all talented in different areas. Some great aneurysm surgeons may not be as adept at removing a spinal cord tumor and vice versa. It does not mean that individuals should not practice neurosurgery, but the prudent practioner will delegate high-risk procedures to those more skilled with better results. For years I referred posterior circulation aneurysms, i.e. those on or around the brain stem, as did many of my colleagues, to Charles Drake of London, Ontario, Canada who pioneered the approach to these hazardous lesions. Although Dr. Drake had the greatest experience he also had a graveyard of adverse results. Certainly his results would be far better than a community or average university surgeon who performed this operation infrequently. The egos in medicine in general and in neurosurgery in particular can be enormous. It is a challenge for a neurosurgeon, who by nature has an inflated ego, to look in the mirror and realize his limitations on a particular case. I know one individual who had amassed a *fifty percent* mortality rate before he eventually gave up operating on aneurysms, because his ego would not allow him to confront his inadequacy. Meanwhile, unknowing and trusting families lost their loved ones.

In universities today, they will have a cerebrovascular division and a tumor division, where individuals sub-specialize, and that is the prudent approach. There also has been a trend in groups of neurosurgeons to have the one surgeon in the group who does the best aneurysm do that high-risk procedure. But for most of my career, these approaches did not exist. There is no question that the best results are seen in high volume centers for high-risk procedures, so I am a strong advocate for centralizing high-risk procedures so that a few people can have a great experience. Under this approach, it is not only the surgeon who gains invaluable experience in high-risk cases, it is the whole operating team — the scrub nurses, the postoperative unit, the intensive care unit, the nurses on the floor. Everyone gets an intense, hands-on experience as opposed to anecdotal experience, which is the case currently in community hospitals. The previous model did not lead to optimal results for high-risk procedures. But to get neurosurgeons to give up income and refer a patient for the good of the patient is not easy. There are significant financial considerations in addition to the ego considerations — and that combination can be catastrophic for patients. I have seen some very good young surgeons with high-risk cases do very skilled work. And I have seen older experienced surgeons who never improved with time, and who should not be doing those high-risk cases.

In my practice after more than twenty-five years of intracranial aneurysm surgery I decided to abandon the procedure. My decision was based upon the perfection of a minimally invasive procedure originally developed in Italy by di Gugliemi which encompassed threading a small catheter via an arterial puncture site such as the femoral artery into the intracranial arterial vasculature and releasing platinum coils into the aneurysm which would promote thrombosis rendering the aneurysm unlikely to rebleed. It was only fair for patients to receive the least invasive procedure, although not necessarily the less risky procedure, depending upon the skill of the intracranial aneurysm surgeon as well as the endovascular surgeon. The number of aneurysms eligible for craniotomy and clip application would be too few in the community to afford maintenance of operative skills if more than fifty percent of these patients were referred for endovascular coiling.

I recently evaluated a middle-aged woman who leaked from an internal carotid artery aneurysm. Of significance was the fact that twenty years ago I performed three craniotomies on this unfortunate woman and clipped six intracranial aneurysms from which procedures she emerged remarkably without any impairment. I referred her to Dr. Erol Veznedaroglu, an excellent fellowship trained endovascular neurosurgeon, for the minimal invasive procedure of aneurysm coiling which was successful. She was discharged from the hospital after forty-eight hours.

Again, your skill and results are directly tied to your training as well as your surgical ability. And it is critical to note that a physician's academic ability and his surgical skill are poorly correlated. You may have doctors who are very well-known because of their research and publications in the field, but yet in the operating room they lack the skill of many junior residents, because it is often not their primary interest. Their inherent capabilities may not necessarily lie in manual dexterity or judgment in manipulating tissue. They can be absolute butchers. I have seen this numerous times, with drapes covered in blood. George Perret was significant in my career because he instilled in me that nothing bad should happen to a patient, and that you have to be absolutely paranoid about everything you did. He made you justify putting a foley catheter in someone's bladder. He made you justify putting in a central line. He made you think about what was on the film. I can remember him saying "So what?" over and over, so you would not leap to a conclusion that was not valid. In other words, he instilled that association is not causality when evaluating patients and films, and that you had to be very specific in everything you did with an excellent reason for doing it. Your reasoning and your actions based on that reason had to be rigid, exact and defensible.

As a neurosurgeon, it is critical to hold yourself to the highest standards because the consequences of your work are so vital. I think in his later years, George Perret grew weary of all the pain, suffering and death he had seen. The trauma was enormous. The number of patients who would come in with quadriplegia —young and old— was staggering. It was hard to interact with. I saw a resident leave the program because he just could not face the next quadriplegic who presented. These patients would typically ask, "When am I going to move my legs again, doctor?" And you, of course, knew the answer was "never." But we didn't say that. We would say things like, "Well, we have to wait and see. We have to give it some time and see if the spinal cord recovers." But we knew that was absolute rubbish, that this was quadriplegia forever. I have never seen anybody come back from complete quadriplegia. However, we tried not to destroy hope and we allowed time for psychological adaptation.

Years ago I received a call from Barbara Johnson, a friend I knew from the Princeton Boathouse who was a fellow avid sculler. She also happened to be the mother of Christopher Reeves. Chris had fallen off a horse at an equestrian event fracturing C1 and damaging irreversibly his spinal cord causing quadriplegia. His mother did not quite comprehend this type of injury, which I explained to her over lunch at Winberie's café in Princeton. Like most families of patients with this injury, they entertain that a more favorable outcome might be death. However, Barbara told me she received hundreds of letters from Chris' fans throughout the world wishing him recovery and encouragement. Her despondency over this tragedy was difficult to console.

It was déjà vu after years of managing patients and families with this devastating injury.

The most common cause of quadriplegia, which is due to dislocation of the cervical spine, is high-speed auto trauma. The second most common cause is diving into shallow water, which caused so much injury that the American Association and the Congress of Neurosurgery instituted a "Feet First" lecture series throughout the country. I think the worst injury to man is a dislocated neck and quadriplegia. Patients cannot breathe. They are on a ventilator initially until their diaphragm strengthens in order to make the ventilatory effort competent. Their skin breaks down so they have to be rotated every few hours. We used to have Stryker circle electric beds to make these patients prone then supine hourly to keep the skin from breaking down. Quadriplegic patients develop an enormous number of complications, including deep venous thrombosis and pulmonary infection as well as kidney stones, but the worst sequela is the severe psychological stress of not moving your arms and legs. This is why a multi-disciplinary approach of various specialists is necessary to treat these patients and why the best care is in a spinal cord injury center. Psychiatric care is also necessary. There was a case in New Jersey about thirty-five years ago in which the brother of a quadriplegic snuck a shotgun into the intensive care unit and killed his brother because the patient did not want to live completely paralyzed maintained by a machine.

As a neurosurgeon who has to deal with these instances of human tragedy, you have to come to terms with yourself as to whether you can stay in this career choice. In this field, you develop a certain callousness after years of tragedy, like treating young mothers with malignant tumors or young fathers with sudden aneurysm rupture. You see them come into the hospital with severe brain damage or brain death. This is the harsh reality of life as a neurosurgeon — having to sit down with the families and try to make these poor people understand what happened. Sometimes you have to make the families understand that it is not their fault, because they will remember that the patient complained to them of a headache a week ago but they did not think treatment was necessary. This causes tremendous guilt and self-inflicted blame.

A sudden headache can be a warning of an aneurysm leak, but these family members are not doctors, they are not supposed to be able to diagnose something like that.

A neurosurgeon sees life in its cruelest moments. I did not really know how difficult neurosurgery would be until I was immersed in it. But I loved neurology from the time I was exposed to it at Jefferson as a medical student. I absolutely loved it. It was like Latin and Greek. There was a specific reason why the patient had the symptoms, and it had to deal with a certain location in the brain, spine, or peripheral nerve. Unless you knew neuroanatomy perfectly, you would not be able to figure out the puzzle. That intellectual challenge today is gone because of MRI scanning. Frankly, it is not as much fun. Perhaps this is the reason why neurological societies for the most part have become defunct. In 1975, I was an active member and enjoyed The Philadelphia Neurological Society where intense discussions were held regarding a patient's presenting symptoms and signs followed by the ultimate answer—the autopsy findings. These discussions were outright aggressive arguments and reminiscent of residency training where combined neurology and neurosurgery conferences would often represent an imbroglio. MRI scanning, for the most part, has rendered intellectual discussion obsolete and these respected societies as well.

Neurosurgery is a field for the aggressive in nature. When I was finishing my military obligation with the U.S. Public Health Service, there were only about ninety neurosurgical residency spots in the United States. To get one of those coveted spots, you had to be at the top of your class because neurosurgery attracted the best and the brightest. It required a strong personality and a sense of urgency that when a situation arose, you had to get there *yesterday*. Get that head open *yesterday*. You had to be willing to tell anyone, "Get out of the way, I'm taking this patient to the operating room." If you don't have that fire, you don't belong in neurosurgery. And I've seen so many people that don't have it. They don't belong! And because of them, people will die or be maimed.

For instance, I remember being called for a student from Trenton State College who had come in from the gym, went to his room and collapsed. He was nineteen years old. His roommate called the ambulance, and he was brought to the Mercer Hospital emergency room. I was told he had a hemorrhage in the cerebellum with brain stem compression of the medulla, which is the respiratory center. So I went down Route 1 at eighty-five miles an hour or more knowing time was critical. I got to the emergency room having had the operating room set up for an emergency craniotomy. The family told me they would like another opinion. I didn't even give them the time of day. I said, "Lady, your son is going to the operating room or he is going to be dead in about an hour." The kid was comatose, intubated on a ventilator with severe brain stem compression. I just grabbed the bed and headed to the O.R. In that situation, you get everybody out of the way, take the bed personally onto the elevator, get him onto the operating table yourself and get that head open. I saved that student's life. But that was not the end of the story.

I had removed his subocciput, i.e. the back of his skull, and taken the hemorrhage out of the cerebellum and the fourth ventricle. The next morning, he was moving around and actually following commands. He came back from the grave. I had a drain in his lateral ventricle, so spinal fluid was running into a bag known as external drainage. I told the family I wanted to run the tube under the skin into the belly and just let it drain internally because I said there is a risk of infection if I just keep it out to the open. His family responded that they wanted to move him to a trauma center. I said, "This is not trauma. He has ruptured a malformation of blood vessels. We need to evaluate that after we first stabilize him." Still, they wanted him in a trauma center, despite my protest. So after I saved the patient's life they transferred him to a university in Philadelphia. What did they do at the university? Despite my recommendation to the Chief Resident, they nevertheless pulled the external drainage from his ventricle and he became poorly responsive. They next had to tap the ventricle as an emergency. Then he got an infection in the spinal fluid from replacing the tube, which had to be done. And then he died from the infection.

They subpoenaed one of my records, because I am sure the family sued the university. An inexperienced resident likely was caring for this patient instead of an experienced, seasoned neurosurgeon. The judgment made by his family was that the care provided by a surgeon in the community would not be anywhere near as good as it would be in the university hospital. It appears to have been the wrong call. At the time I had practiced neurosurgery for thirty years treating many similar cases. But this patient died because of the inexperience of the attending resident staff. The postscript to this story is that about ten years later, while sitting in the record room of a nearby community hospital I struck up a conversation with a woman sitting next to me. As many things in life are ironic, this woman turned out to be that patient's mother. She worked at this hospital. After she remembered me we spoke about her son, and she admitted to me it was the biggest mistake of her life to have moved him from my care.

Many times, patients will be drawn to a university or to a particularly well-known surgeon because he has published some renowned papers, but that does not mean he can operate. There is no relationship between intellectual achievement through research and publication, and a surgeon's motor skills and judgment in the operating room. You can be a great researcher and writer yet have completely asinine judgment in a clinical situation or not have the slightest clue as to how to technically approach an aneurysm or a tumor. They are not related at all. Clinical skill is a different issue-- being able to make the right judgment and having the courage to make a decision that, if you are wrong, could mean loss of life. It has no bearing on your ability to write an academic paper. I have seen terrible surgeons in universities and a lot of times they hang there because they know that they are safe. They are protected by the university — if they were in the community, they could not hide their results. So be careful of credentials, because they can be misleading. You can have impeccable credentials and be a complete idiot with a knife in your hand. There is no relationship.

When I entered practice in Mercer County, I came home one evening and picked up the New York Times. On the front page was the headline

"Iowa Surgeon Loses in Supreme Court." I saw a familiar face in the photograph that was a former associate professor at Iowa whom George Perret dismissed during the first year of my residency. I never quite understood why, but I did after reading the article. He went into private practice in Cedar Rapids, Iowa. He opened the wrong side of the head several times in his first year in practice among other misgivings. Subsequently, the anesthesiologists at both hospitals in Cedar Rapids refused to work with him and would not anesthetize his patients. He subsequently sued the anesthesiologists and the hospitals involved. The case eventually arrived in Supreme Court, where he lost. The issue I wish to present is the unreliability and false sense of security patients can have in a surgeon's credentials. This individual was a graduate of Harvard and Harvard Medical School, interned at Peter Bent Brigham and finished a residency in neurosurgery at Massachusetts General Hospital. He did a fellowship at Queen's Square in London. His credentials were absolutely impeccable. He looked like Clark Gable and married an English wife. Yet, despite impressive, impeccable credentials, where was the mind when the hand was pulling the lever? Since this infamous case, and others, I have always viewed credentials with a jaundiced eye.

Another example was a neurosurgeon who was Chief at Sloan Kettering in New York. He opened up the wrong side of the head on an Indian film star's mother and went into the wrong temporal lobe. He then had to re-operate on the opposite side, causing her significant deficit. Because this instance was not his first occurrence of substantial deviation from acceptable standards, he eventually lost his license. Subsequently, after a period of time, he was reinstated elsewhere. If the public does not think that these occurrences exist, they do, and the professions are pervaded by incompetence, perhaps not to the same degree, but to lesser degrees where the names are off the radar and the front page of *The New York Times*. As in the community, famous institutions are not exempt from incompetence.

A few years ago in a Rhode Island hospital, three different neurosurgeons in the same institution opened the wrong side of the head creating network news coverage!

In neurosurgery there is no room for error. If I had driven the speed limit down Route 1 the night I responded to the call on the student from Trenton State, he would have been dead when I arrived. You need that sense of urgency, and I have seen too many surgeons that do not have it. They should not do neurosurgery — they have a country club approach. I think George Perret saw this, too, and that is why he fired so many residents. He knew that it takes a certain personality type. The truth is that not every program director is going to filter out personality types that should not be in the field. If they are academically inclined, these trainees may eventually get to be professor or chairman at an institution and then allow similar personality types to slip through, which, in my opinion, is a major problem in the field. Not every jet pilot can be an astronaut. From the patient's perspective, I look at it this way: If you are shopping for a car, your options are clear. You can get a broken-down Ford with no brakes; or maybe a Honda with 100,000 miles and some worn tires; or you can get a brand-new Mercedes Benz. What you see is what you get. But when you are shopping for a doctor, they can all look alike. They all have diplomas on the wall, even board certification, but how do you know what you are getting? And believe me, the incompetence out there is rampant. A patient can go to a four-man neurosurgery group, each member of which is qualified on paper. However if he sees one of the surgeons it may end in death. Another surgeon may cause paralysis. The third surgeon may render him vegetative, and the fourth surgeon leaves him perfectly fine to resume a normal life. Now, eighty-five percent of doctors do a great job, but there is that fifteen percent who either did not learn, do not care, or — even worse — a combination of both. They are in every hospital.

I have often thought that one of the reasons I went into medicine was because I absolutely feared death, especially the death of my mother and father. Maybe I felt, deep down inside if I was a doctor, I could avoid it or at best understand it to be able to accept the mortality of loved ones and myself. But I have endured so much tragedy in my field. I do not think the average physician can tolerate a field like neurosurgery for a lot of reasons, most notably the severe workload of an average residency and the tragedy that you have to confront. Dealing with quadriplegia, sudden death from aneurysm ruptures, malignant brain tumors — these are not entities the average individual is willing to take on. I think you need to be highly motivated and be driven to be a neurosurgeon.

And maybe a little crazy.

The era in which I entered neurosurgery was brutal. Without CAT or MRI scanning, you had to make decisions and judgments based on a really fine neurological assessment, and have the courage to stand on your convictions. If you were wrong, you were going to wreck somebody's life. You make technical errors in surgery and you had to live with mortality that may be your fault. It was not for the light of heart. You had to be a stoic and emotionally disciplined. On the other hand, there is a major ego factor in neurosurgery. Self-image as "the greatest" pervades the room when you have a group of neurosurgeons in it. It could be likened to a Mohammad Ali convention. There is a tremendous self-image that comes along with saving lives. When you are successfully dealing with acute clots, subdural hematomas, epidural hematomas, aneurysms and the like, you are the hero. But when things go in the shitter, you are the goat. Once you learn the lessons of both sides of the equation, then you can be called a professional. You don't elate at the triumphs and you do not despair with the tragedies. You are a professional. You realize that you are in a high-risk field and there is going to be winning and losing. To survive, you better keep your emotions in a frame that does not interfere with performing your work.

In this field you also will continue to see things you have never seen before. I can vouch for that. I still have cases I have never seen before — and things that should not happen, according to textbooks, but they do. In a long career you must continue to learn. If you think you have seen it all, you become dangerous. Surgeons have big egos and a real trap is to let your ego get in the way of doing the right thing or admitting wrong judgment. You have to remain objective, and I think a great attribute for a surgeon is to be self-critical. I have seen surgeons rationalize a wrong judgment, rather than admit to doing what caused a major complication or death of a patient. If you are in a high-risk field, you are going to have morbidity and mortality. It goes along with the field. No one is perfect, and you can't be right 100 percent of the time. Just as life is imperfect, so is the practice of neurosurgery.

When maloccurrences happen because of a judgment call that was the best that could be made at the time, therein lies the problem with some malpractice litigation. Another expert might come in and say, "Well, I would not have done that, I would have done it this way." At the time, however, someone's judgment may have been the best they could make at the time. It is an art form we practice. I once had a cardiologist come in my office with a benign meningioma spread along the floor of the skull. He had seen five different neurosurgeons. The first suggested radical surgery. The second said to do nothing and follow it. The third said to biopsy it. The fourth said to biopsy and radiate. And the fifth said to just radiate. My opinion was to do nothing and follow it, agreeing with the second opinion he received. But that illustrates the complexity of the field — we don't all see things alike. If someone did act on one of those judgments and there was a major complication, it might go to litigation and trial. Then, on the witness stand, you would have four other opinions. What would the jury believe? Therein lies a problem with some cases of medical malpractice and litigation. The defendant would have his experts saying that this was a reasonable judgment and treatment, and the plaintiff's experts would be saying that they would have done it a different way. But these differences in opinion are very common. This is why I always encourage patients in my practice to get another opinion. I will tell them, "This is my judgment and what I would recommend, but I'm not always right. Someone else may see things differently." And I always suggest getting an opinion from an older surgeon, who has been around for at least twenty years, because your judgment is based upon your experience. Good judgment comes after a series of bad judgment. I think it's prudent to have an older surgeon's evaluation and opinion, particularly in high-risk surgery. This is not to say a younger surgeon couldn't do it well, but there is a learning curve. You are not a seasoned neurosurgeon in the first ten years, unless you are doing one particular subspecialty and you are doing a good volume every year.

In my training at Iowa, we were taught to do the least and look for reasons not to operate, whereas I have seen other surgeons looking for reasons to operate because it generates income. Their judgment is based on self-remuneration, which can cause problems in private surgical practice. On the other hand, if there is no incentive, such as in the VA hospital where everyone is salaried, little gets done after noon. Fortunately, I think most surgeons practice ethically and honestly. But there will always be 10 to15 percent of bad apples in the pile. A good example is when I opened my practice in Princeton, and I was performing microdiscectomies for disc ruptures in the lumbar spine. I saw a group of surgeons in the area performing a fusion on every patient with a lumbar disc herniation. The neurosurgeon would take the disc out and the orthopedic surgeon would perform the fusion. They cross-referred patients to each other. Was this indicated? The current state of the art was not to do a fusion for a disc herniation. This caused the patient with the fusion to be in bed for several days with a foley catheter in his bladder, two units of blood transfused, and excessive pain and an eight inch incision, not to mention the pain from the donor site of the bone autograft, usually from the iliac crest. That pain could last more than a year. The patient who had the simple discectomy went home the same day with a two-inch incision negligible blood loss without restriction. So why were fusions being done? Because it generated income!

One day, I discharged a patient whose lumbar disc I removed that same day. The patient in the next bed had the same condition, only a much bigger operation with an extensive fusion. And he was not out of bed for four days. Finally, I said, "This is unacceptable." I went to the chairman of surgery, and said, "If you do not do something about this, the Board of Medical Examiners will do it for you." I was the representative for neurosurgery in New Jersey to Blue Cross/Blue Shield to negotiate our fee schedule. I had access to data from their computers. In the tri-state area of New Jersey, Pennsylvania and New York, the incidence of fusion with lumbar laminectomy was about two percent, except for three hospitals. One of them was this particular hospital, where the fusion rate was eighty-five percent. Dishonesty pervades every profession, and medicine is no exception. This is especially true since the onset of managed care.

When managed care arrived reimbursements dropped for surgical procedures by as much as seventy percent, down to the Medicare rate. Surgeons would look for any reason to do more. They had mortgages and tuitions to pay. J.T. Robertson, a neurosurgeon from the University of Tennessee, wrote an oft-cited article about this phenomenon, called "The Rape of the Spine." The hospital tissue committee, often the gate keeper of unnecessary surgery when too many specimens from a particular surgeon are not abnormal, cannot discipline a spine surgeon because the gross and microscopic appearance of a ruptured disk is no different than that of a normal disk. Nor is the bone removed abnormal. With the advent of spinal instrumentation in the era of low reimbursement, a bonanza was sniffed by the unscrupulous. Because third party reimbursement is substantial when instrumentation is used in the form of screws, rods, and cages, the average spine surgical candidate began to look like a hardware store.

But, fortunately, most surgeons practice ethically and honestly. There will always be a few bad apples, whether it's Harvard or Philadelphia General. Sometimes unethical behavior comes from greed, and other times it occurs from stupidity. I recall operating on a patient who allegedly had previous surgery. He had in the past a simple herniated disc, which is performed unilateral (from one side). This patient had had it done from both sides and the level above — all unnecessary procedures to run up the bill. Clearly this situation represents unethical behavior and not an uncommon occurrence.

The words of Shakespeare ring true, "Find me an honest man, find me an honest man."

The other blight on our profession is the non-caring surgeon. There was a surgeon in our county who was called for a gunshot wound through the head, and he showed up two days later. This same surgeon had a patient admitted with severe back pain, and he again showed up two days later. The patient was found dead in bed because he had ruptured an abdominal aortic aneurysm, which is what had caused the back pain. A third instance with this particular surgeon occurred when I was asked to give a second opinion requested by his patient whom he scheduled for a cervical laminectomy after the patient was admitted for low back pain after lifting a keg of beer. Even the patient could figure out that he had terrible low back pain but was getting his neck operated on and that did not correlate. This surgeon was produced from a prominent university neurosurgery residency in New York. The professor who trained him, though famous, should have been held accountable. I have seen my share of complete incompetence in practice, and it should not be tolerated. I think the greatest compensation patients have is the ability to seek retribution through the court system. Medical malpractice lawyers are necessary. Patients have to be protected from incompetence and indifference. They have to have recourse.

The combination of stupidity and greed can be lethal. Thankfully, the bad apples are just a minor percentage of the people who make up our profession.

CHAPTER XII:
THE ORIGIN OF LIFE

"If I were to give an award for the single best idea anyone ever had, I'd give it to Darwin, ahead of even Newton or Einstein and everyone else. In a single stroke, the idea of evolution by natural selection unifies the realm of life, meaning and purpose with the realm of space and time, cause and effect, mechanism and physical law."
— Daniel Dennett

As a student of science and medicine, one of my greatest sources of frustration is seeing educated, seemingly intelligent people duped into believing that life as we know it the product of divine creation. The marketing of religion is one of the greatest scams perpetrated on the human race—and lucrative to say the least. And I believe a major factor in the spread of preposterous ideas about religion is a lack of knowledge about cell biology and the origins of life on Earth. It is critical to understand the scientific foundations of our existence before engaging in a discussion of the fallacies and manipulations that are employed in spreading the "word" of religion.

A simple analogy for the reader to understand on the origins of religious dogma and in particular the Bible, would be good men coming together to provide a framework for society to have a moral code to live by. In 1776 good men came together in similar fashion to form a code of conduct called the Constitution of the United States and the Bill of Rights. I t is understandable that thousands of years after the mutation in neural tissue, which allowed cognitive thought to the degree present in homo sapiens that moral chaos more likely than not existed in an uncontrolled environment with murder, rape, theft and other unsavory actions of which a human is capable. In order to instill and create an orderly society, the Code of Hammurabi around 1760 B.C. created a foundation for the social evolution of law and order. In similar fashion, the Bible was written with parables endorsing a moral code much like the Ten Commandments, which were composed more than 3,000 years ago. I was reminded of the New Testament endorsing and promoting the philosophy and miracles of the Christ when the recent dictator Kim Jong-il expired. The North Korean regime promoted his great achievements including scoring a hole in one from every tee on the golf course, composing a magnificent opera, etc. in attempt to impose the status of an immortal deity. In my childhood I loved reading *The Adventures of Superman*, where he fought crime and helped those in need through his superpowers. Writing about Christ in my opinion is comparable to writing about Superman.

I have read with interest the works of Dawkins (*The God Delusion*), Hitchins (*God Is Not* Great) and most recently Bugliosi (*Divinity of Doubt*) bespeaking anti-religious sentiment and the rationale for atheism based on a dismissive attack of scriptures, the Bible, and other aspects of religious thinking. Bugliosi's position is one of agnosticism, meaning "not to know." He allows the possibility of the existence of a God. Yet, there is absolutely no objective evidence with current knowledge. To assume the possibility of this existence is contrary to the scientific method. Every high school student of biology knows that to assume (ass-u-me) is to make an ass of you and me. Current best-selling atheist literature in my opinion is not optimal and insufficient to give people an explanation so they can understand how life could occur other than what has been programmed through religion.

Our neural tissue, the human brain, is "the hardware" eligible for programming. The programming or "the software" is installed from the time of birth. We observe programming in lower forms of life, such as our canine and feline pets. Pavlov's experiments are an excellent demonstration. The software installation occurs by inculcating beliefs from parents, teachers, religious leaders and others in homes, schools, and in churches. Unfortunately, as we will see in subsequent chapters, the hardware systems differ in capability i.e., storage (RAM), speed of processing and computation, conduction, size, number of neurons and synapses. There is also a difference in head size and subsequently brain size contributing to this difference. The differential occurs among human beings both individually as well as in race. It also has a significant genetic composition. It is the unfairness of evolution that some of us are born with a simple calculator or a laptop, and others have supercomputer capability with everyone else in between. To acquire change in the programming is difficult and sometimes impossible unless attacked by a "computer virus." The Jesuit adage "Give me a lad by the age of seven and I have him for life," is absolutely true for most individuals raised with religious programming. It becomes an indelible imprint in an individual's hardware and more often than not it is permanent and to the grave.

An excellent example occurred at dinner in 2005 with classmates from St. Joseph's Prep prior to departure to compete at the Royal Henley Regatta in England. I mentioned over coffee my choice of a political candidate who was pro-choice and condoned abortion. One of the crew members was appalled that I would favor termination of a pregnancy if, for instance, my daughter was date raped at a party and got pregnant without her consent. He stated if it happened to his daughter she would have to have the child and they would have to raise it no matter who fathered it. I asked him if he was willing to interfere with his daughter's life choices, career, and happiness over such an issue and his answer was, "Absolutely, our life on earth is a trial." This man was a pediatric orthodontist and educated in the biological sciences. He reflects the control of the hardware with thought processes having been programmed by the Catholic Church and at the age of sixty-five had been unable to break this programming. Education per se is not necessarily a "computer virus" that interferes with the original software.

"Give me a lad by the age of seven and I have him for life" could not be more true!

In contradistinction to arguments made by Dawkins, Hutchins, and Bugliosi I wish to present in as simplistic language as I am able, scientific fact extrapolated from current knowledge divorced from religion. I request that the reader approach the presentation with an abandonment of previous programming and with an open mind, which will enable one to understand the basis of human interactions and allow a rational explanation of life on Earth as we know it, dismissive of mythology and divine providence.

Some areas of the following basic science presentation have been extracted and paraphrased from *Campbell's Textbook of Biology Ninth Edition*. **A table of definitions of scientific terms is provided for the reader uneducated in the biological sciences at the end of this chapter to implement an understanding of basic scientific concepts.**

Georges Lemaitre was a Belgian priest, astronomer, and professor of physics at the Catholic University of Louvain. He was the first person to propose the theory of the expansion of the Universe and made the first estimation of what is now called the Hubble constant, which he published in 1927, two years before Hubble's article. He became a graduate student in astronomy at Cambridge. In 1925 he presented his new idea of an expanding Universe in contradistinction to Einstein's own finite-size static Universe model. Initially rejected by Einstein, Lemaitre proposed the Universe expanded from an initial point, which he called the "Primeval Atom." He described his theory as "the Cosmic Egg exploding at the moment of the creation." It became better known as "the Big Bang theory." This theory was ultimately proven correct as explained by the redshift of galaxies and the detection of cosmic radiation. Lemaitre's theory changed the course of cosmology. Though worthy of the Nobel, that prize allegedly has never been awarded to a cosmologist because Nobel's wife at one time had an affair with one!

Can science and religion co-exist? We are free to make that choice and I leave it to the reader to decide.

Scientific evidence exists that Earth and other planets of our solar system formed about 4.6 billion years ago, condensing from a vast cloud of dust and rocks surrounding our star, the Sun. However, recent discovery reveals that the universe dates back 13.5 billion years. Earth's early atmosphere was more likely water vapor with various compounds released through volcanic eruptions, including nitrogen, carbon dioxide, methane, ammonia, hydrogen and hydrogen sulfide. As the Earth cooled, water vapor condensed into oceans and much of the hydrogen condensed into space. Russian biochemist Aleksandr Oparin and British evolutionary biologist J.B.S. Haldane independently hypothesized that the Earth's early atmosphere was a reducing (electron-adding) environment in which organic compounds could have formed from simple molecules. Experiments have shown that electricity passing through water, such as lightning or intense ultraviolet radiation, could have caused hydrogen to link with nitrogen and form an amine, which is the basis of amino acids and, ultimately, proteins. The early oceans represented a solution of organic molecules, or what Oparin called a "primeval soup," from which life arose. In 1953, Stanley Miller of the University of Chicago — considered the father of prebiotic chemistry — conducted a pioneering experiment in which he created laboratory conditions comparable to conditions thought to have existed on early Earth. Miller's experiment yielded amino acids found in organisms today, along with other organic compounds. Subsequent experiments have documented that numerous amino acids have formed under conditions that simulated a volcanic eruption.

An extra planetary source of the basic elements needed to begin life cannot be excluded. Fragments of the Murchison meteorite — a 4.5-billion-year-old chrondrite that fell to Australia in 1969 — contained more than eighty amino acids, some in large amounts. These amino acids cannot be contaminants from Earth because they consisted of an equal mix of D and L isomers. Organisms make and use only L isomers, with rare exception. This meteorite also contained other key organic molecules, including lipids, simple sugars and nitrogenous bases such as uracil.

It is known that amino acids form the basis of proteins and proteins, in turn, form the basis of genes, RNA and DNA. The presence of organic molecules such as amino acids and nitrogenous bases is not sufficient for the emergence of life as we know it. However, every cell has a vast assortment of macromolecules, including enzymes, which are made of protein, as well as other proteins and the nucleic acids essential for self-replication. In 2009, a study demonstrated that one key step, the abiotic synthesis (non-living) of RNA monomers, can occur spontaneously from simple precursor molecules. In addition, by dripping solutions of amino acids or RNA nucleotides onto hot sand, clay or rock, researchers have produced polymers of these molecules. The polymers form spontaneously without the help of enzymes or ribosomes. Unlike proteins, the amino acid polymers are a complex mix of linked and cross-linked amino acids. Nevertheless, it is possible that such polymers may have acted as weak catalysts for a variety of chemical reactions on early Earth.

Life cannot persist without the functions of reproduction and energy processing (metabolism) that all organisms must be able to perform. DNA molecules carry genetic information, including the instructions needed to replicate themselves accurately during reproduction. The replication of DNA requires elaborate enzymatic machinery, along with copious nucleotide building blocks provided by the cells' metabolism. This suggests that self-replicating molecules and the metabolism-like source of the building blocks may have appeared together in early protocells. How did this happen? The necessary conditions may have been met in vesicles, fluid-filled compartments bounded by a membrane-like structure. Recent experiments show that abiotically (non-living) produced vesicles can exhibit certain properties of life, including simple reproduction and metabolism, as well as a maintenance of an internal chemical environment different from that of their surroundings.

Vesicles can form spontaneously when lipids or other organic molecules are added to water. When this occurs, the hydrophobic (water repelling) molecules in the mixture organize into a bilayer similar to the lipid bilayer of a plasma membrane. Providing a clay, which existed on early Earth can produce the surface on which organic molecules become concentrated, increasing the likelihood that the molecules will reach each other and form vesicles. These vesicles can reproduce on their own and increase in size without dilution of their contents — what is better known as "growth." Vesicles can also absorb particles, including those on which RNA and other organic molecules have been attached. This suggests a process of primitive cell formation. Finally, experiments have shown that some vesicles have a selectively permeable bilayer membrane that can perform metabolic reactions using an external source of the agents — another important trigger for life and origin of the cell—the basis of all living things both in the plant and animal kingdom (see Diagram I). Once a cell has formed capable of self-replication, much like a bacterium, the process of life on Earth has begun and what followed over hundreds of millions of years is life as we know it today.

The first genetic material was felt to be most likely RNA, not DNA. RNA plays an essential role in protein synthesis and carries out catalytic functions. Natural selection on the molecular level has produced ribosomes capable of self-replication in the laboratory. These ribosomes are RNA catalysts. A vesicle with self-replicating catalytic RNA could grow, split and pass its RNA molecules to its daughters. Although the first such protocells must have carried only limited amounts of genetic information passed to the daughters from the parent, their inherited characteristics could have been acted upon by natural selection. The most successful of the early protocells would have increased in number because they could exploit their resources effectively and pass their abilities on to subsequent generations.

Once RNA sequences that carry genetic information appeared in protocells, many further changes would have been possible. RNA could then have provided the template on which DNA nucleotides were assembled. Double-stranded DNA is a more stable repository for genetic information than the more fragile single-stranded RNA. DNA can be replicated more accurately. After DNA appeared, perhaps RNA molecules began to take on their present-day roles as regulators and intermediates in the translation of genes. The stage was now set for blossoming of diverse life forms — a change we see documented in the fossil record.

As substantial and significant as the fossil record is, we must keep in mind that it is an incomplete chronicle of evolutionary change. *Many of Earth's organisms did not die in the right place at the right time to be preserved as fossils.* Of the fossils that were formed, many were destroyed by later geologic processes, and only a fraction of the others have been discovered. As a result, the known fossil record is biased in favor of species that existed for a long time; were abundant and widespread in certain kinds of environments; and had hard shells, skeletons or other parts that facilitated their fossilization. The fossil record is a remarkably detailed account of biologic change over the vast scale of geologic time. Furthermore, as shown by the recently unearthed fossils of whale ancestors with hind limbs, gaps in the fossil record continue to be filled by new discoveries.

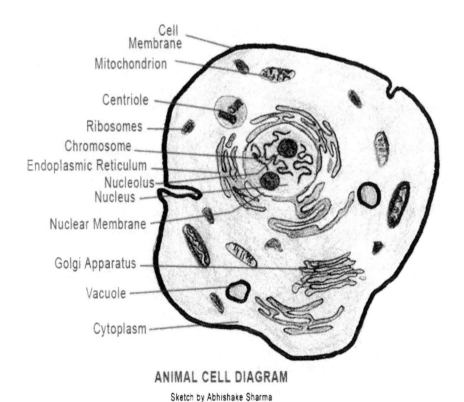

ANIMAL CELL DIAGRAM

Sketch by Abhishake Sharma

The cell of which all living things are composed (courtesy *Campbell's Textbook of Biology 9th Edition*)

The rise and fall of groups of organisms reflect differences in creation of species and their extinction rates. Continental plates moved gradually over time, altering the geography and climate of Earth. These changes led to extinction in some groups of organisms and bursts of new species in others. Evolutionary history has been punctuated by mass extinctions that radically altered the history of life on Earth. Some of these extinctions may have been caused by changes in continent positions, volcanic activity or impacts from meteors or comets. Large increases in the diversity of life have resulted from adaptive radiations that followed mass extinctions. These radiations have occurred in groups of organisms that possess major evolutionary innovations or colonized new regions in which there was little competition from other organisms.

The evolution of new forms can be caused by changes in the nucleotide sequences or regulation of developmental genes, which influence the rate, timing and spatial patterns of change in an organism's form as it develops into an adult. Novel and complex biological structures can evolve through a series of incremental modifications, each of which benefits the organism that possesses it, or in the opposite direction causes changes that preclude an organism or species survival in the environment in which they occurred. The basis of evolutionary change is a modification in the structure or timing or any of these complex processes in the cell through mutation of genes. The word "mutation" is from the Latin *mutare,* meaning "to change." As organisms grew more complex through multicellular stages, the progression of mutation occurred over millions and millions of years. This is not an overnight process or even something that a human can observe over the course of a lifetime.

To put the concept of evolution in clearer focus, you can create an analogy with amino acids and the English alphabet. We have twenty-six letters in the English alphabet, and twenty amino acids. From the English alphabet we can form, for practical purposes, an infinite number of books, based upon the combination of letters forming words, words forming sentences, sentences forming paragraphs, paragraphs forming chapters, and chapters forming books. Nitrogen and hydrogen combining to form an amine, then linking up with carbon, produce amino acids. Amino acids link up to form a protein. Different proteins link up formed from a gene. Genes link up to form a genome. The human genome contains about 25 thousand genes. The average gene size is about three thousand base pairs long. In base pairs adenine is always linked to thymine, and cytosine is always linked to guanine. There are three billion base pairs that make up human DNA. Less than two percent of the genome contains the code for proteins and RNA molecules. Ninety-eight percent of the human genome contains DNA (non-coding DNA) whose function is largely unknown. Non-coding DNA, the DNA that is outside of genes, is thought to play an important regulatory role in controlling how and when genes are used. The greater the similarity between two genomes, the closer the relationship between species.

Much like the analogy with the alphabet, whereas a near infinite number of books can be written from twenty-six letters, likewise with twenty amino acids forming proteins and proteins forming from genes and genes forming the genome, a near infinite number of species is possible. The bigger genome and more genes does not necessarily mean a more complicated organism. Organisms that are very similar to each other can have very different genome sizes. Another analogy can be made from the musical scale *A, B, C, D, E, F, G*. A near infinite number of songs can be composed from these seven notes. Regulatory genes in this analogy could vary the amplitude, pitch, rhythm, etc. of the song played. If we add lyrics to the songs we can conceive how infinite the possibilities are for life forms. *The same structure—the cell—is the basic structure of all life forms.* Life becomes more complex as we ascend the phylogenetic scale. We share thousands of genes with lettuce. Chromosomes are still under intense investigation. The Human Genome Project, a thirteen-year international effort completed in 2003, endeavored to discover all the estimated 20,000 to 25,000 human genes and make them accessible for further biological study. Another goal of the project was to establish the complete sequence of the three billion DNA sub-units in the human genome. Analyses of the data collected by the Human Genome Project will continue for many years to come. Through these investigations, we have learned, for example, that an ape and a human have an almost ninety-seven percent genomic compatibility. The comparison between the human and chimpanzee genomes shows differences in genes that control inflammation and a gene that protects chimpanzees from Alzheimer's Disease. Understanding the effects of these differences may help treat disease in the future.

Looking at comparative genomics the fact is that all life on Earth is very similar. Your DNA sequence shows our close relationship with our earthy neighbors. Your genome is 99.9% identical to that of other humans and about 40% identical to that of mice. So why, then, are ninety percent of species extinct? Because as the genes mutate, they create an organism that is either adaptable to its environment or not. If the organism is adaptable to its environment, it survives through natural selection. This is the foundation of Charles Darwin's groundbreaking *On the Origin of Species* (1859), in which he argued that new species evolved from earlier ones. Darwin's work is the single most important contribution ever made to our understanding of mankind. Organisms that are not adaptable to their environment, as Darwin's work makes clear, become extinct. *Evolution is not necessarily linear and continually producing improved products—it can proceed in the opposite direction.*

Whereas mutation of genetic material, DNA, is the fundamental process producing marked diversity in plant and animal species and their organs rendering survival or extinction, it is also the basis of carcinogenesis. If the problem of cancer is solved by attacking the genetic activity in cellular processes could we stop evolution or alter it?

When I see animal activists campaigning for preservation of certain species like "Save the Whales" it is seemingly disconcerting in some respects because new species will never cease to originate as existing species disappear. *Despite consideration of ecological concerns the overwhelming number of species that ever lived are extinct.* It gives wonder to their crusade.

Fuck the spotted owl.

Mutations that occur in the genetic material contained within the DNA can produce an organism that is more friendly or suited to its environment. For example, the emergence of needle-like skin in a porcupine to ward off predators is a favorable mutation to permit survival of the species. Perhaps the mutation that produced an extremely long neck in a giraffe was a friendly mutation, allowing survival in times of failure of crops on the ground through the ability to graze from trees. If you look at an elephant's ears, perhaps their size reflects the animal's need to better hear predators. Likewise, the mutations that produced powerful thigh and jaw muscles in terrestrial animals, allowing speed in running or biting their prey, permitted survival. If you have ever watched a program on Animal Planet, you see the evolutionary food chain in action. You can watch a lion strip a wallaby down to the skeleton in fifteen minutes. A wallaby that is slower than the rest of the herd is going to be eaten — it is survival of the fittest, as Darwin so eloquently explained.

Certainly the greatest mutation ever was that which took place in neural tissue in primitive ape-man creatures, which allowed advanced cognitive function not seen to this degree in other species, and allowed the complete takeover of the planet Earth. For anyone who has seen the film *Rise of Planet of the* Apes, it is not inconceivable that the high level of cognitive ability of humans could have been induced by a virus changing the DNA of neural tissue. Primates all have a common ancestor. We did not descend from monkeys or apes — we shared a common ancestor. Somewhere in time, probably several hundred thousand years ago, when progressive and ongoing mutations occurred in neural tissue, it gave us advanced cognitive thought processes. This is a concept that today remains difficult for people to understand, because they have not been exposed to enough science and instead have been programmed by religious teachings about how God's will shapes our destiny. But the evidence of Darwin's work is visible in everyday life. Our world is predicated upon survival of the fittest. After millions of years of mutation in genomes allowing natural selection of the fittest and extinction of the less able, species and races and individuals within a particular race survive or die. Look at athletics: Not everyone can play in the NFL or compete in the Olympics. You have to be physically better than the competition. That is why there are gold, silver and bronze medals — the evidence that there are comparative differences and strengths in all humans. Training and working hard are, of course, important aspects of success, but they are not the fundamental aspect because if you are not gifted genetically, you are not going to excel. The results of evolution are staring us in the face, but most people have a hard time comprehending this without understanding the science.

Cognitive thought exists to a degree in many species, such as canines, or dolphins, or chimpanzees and throughout the animal kingdom. They have intelligence and emotion but not to the degree of Homo sapiens, which in Latin means "wise man." The evolution of Homo sapiens gained worldwide attention with the discovery of the skeleton of "Lucy," a three-million-year-old hominid found in 1974 by anthropologist Donald Johanson and his student Tom Gray in northern Ethiopia. Subsequent findings have shown that ape-like specimens with human characteristics date back nearly five million years ago. If you understand that the human brain is a result of mutation, not creation by a supreme being, it explains much of what we know about humans today. It explains why we have retardation; why SAT scores vary; why some people are more creative than others; why there are A students and D students; how people can be sociopaths or psychopaths. All of this relates to the variations in gene expression — in combination with the environment, of course.

Because evolution is based on mutation of the genome — the segment of the chromosome that gives the characteristics of a species — it is worth exploring questions about whether evolution treats all racial genomes equally. While this is certainly a controversial topic in today's politically correct world, from a scientific standpoint it is impossible not to notice that certain traits have evolved among certain racial groups among the human species. Observing trees in a forest, they exhibit a basic structure, namely, a trunk then limbs, which divide into smaller branches, which terminate with leaves. More often than not the identification of the particular tree is made by looking at the character of the leaf and the façade of the bark on the trunk as well as the particular architecture of the tree. Humans like tree anatomy have a torso (trunk), extremities (limbs), fingers (branches), then external facial characteristics (leaves). If one observes a person with blonde hair, blue eyes, white skin would you call him an African? Of course not, he has classic northern latitude features and more likely Scandinavian. If you observe a man with black skin, kinky hair, enlarged lips, and a wide nasal base would you call him an Eskimo? Of course not, he would have the classic appearance of a sub-Saharan African. Also visualizing the average East Asian the eyes are a dead giveaway. You would not call someone with the facial appearance of an East Asian an Italian. The truth is we did not evolve identical in either our external structure or internal physiology. We share a basic structure of human anatomy, but the differences are not quite subtle in skin or color, hair texture, ocular design, lip and mouth architecture, not to mention variation in physiological ability of various organs or pathology in those organs.

Why is it that when I was in medical school at Jefferson the Jewish students were at the top of the class? The politically correct answer would be that they work harder. Or it is cultural. Is the latter the reason why over twenty percent of all CEOs of Fortune 500 companies in America are Jewish, or that twenty-five percent of all Ivy League students are Jewish? Thirty percent of all Nobel Prize winning scientists since 1950 are Jewish. One half of the world's chess champions are Ashkenazi Jews. Eighty-five percent of American Jews are of Ashkenazi descent. Yet they make up less than three percent of the population in the United States. Moreover, the Jewish race comprises less than one percent of the world's population. To claim that this phenomenon is based on work ethic or culture is delusional. It is my belief that Adolf Hitler viewed the Jewish population as a threat. They were brighter and as a consequence, controlled much of banking and industry. A good example in the United States is how the great talent and business sense of the Jewish seed control Hollywood, make no mistake about it. It is not unlike anti-Semitism today, which in my opinion is commensurate with envy. If one reads Jerome Karabel's *The Chosen The Hidden History of Admission and Exclusion at Harvard, Yale, and Princeton* admission criteria had to be changed from an achievement basis to a meritocracy or else the classes would be over ninety percent Jewish which actually occurred at Columbia University in New York. They feared losing the Anglo-Saxon clientele.

When I watched the world track championships while vacationing in Europe, I asked myself why the running and jumping events were dominated by Africans and African-Americans? There were occasional "token" Caucasian athletes. Why are NBA and NFL players predominantly African-American? Is it because they work harder? Or because there are not as many Caucasians who want to make $20 million a year playing a sport? The politically correct answer is that this is due to individuals' hard work. Yes, of course, hard work plays a significant role. But from a scientific standpoint it would be foolish to ignore the facts. *Three months before the London Olympic Games I accurately predicted that there would be no one white on the starting line in the finals of either the men's or women's 100 meter dash.* One might attempt to argue that there are cultural factors at play. That may be true to some extent, but the overwhelming evidence points toward genetic expression. Does this mean a Jew cannot play in the NBA or a sub-Saharan African cannot win the Nobel Prize in science? Of course not. A shift in the Bell curve represents a relative propensity for achievement in an area of human endeavor—it has shifted to the right with academic intelligence among Jews of Ashkenazi descent and with athletic ability in track and field with sub-Saharan Africans and their descendants, African-Americans. These are not absolute conclusions that apply to every human, but the trend is empirically clear in my opinion.

Discussions about how racial genomes have evolved can be uncomfortable or unsettling. But in my view they are perfect examples of how science provides answers to questions that mankind might label as "racist" and often seeks to obfuscate through political correctness or, in the case of religion, through manipulation, avarice and hunger for power. In my own case, science saved me from the brainwashing that was attempted on me by the Catholic Church and the charlatans who masqueraded as teachers.

DEFINITION OF SCIENTIFIC TERMS

Abiotic — Non-living.

Adaptive Radiation — Evolution of a number of divergent species from a common ancestor, each species becoming adapted to occupy a different environment.

Amino acid — A molecule consisting of the basic amine group (NH2), the acidic carboxylic group (COOH), a hydrogen atom (H), and an organic side group attached to the carbon atom. Amino acids are over 100 in nature and are the building blocks of protein. In the human there are 20 involved in making up proteins, 11 non-essential (synthesized in the body) and 9 essential (only obtained from food).

Catalytic — A substance capable of initiating or speeding up of a chemical reaction.

Cell — The basic structure of all living things. An autonomous membrane bound structure, a self-replicating unit that may exist as a functional, independent unit of life containing biomolecules such as nucleic acids, proteins, and polysaccharides.

Chromosome — A linear thread-like strand of DNA that bares genetic material in the nucleus of the cell.

DNA — A double strand of nucleic acid, a ladder-like helical structure that contains the genetic information for cell growth, division, and function.

Enzyme — A substance protein in structure that facilitates a biochemical reaction, making the reaction faster as a catalyst. It is not wasted during the reaction.

Gene — A segment of DNA that is the fundamental, physical, and functional unit of heredity.

Isomer — One of two or more molecules that have the same chemical formula but have a different stereochemical arrangement of their atoms.

Macromolecule — A large complex molecule such as nucleic acids, proteins, carbohydrates, and lipids with relatively large molecular weight.

Metabolism — The process involving a set of chemical reactions that modifies a molecule into another for storage or for immediate use in another reaction. It includes processes for cell growth, reproduction, and response to the environment.

Molecule — A small particle at the cellular level such as a biomolecule.

Mutate — A permanent hereditable change in the nucleotide sequence in a gene or a chromosome.

Nucleic acid — A compound composed of linear chains of nucleotides with phosphoric acid, sugar, and nitrogenous bases involved in preservation, replication, and expression of hereditary information in every living cell.

Nucleotide — The basic building block of nucleic acids such as DNA and RNA. It is made up of a nitrogenous base, a sugar, and a phosphate group.

Organism — An individual living thing that can react to stimuli, reproduce, grow, and maintain homeostasis. It can be a virus, bacterium, fungus, plant or animal.

Polymer — A compound made up of several repeating units (monomers).

Protein — A molecule composed of polymers of amino acids joined together by peptide bonds, distinguished from fat and carbohydrate by containing nitrogen (N2). Other components include carbon (C), hydrogen (H2), oxygen (O2), sulfur (S), and phosphorous. A regulator of gene expression.

Protocell — A large ordered structure enclosed by a membrane that carries out some life activities such as growth and division.

Ribosome — A minute particle composed of protein and RNA that serves as a site of protein synthesis.

RNA — A single strand of ribonucleic acid that plays a role in transferring information from DNA to the protein forming system of the cell. A molecule of nucleotides composed of sugar, phosphate, and a nitrogenous base.

Species — An entire group of organisms having common characteristics capable of mating with one another to produce fertile offspring.

Vesicle — A small sac containing gas or fluid. A membranous structure that stores and transports cellular products and digests metabolic wastes within the cell.

CHAPTER XIII:
THE PATH TO ATHEISM

"Surely a church that expels a priest for advocating women's ordination faster than it does men who have been credibly accused of raping children is in some kind of trouble."
— *Margaret Talbot*

I reflect with dismay at the religious teachings I endured in my elementary, secondary and college education. As I wrote in the previous chapter, the human brain can be viewed as hardware eligible for programming, and religion is one of the most notorious efforts to program young minds. From this notion springs the infamous Jesuit adage, "Give me a lad by the age of seven and I have him for life." Religious programming is no different than television advertising for fast food or sugar-laden cereals: It is an effort to hook consumers, from the youngest age possible, on something that feels good but ultimately can be harmful — not unlike a vagina harboring a sexually transmitted disease.

Man necessarily created the concept of religion. Once genetic mutation occurred creating rational cognitive thought as the human race evolved from earlier species, man needed an explanation for observed phenomena, whether thunder or lightning or other natural occurrences. A rational mind will seek an explanation, a cow will not. And in the absence of scientific knowledge, an explanation was created in the form of a supreme being. Even today, this fabricated explanation is still espoused by supposedly educated people. It is important to note the etymology of the word educate, which comes from the Latin *e-* out of and *ducere-* to lead, meaning "to lead out of" (darkness). But, amazingly,

I still hear educated people attributing the creation of life to a Supreme Being. This is completely irrational. Catholic theologians tell you there is a "soul." Where did that come from? They claim the soul has the attributes of intellect, memory, and will (I am a product of eight years of Jesuit "education"). According to Catholic theology at death the soul leaves the body—now where did it go? Is this like hide the salami? They say it goes to heaven or descends to hell or if there is a chance of salvation you go to Purgatory to pay down sinful debt. And don't forget limbo if you forgot to get baptized on the way to the grave. Then there is the triumvirate- the Father, the Son, and the Holy Ghost. All three are one! Moreover, as the Father is the Son and the Son is the Father, the Father and the Son "spirate" the Holy Ghost. The mental masturbation of these snake oil salesmen called theologians represents fabrication created with smoke and mirrors. It is almost a comical farce.

Most people struggle with trying to understand the world around them. The idea of God or a supreme being is a convenient explanation for everything. And it has turned out to be lucrative as well as prestigious for people who created followings in every culture, from the Incas to the Christians to the Muslims, and on and on. Religion was a way to unite society under some code to live by, but provided significant wealth to the providers and the organizers. William Manchester's brilliant book, *A World Lit Only by Fire*, offers a history of the European Middle Ages, and describes the absolute depravity of the Catholic Church. From debauchery to murder to incest, depraved behavior was routine in the Vatican during the Middle Ages — and it's still occurring today. I think the Catholic Church could be among the most immoral and sordid institutions ever to surface on Earth.

In his book *In God's Name*, the journalist David Yallop contends that Pope John Paul I, who died just 33 days into his papacy in 1978, was murdered because he uncovered corruption in the Vatican bank. According to Yallop, the Vatican bank had floated $100 million in fake bonds and was laundering money from illegal operations by the Mafia. John Paul, who was from a poor parish in Italy where the local bank collapsed due to Vatican bank operations, prepared to institute change when he assumed the papacy. Farmers from his hometown could not get loans and some lost their farms. Yallop's research contends the new Pope was poisoned before he could do so, probably with digoxin in his tea, which he routinely enjoyed prior to bedtime. This relatively young, healthy individual failed to wake up one morning. The Vatican claimed that the sixty-five-year-old John Paul died from a heart attack. There was no autopsy. He was into the ground as soon as possible. But *In God's Name* contends that the Vatican's old guard let John Paul be murdered because he was an intellectual who had designs on making broader changes to the Church. According to Yallop, John Paul was going to change Pope Paul VI's *Humanae Vitae*, which a decade earlier had affirmed the Catholic Church's traditional teachings, including the rejection of birth control. Birth control, of course, is not conducive to the Church's program, because that would create fewer "souls" and, more importantly, less money. The Muslims are no different — they forbid birth control as well, which is why they are proliferating in Europe while other populations across the continent are experiencing lower birth rates. It is expected that by 2050 that Muslims will account for twenty percent of Europe's population, up from four percent today.

Islam and its origins are also disconcerting. According to Zaki Ameen, a Muslim and Imam, he realized how the teachings of Muhammad and the Quran were used to deceive followers in order to gain control, money, and power. In his book *Living by the Point of My Spear* he reveals shocking evidence against Muhammad: He married a child Aisha and deflowered her at age nine (Bukhari 7: 62: 88). He helped behead nine hundred captives in one day (Quran 47: 4). Muhammad was known to rob caravans and received twenty percent of the booty. He had fifty wives and sex slaves while creating Islam, the religion of peace. Yet it was death to apostasy and death to anyone insulting Muhammad or the Quran. And don't forget misogyny, which persists today throughout Islam. Islam is based on hate, violence, rape, war, bloodshed, etc. Look at Islam and Muslim countries today, they are economic failures.

Religion makes me think of the catchphrase from the movie *Jerry Maguire*: "Show me the money!" Think about the whores on Wall Street in recent years who came up with various schemes to make money, such as the credit default swaps that put AIG under. The Catholic Church invented the credit default swap in the Middle Ages: Selling indulgences to gain salvation. It was an insurance policy for the wealthy who could pay for indulgence and continue to sin as they pleased with confidence that salvation and eternal life were guaranteed. For the less well-to do there was the creation of confession, where one could be absolved of their sins with a penance. Selling comfort is a winner! And don't forget to drop some money in the basket on the way out. Anyone who has ever visited St. Peter's Basilica in the Vatican and visualized the Sistine Chapel has to be overwhelmed at the human effort to create one of the most astounding structures ever built. It took one hundred and twenty years and another twenty years to furnish. How do you think the artists for all those magnificent and priceless paintings were paid? This type of behavior is what eventually led Martin Luther and John Calvin to split off from the Catholic Church and form Protestant movements. The Catholic Church's behavior historically is both egregious and abominable. Has anything really changed? As late as 2013, the Vatican Bank continues to be under scrutiny for deceptive practices as a direct consequence of the Lateran Accords of 1929, which were incorporated into the Democratic Constitution of Italy in 1947. It recognized the Vatican as an independent state, with Mussolini agreeing to give the church financial support in return for public support from the Pope at the time. The subsequent sovereign state of the Holy See which was created by the Lateran Pacts of 1929 rendered the Vatican Bank independent from examination and regulation by the Italian government.

It is difficult for me to understand how a rational mind could contribute to the type of delusions that the Catholic Church and other forms of organized religion have promulgated for centuries. What a scam! Take another example: Joseph Smith, the founder of the Latter Day Saint Movement and publisher of the Book of Mormon, was another "visionary" who realized there was money to be made in religion. The Mormon faith, created in the first half of the 19th century, is now one of the wealthiest religions in America. And not only did Smith use religion as a way of creating wealth, he also used it for his personal indulgences by making polygamy legal among Mormons so he could have as many women as he wanted. Smith's life ended after a falling-out with his closest associates who became critical of Smith's power and split to form their own church. He was shot to death in 1844 when a mob invaded the jail where he and his brother were being held for polygamy and other crimes. Smith was a real thinker — he competes with the best of them in the Catholic faith.

All religions are an offshoot of man's attempt to explain his surroundings. The most important product they have to offer is comfort. But the truth is, people need comfort as well as they need hope. Life is awful for most individuals at some time or another because of sickness, death and loss of love so they need comfort and hope. Selling comfort certainly is lucrative, and it ensures the longevity of these religious institutions. This is why I think the Catholic Church, in particular, preys upon the uneducated and the indigent and why their growth is in Latin America and third world countries and declining in the more educated western world. In Britain, the 2011 national census revealed that a quarter of the population claims to have no religion, almost double the figure ten years ago and though the United States remains the most religious country in the West, twenty percent claim themselves to be without religious affiliation—double the number a generation ago. So while I am critical of organized religions, I do see that they provide a way for people to find some solace in their life. Religion can be a powerful community builder and bind individuals through habits of altruism. That solace, however, is based on delusion. It is not in the best interest of any religion to educate people as to how life really evolved on Earth. What is in their best interest is to program people right out of the womb. In relation to the Catholic Church, in which I was raised, this is where the concept of parochial schools comes in. Going back to first grade, we were taught to recite the Baltimore Catechism:

Who made me? God made me.

Who is God? God is the Supreme Being, infinitely perfect, who made all things and keeps them in existence.

Why did God make me? God made me to know him, to love him, and to serve him in this world and be happy with him forever in the next.

What must we do to gain the happiness of heaven? To gain the happiness of heaven we must know, love, and serve God in this world.

The above answers are from rote memory from my early stages of programming in the first grade.

This is how the programming starts. Get them addicted early! The cigarette industry recognized the same strategy — let's hook the kids with Joe Camel. McDonald's uses the same marketing concepts. Put the playground next to the restaurant because the families will come. While they are eating, the children can play on the jungle gym. Then those children will be eating at McDonald's when they are adults with their own children. It is really no different than the Catholic Church. Parochial schools were created to institute the software by age seven. And the Catholic Church took it one step further and, being that it is infested with pedophiles, came up with another brilliant idea: Altar boys. The Catholics made it easy for the church to become a playground for pedophiles. There have been multimillion-dollar settlements in clergy abuse cases across the country — it is a true epidemic. In the United States, more than 6,900 priests have been accused of sexual abuse since 1950 and more than $2.5 billion has been paid in settlements and therapy bills for victims, attorney's fees and costs to care for priests pulled out of ministry from 2004 to 2011 — with major cases from Alaska to the Pacific Northwest to Boston. This total includes the stunning $660 million paid by the Archdiocese of Los Angeles to more than five hundred victims in 2007. And, really, that is just scratching the surface. The global extent of abuse is immeasurable: Ireland, Australia, Germany, and so on and so on.

The church will argue that only four or five percent of priests have been accused of molesting children, which is comparable to the percentage in the general population. More sex, lies without the video tape— it is a corrupt institution. In my youth homosexuality was condemned as abnormal and pathological. You never heard of anyone "coming out of the closet." The priesthood and/or convent offered an option for an alternative lifestyle. Homosexuality has been estimated to be approximately five percent of the general population, not to mention three percent of sheep are gay! I am not against homosexuals, but no one should ever touch a child. Neither homosexuality nor pedophilia is treatable. I repeat: Neither homosexuality nor pedophilia is treatable. If I were running things, I would tax the church and similar institutions out of existence. The entire system is built upon a tradition of corruption, greed, hypocrisy and immorality. Take the most recent Pope, Benedict XVI, who retired in February 2012 due to ill health. In *The New Yorker*, Margaret Talbot reported:

"When Cardinal Joseph Ratzinger assumed the papacy, in 2005, it seemed that he might take on the abuse scandal in a way that his predecessor had not. He met with victims in the United States and the United Kingdom, apologizing and expressing 'shame and humiliation.' In 2011, he instructed bishops to make a priority of rooting out sexual abuse by clerics. But he did not dismiss bishops who had looked the other way, and he did not inaugurate an accountability at the highest levels, as the abused and their advocates had hoped.

Benedict's term, in fact has been characterized by an intensifying disapproval of would-be reformers. In a homily last spring, the Pope denounced the efforts of a reforming priest in Austria, where a hundred and fifty thousand Catholics have left the Church in response to revelations of sex abuse in that country, and called upon Catholics to embrace instead "the radicalism of obedience."

The Catholic Church has brought upon itself the obloquy of society.

Catholic leaders hide behind a pretentious façade of humility and forgiveness, when in reality the Church is a haven for criminal behavior. Cardinal Law from Boston oversaw innumerable cases of priests accused of pedophilia. He transferred these criminals to other parishes where they could continue molesting innocent children. Cardinal Law was transferred to the Vatican and given a high post before he could be indicted for failing to act in negligence of his responsibility.

I attended a Jesuit college because it was all I could afford, since I was paying for it myself, but I was not fond of my education because they bulldozed religion down my throat into my esophagus, stomach and intestines until I was finally able to defecate. Even in our science classes, they would refer to God working in indirect ways. In my biology class, I was taught that God created the first protein molecule. Why would God create man indirectly? The whole concept of religion is a delusion and concomitantly you have to be delusional to hang your hat on it or give a dime to it. In fact, it has been demonstrated that the deeply religious have lower IQs. These religious institutions have caused more death and misery than any good they might have done. Here is a great example: Recently in Dublin, Ireland, a hospital staff refused to give a patient an abortion even though her fetus had no chance of survival, citing the country's Roman Catholic social policies against abortions. The staff waited three days until the seventeen-week-old fetus had died. By then the patient was in an advanced state of septicemia (blood born bacterial infection), and she died four days later. The doctors refused to perform a termination while the fetus had a heartbeat despite the critical state of the mother because of religious belief.

Here is another example: In 2006, a study by the Mind/Body Medical Institute near Boston, concluded that prayers offered by strangers not only did not benefit the recovery of heart surgery patients, those patients who were being prayed for actually suffered higher rates of postoperative complications. The researchers suggested that these complications, such as abnormal heart rhythms, could have been due to expectations created by awareness that prayers had been made on behalf of those patients. This was a major survey of 1,800 patients and, following years of mixed results from studies of prayer, finally made clear that praying has no bearing on healing, and in fact might have a negative effect.

Let us not forget that the Pope is self-proclaimed as infallible in matters of faith and morals which doctrine originated with Pope Pius IX

(1846-1878) and dogmatically defined by the First Vatican Council but originated in medieval theology at the time of the Counter-Reformation. Recall Pope Benedict's condemnation of the use of condoms in Africa where one third of the male population under age forty is infected with the HIV virus. The self-righteous demeanor and arrogance of the Catholic Church in general and the papacy in particular has no boundary even to the detriment of the health, welfare, and potential lives of individuals of an entire continent.

In the neurosurgical field, where you deal with life and death on a regular basis, I have seen many physicians react to the tragedies of life by receding into the solace of religion or alcohol. The other option is to become a hardcore realist, which is what occurred to me over months and years of observing and treating in human tragedy. It became clear to me that no possible creator could allow such a situation. In his book, *Blood and Soil: A World History of Genocide and Extermination from Sparta to Darfur*, Ben Kiernan of Yale University's Genocide Studies Program details the atrocities of humanity in places like Armenia, Germany, Cambodia, Yugoslavia and Rwanda. Researchers have attributed between 150 and 200 million deaths in world history to genocide. In the Central African Republic alone in the past ten years eight million have been slaughtered—more than the Holocaust! Every ethnic group is capable of this type of behavior. *Today,* Eastern Congo is known as "the rape capital of the world" by the United Nations, with reports that forty-eight women are raped every hour. The ancient Romans were cruel. Stalin slaughtered twenty million of his fellow Russians. Read *The Rape of Nanking* to learn the cruelty demonstrated by the Japanese in China, where 300,000 people were killed amid beheading contests and babies were cut out of pregnant women after they were raped. These are examples of what the human animal is capable of doing. And do not forget Hiroshima and Nagasaki.

For any reasonable observer of human life to say that these atrocities are "God's will" — the favorite expression of the fervent believer — is baffling. Is this what a creator wanted? Masterful theologians will take you back to the fall of man and the mythology of the Garden of Eden for examples of man's ego and disobedience. Nice try. What reasonable person with average intelligence could think that this life could be a divine creation? Show me a sprout (the beginning of regeneration of a nerve after transection)!!!

In contradistinction to genocide are natural occurrences eliminating mankind. The recent tsunami in Asia eliminated three hundred thousand people. The recent earthquake in Haiti removed two hundred and fifty thousand. Historically, the Bubonic Plague removed one-third of the population of Europe. Other examples are the Influenza Epidemic of 1918 which eliminated millions around the world and the AIDS virus which has claimed thirty seven million lives so far.

I realize some may read this and think I am an ogre. But, really, you have to be delusional to think that mankind and its actions are the result of a supreme being's creation. But I think most people are afraid to step out of their shells of conventional wisdom. It is toasty in their cocoon. To step outside of that comfort zone and think, "This is it? There is no afterlife?" is an absolutely frightening concept. The old saying "There are no atheists in foxholes" is a good example of the need to believe in religion — it reinforces the notion of a supreme being as salvation in the face of reality, life and death. This is why religion will always persist. It is brainwashing! Religion is the greatest survivor of them all. Superpowers tend to last a century; the great faiths last millenniums. I was fortunate to have a medical education to help overcome the programming of my education in the Catholic Church. I have observed the world. I read books. I think independently. This is how I escaped becoming trapped in these ridiculous beliefs.

The prevalence of religious dogma in so unsettling, particularly in our political and legal debates, where they do not belong. In *Freakonomics*, Steven Levitt presents data proving that after the passage of Roe vs. Wade there was a dramatic drop in crime rates over the next 25 years, supporting the hypothesis that the reduction in unwanted pregnancies resulted in fewer children born into lower socioeconomic groups who would become criminals. Of course this is not to say that an unwanted child born in an inner-city ghetto will become a criminal — there are some great people born under these circumstances. But there is a clear trend toward criminal behavior in lower socioeconomic groups. This is why I think the demands for the outlawing of abortion by the Catholic Church and the right-to-lifers in America are harmful to society.

In 2011, U.S. Health and Human Services Secretary Kathleen Sebelius overruled the Food and Drug Administration and forbade the sale of Plan B One-Step emergency contraceptives to be sold over the counter. While this was billed as a safety issue, the decision came during an election season in which discussions of contraception would galvanize the religious right. Plan B is not even an abortion pill — it's a contraceptive. But to members of the religious right, with their programmed blinders on, it is akin to murder. In my years in neurosurgery, I have unplugged many people from respirators who were brain dead and had no respiratory effort, but had a heartbeat and blood pressure. Was I committing murder? In that same vein, if a doctor scrapes out a group of cells growing on the uterine wall, is that murder? These are not questions for those programmed by religion to answer. I do not want someone on the U.S. Supreme Court carrying religious dogma into his or her interpretation of the Constitution to determine how people should live in America. I would prefer nine atheists on the bench to prevent this from happening, because the Constitution could be interpreted toward an individual's religious beliefs and programming. Just because someone is extremely intelligent, even brilliant in his or her field, does not mean he or she cannot fall prey to the psychological benefits of religious belief. Some of the brightest people in their fields are fervent believers in religion and a creator and vice versa. But among those who are educated as to the origins of life on Earth, the numbers tell a different story. A 2009 poll by the Pew Research Center for the People and the Press revealed that fifty-one percent of members of the American Association for the Advancement of Science expressed belief in a higher power, compared to ninety-five percent of the general American public. However, in a 1998 survey of members of the National Academy of Science that provided insights by fields of specialty, just 5.5 percent of biologists and 7.5 percent of physicists and astronomers affirmed a belief in God.

Around 1995 the first planets outside our solar system were discovered, and now number as high as seventeen hundred. About four Earth-like planets have also been discovered which offers the possibility and more likely probability of life existing outside our solar system as quite high. When you look at the sky and realize all those stars are suns to the planets around them, I think life on Earth is a chance occurrence. Earth is the precise distance from the sun, our star, providing the temperatures necessary to allow life as we know it to evolve. However, we are expendable. The right size meteor or asteroid hitting Earth could extinguish life as we know it. This is what people need to understand: We are expendable.

I worry about my children falling victim to religious propaganda. I want them to be intelligent, objective observers of life. In their childhood I explained to them that their teachers are fervent believers in the religion in which they were programmed. I explained that the tenets of their faith are not necessarily true. If you are a child growing up in India more likely than not you would be a Hindu and believe in reincarnation. If you grow up in Pakistan you would likely be a Muslim and believe in Muhammad and the teachings of the Quran. If you are born and raised in Japan you would read the teachings of the Buddha and practice Shintoism. In Israel you would be raised with the Torah and believe that Jesus Christ was nothing more than a carpenter. In China, knock yourself out with Confucius. If you are not so intelligently endowed you might adopt Scientology, a body of beliefs created by L. Ron Hubbard. Scientology teaches that people are immortal beings who have forgotten their true nature. Its method of spiritual rehabilitation is a form on counseling known as *auditing* in which one re-experiences painful events in their past in order to free themselves. Such auditing courses are made available for specified donations. It is the most controversial new religious movement of the twentieth century described as a cult that brainwashes, financially defrauds and abuses its members charging exorbitant fees for its spiritual services. Further controversy has focused on the belief that souls, *thetans,* reincarnate and have lived on other planets before living on Earth.

A moron would be a euphemism for a Scientologist.

I have been a physician for more than forty-five years. You want to talk about life? Go back to 1967, when I was an intern at Pennsylvania Hospital. I was on an obstetrics rotation and one evening I took a young girl from the inner city up to the delivery room. I delivered her baby in the elevator on the way up! She screamed, "What's that thing, what's that thing?" I said, "Honey, that's your baby!" "Baby?!" she yelled, "I thought I had gas!" Tell me, was this God's will?

My thoughts often return to the early days on the neurosurgery service at Iowa, when I was called to the emergency room to see that twelve-year-old girl who fell on an escalator while shopping with her mother. She had beautiful long hair that got caught in the escalator teeth. It ripped her entire scalp off. So she came in with no scalp — just her skull showing. But the horror was more than that. The fall broke her neck, and she would be quadriplegic forever. What did that poor child do to deserve this? Where is the creator when you need him? If the creator appeared perhaps in the form of Christ I would consider pushing in his crown of thorns a little deeper hoping to alter his judgment through partial frontal lobotomy. With tears running down her eyes, never going to move her arms and legs again, you want me to believe that somebody or something created this? That she is paying for somebody's sins? Whatever you are smoking—pass it on!

CHAPTER XV:
SAILING

"Ah! The good old time—the good old time. Youth
and the sea. Glamour and the sea! The good, strong
sea, the salt, bitter sea, that could whisper to you and
roar at you and knock your breath out of you."
— *Joseph Conrad*

It was a crisp, clear fall day in late October around 1987 when I set sail from Newport Harbor, Rhode Island to return *Aeolus*, a Swan 47, to her home berth in Annapolis, Maryland. I had followed this routine for many years after the summer racing season in New England. I purchased Aeolus in 1981. On odd years, I would come to Newport with the Annapolis to Newport race. On even years, I would enter the Bermuda race, which ran from Newport, Rhode Island to the island of Bermuda.

While *Aeolus* made passage out of Newport Harbor I noticed the small white caps beginning to form on the ocean surface, indicating the breeze was now approaching thirteen to fifteen knots. I had checked the weather forecast and there was no suggestion of foul weather for our passage. Although I thought it unusual that the wind was out of the northeast on such as beautiful day, which appeared to have high pressure over New England as winds typically come from the west-northwest with a high-pressure system. We finished our morning coffee as we passed Point Judith en route to the rhumb line to Cape May. The plan for arriving in Annapolis was via Delaware Bay and the Delaware-Chesapeake canal into upper Chesapeake Bay. While passing Point Judith to starboard,

I noticed the wave height increasing from what was previously about one foot in Newport Harbor past Brenton Light to now two to four feet with white caps building. We were soon passing Montauk to starboard thirty miles off shore when the wind strength was approaching a fresh breeze at twenty-five knots, sometimes gusting to thirty-two knots. We reduced sail. We were on a broad reach on starboard tack and I reduced the foresail to a #4 jib. Our boat speed was nine knots. Our apparent wind was fifteen to twenty knots. The sea state and wind strength early on and the minimal number of crew, namely four of us, precluded setting a spinnaker out of Newport Harbor. Within the next two hours, the wind gradually began to howl and whistle through the rigging. I had one reef in the mainsail when I realized we were in a full gale. The wind was averaging thirty-five to forty knots with gusts to forty-five knots. I reduced sail to a triple reefed main and kept the #4 head sail to balance the rig. The Swan was one of the finest production yachts made and certainly in the era in which *Aeolus* was built, she could take a battering sea and the fear of losing the rig was not a consideration at that time since Swans rarely lost their rig even in violent storms. I soon realized we were in trouble. Despite continued sunny skies, there was an apparent intense low-pressure coming up from the Bahamas, which was now just south of Cape Hatteras and sucking the air out of New England. The white capped waves now reaching six to seven feet in height were whipping against the hull, making a great thud as the boat tried to force its way through peaks and troughs. We were taking the waves on the starboard quarter. We donned our life jackets. We cleated ourselves with a tether onto strong deck fittings. I did not trust lifelines. As the wind picked up to over forty knots steady with gusts of forty-eight knots, I removed the #4 head sail and put up a staysail on the baby stay as *Aeolus* was cutter rigged. Taking the helm, the boat felt balanced with a triple-reefed main and the staysail. It is noteworthy that years later reading John Rousmaniere's fascinating account of the 1979 Fastnet race, the boat on which he sailed, a sister ship Swan 47, in that horrific storm carried the same sail combination of a triple-reefed main and a staysail. I was worried. Fear was part of it. I was concerned for our crew's safety. We were significantly away from land and in the preferable deep water which allowed less of a wave height than if we were in shallow water. There was no fear of a lee shore since the New England coast was to weather. I went below to check the charts to see where we might be able to duck in if things worsened. The Long Island coast did not afford water to accommodate a nine-foot draft.

The wind was now gusting over fifty knots.

I was angry at myself for not having been able to forecast what lay ahead when we departed Newport. I always check the weather meticulously, and this was not forecasted. My mistake was not getting the updated forecast once we were underway. The next tactic was to seek shelter. I considered going under bare poles since we were running with the wind, but now feared for the rigging. Hoving to was another option, but I needed some sail area to balance the boat in the gusts. During the act of reducing sail and getting the baby-stay up with the staysail, I put Bucky Katzenbach on the helm because we needed muscle on the foredeck. At the time Bucky was a retired surgeon about age seventy-two and was a decent sailor. His cousin, Nick, was President Richard Nixon's attorney general. Bucky was doing a reasonable job holding the yacht steady in the waves. All of a sudden, I saw a ten-foot wave come over the stern of the yacht and strike Bucky and throw him against the pedestal. We later learned that in that collision, Bucky broke five ribs. As a true stoic, he never said a word. He stayed at the helm because he knew we were in trouble and the weather could develop further into survival seas.

A well-built boat like a Swan will certainly take more punishment than the crew. Our goal was not to become exhausted where we could not fight the weather any longer. In the 1979 Fastnet race, the yachtsmen gave up before their boats did. Most of the seventeen sailors who died, abandoned their yachts, which were later found floating. The old adage, "always step up into a life raft," holds true. Most of the yachts were recovered still floating after the Fastnet storm and those sailors who stayed with the boat remained alive. Another factor in this type of weather is allaying the fear which grows like a fungus among the crew coupled with fatigue which will often sap the crew morale. The strain on the helmsman was substantial. We had to alternate the helm every twenty minutes. Crashing waves would sweep across the deck. The cockpit would fill and then empty. We were helping with buckets, trying to keep the cockpit free of water as water found its way below the rear cockpit hatch into the rear cabin. I decided not to lie ahull. In this state, the yacht is left to find its own position in the waves under bare poles. The wave height could induce a broach or worse yet, a one hundred and eighty degree roll leaving us upside down as a rogue wave could cause. I was not a fan of sea anchors at that time. I kept the crew weight abaft the beam to try to prevent the bow from digging in and the boat broaching or pitchpolling. I started to question why I ever left shore and got involved in the sport of sailing because I certainly did not want anything to do with the situation I found myself and my crew in. We started to be concerned for our lives as the whistling of the wind through the rigging with the waves crashing and our exhaustion building. In the back of my mind "how big will this get? How long will this last? How near is the nearest land and safe harbor?" The wind was gusting to fifty-six knots.

In the summer of 1961, I took over as the manager of the Fairways Swim Club in Somers Point, New Jersey, where I had spent previous two summers as a rotating lifeguard between Somers Point and Cape May. The manager's job allowed me to make sufficient funds not only for my college education but for medical school as well. As pool manager, I would close up at seven o'clock every evening. One night as I was cleaning up after closing, a gentleman approached me to ask if his son who was a collegiate swimmer could use the pool to train while I cleaned up. I agreed and each night he would swim laps while I finished my work. One night the man asked if I would like to join him and his son for a sail. I had never been sailing. I had done power boating as a teenager and in my early twenties, secretly taking out my uncle Stan's thirty-two-foot Chris-Craft for fishing and joy riding with my friends. The closest I had ever been to sailing was seeing sailboats on the bay while going by them under power.

I readily accepted the offer.

They took me down to the dock at Somers Point and brought me onto their eighteen-foot sailboat. I was instantly fascinated by the aesthetic, peaceful, and thrilling sensation of a boat moving through the water under the power of the wind without the sound of an engine. Moving along the bay at seven knots guided by the wind and the sound of the water hitting the hull was addicting, but it would be more than a decade before I set sail again on Lake McBride in, of all places, Solon, Iowa. At that time, in the early 1970s, chasing Elke Hunter, the Bavarian beauty, who unknown to me was married, was the fortuitous event that allowed my sailing lessons to begin. Her husband, Chase Hunter, a former chopper pilot in Vietnam, taught me to sail—which event I discussed in a previous chapter during my neurosurgical residency at the University of Iowa.

After I moved into practice in New Jersey, I took advantage of any opportunity to sail. I still maintained contact with Oliver Grin, a fellow neurosurgery resident at Iowa, who practiced in Grand Rapids, Michigan. Oliver also developed an interest in sailing and had bought a boat. He told me that he had taken courses at the Offshore Sailing School in Captiva Island, Florida. He suggested that I do the same. Subsequently, after my daughter was born in 1978, we looked for a place to go for spring break and I decided to take a course at Captiva Island, Florida. I took their learn-to-sail course at Offshore and became qualified to take a small boat out on my own. Captiva Island is a barrier island, having been named by pirates who kept their women in a location they could not escape. I continued to sail and annually took courses. After "Learn to Sail," I took "Learn-to-Cruise," then "Learn-to-Race," then "Advanced Racing." In Princeton, Lake Carnegie had Sunday afternoon sailing events. I bought myself a Laser and competed every Sunday afternoon at the Kingston end of the lake.

After one of my weeklong courses at Offshore, I met Steve Colgate one day on the dock. Steve was a member of the family behind the Colgate toothpaste fortune and he was the very first person to start sailing schools in the United States. He is one of the world's best-known sailing instructors and author of multiple books on sailing and cruising. Along with his wife, Doris, they started the Offshore Sailing School, which has taught thousands to sail and race. Steve was a former Olympic sailor and America's Cup competitor. He has pioneered sailing instruction not only nationally, but internationally. I wanted to learn more from Steve and as my family enjoyed Captiva Island, I bought a timeshare so we could go there annually during spring break.

After completing all the courses offered at Offshore, I was crewing on small boats at the Jersey shore, crewed at Atlantic City race week or on Barnegat Bay racing out of the Toms River Yacht Club. By the early 1980s, I decided to buy a boat. I was doing well financially and my practice was successful. I was attracted to ocean racing and therefore I needed a larger seaworthy boat. I realized that the cost of yachting and racing large boats in particular was formidable. I decided to take on a partner who might like to share the boat as well as the expense. My sights focused on Bill Hardesty, a vascular surgeon at Mercer Medical Center whose father was an admiral in the US Navy and taught at the Naval Academy at one time. Prior to the 1986 tax law change, one could own a yacht and put it up for charter and then have a five-year straight line depreciation so the tax dollars would offset a lot of the expense. Bill Hardesty was in agreement, we purchased a new Swan 47 made in Pietarsaari, Finland. The yacht was transported to Annapolis and now we were ready to go. Since I read Homeric Greek for several years in prep school and had read *The Odyssey* as well as the *Iliad* and Xenophon's *Anabasis*, I was familiar with the story of Odysseus arriving on the island of Aeolia where the king, Aeolus, gave him a gift of a bag and told him not to open the bag unless he was in trouble at sea. After he departed from Aeolia, Odysseus could not stand the suspense and opened the bag. The bag contained winds, which blew him back to safety to Aeolia where the king was highly displeased that Odysseus disobeyed him. On christening day, I read this passage from Homer in the original Greek. I suppose the witnesses viewed this as perhaps eccentric, but it was hard to abandon my classical education. The yacht was absolutely spectacular and dressed for the christening at the dock in Annapolis Harbor.

I was ready to go racing.

What follows is a brief representative example of each of the numerous ocean races in which I participated over the next thirty years:

THE ANNAPOLIS TO NEWPORT RACE:

The Annapolis to Newport race is biennial and one of the most historic and well known of the United States east coast blue water races. It provides a contrast between the country's largest estuary, the Chesapeake Bay and the Atlantic Ocean. The race course heads south from the starting line in Port Annapolis for 120 miles to Chesapeake Bay bridge tunnel. This represents typically the windward leg of the race. Once rounding the Chesapeake Light at Virginia Beach the second leg is northeast in the open ocean to Newport, Rhode Island. Depending on wind and tactics Block Island can be left to starboard or port. It is a favorite for first time offshore competitors like myself as well as experienced blue water racers. It is a challenge for weather, tactics, boat handling, and skill along the 475 mile race course. As southwesterlies are the prevailing breeze in June, the time of the race, the Chesapeake Bay leg of the race is usually the windward leg and once you round Chesapeake Light into the Atlantic Ocean, it is a downwind spinnaker run to Newport. As you had to be qualified to enter this category of ocean race, I did fudge my application a bit saying that I had been sailing on the ocean for many years. This was true, of course, but in a power boat rather than a sailboat, but I did not specify. My application for the race was accepted and with a crew of fourteen, I went to the starting line with some trepidation, but with an unsurpassed sense of adventure. Prior to the race, the chairman of the board of Mercer Hospital, Jodie Comley, called and asked if I could bring along the son of a business associate. Although I had a full crew, as a favor to Jodie, I made room. His name was Billy Nettles and as it turned out, he was a terrific sailor. He sailed for the Citadel in South Carolina. He was a wonderful young man. At the time of this writing thirty years later, Billy Nettles was just named the US Attorney for the State of South Carolina. When Billy first came aboard, I showed him an

Exxon roadmap that showed the east coast and told him, "This is what I am using for a chart." He assumed we did not know what we were doing and thought about leaving, until I said, "Billy, we are only kidding you." So, he caught on to our sense of humor and pretty soon we found out that his sense of humor was even greater. He had us laughing all the way to Newport. Peter Vielbig was our chef and lifelong friend who cooked on most of my offshore excursions. He was a former coast guardsman and a knowledgeable sailor. Even in high winds and heavy seas, Peter would be strapped in the galley cooking gourmet meals while crew members were seasick and vomiting off the transom.

A race like Annapolis to Newport in a forty-foot monohaul takes about four days with average wind strength. You have to continually trim sails, optimizing your course to the wind while observing the sea surface to see where the breeze might be stronger. It is interesting that once you enter the ocean often competing yachts have disappeared as they are spread out beyond the seven mile visual limit to the horizon. Analyzing and battling the weather is an aspect of sailing that has always fascinated me. For example, if the high pressure was coming across the race course, you know that the breeze will start from the west northwest and then clock to the right. You have to position the boat so that as the wind changes direction your bow is headed toward the destination on the most optimal wind angle. You would sail toward the anticipated shift going upwind and away from the anticipated shift going downwind so that you tack or jibe favorably when it does shift. These are the tactics of yacht racing and ocean racing. It was like Latin and Greek - an intellectual exercise. Yacht racing in many ways is like chess on water and a totally cerebral as well as physical sport. There are no dumb good sailors.

We did reasonably well for my first ocean race, finishing in the upper third of the fleet. The record time for this race is held by *Carrera*, Joseph Dockery's Farr 60, which set a new course record in 2001 of 42 hours, 58 minutes, 12 seconds.

THE NEWPORT TO BERMUDA RACE:

2006 marked the 100th anniversary of the Newport to Bermuda race. This historic race began in 1906 as the first ocean race for amateur sailors. It has attracted almost 4,500 boats crewed by 46,000 men and women who have raced nearly three million miles to Bermuda. The Brooklyn Yard Club started the race in New York Bay in 1906 and the Royal Bermuda Yacht Club finished it off St. David's Head. In the very first race, critics predicted disaster and it was rumored that funeral wreaths were delivered to the fleets so the sailors will be prepared to make a decent burial at sea. Three boats, forty feet or smaller, started at the first race, but eventually the Bermuda race became a major national and international event currently with more than one hundred entries from around the world.

As Annapolis to Newport race occurs on odd years, the Newport to Bermuda race occurs on even years. Newport to Bermuda was the mother of all races and was now in my sights, having got my feet wet literally with the Annapolis to Newport race. The 100th anniversary of the Newport to Bermuda race occurred in 2006. It is arguably the greatest classic ocean race in the world. It is 683 miles on the rhumb line from Newport harbor to the St. David's Lighthouse in Hamilton, Bermuda. Historically, three significant factors in this particular ocean race are the weather, the gulf stream, and the last thirty miles. Prior to 1980, the race would take place without the aid of any modern navigational instruments such as LORAN. Satellite navigation had not been invented, nor had GPS come on the scene. It was a Corinthian race historically and traditionally. Navigators had to use a sextant to determine the boat's position. Bermuda is only thirty miles wide, and if it is overcast you could miss the island. In the late 1970s and 1980s, LORAN became popular, which stood for Long Range Aid to Navigation. There would be a master station and two slave stations to receive the signal, and based upon your reception of signal and the time interval between the master and slave stations, you could calculate your position. The trouble was LORAN was inaccurate beyond 200 miles offshore and the island of Bermuda lies four hundred miles off the coast of South Carolina.

Today yachts utilize GPS (global positioning system), which is accurate to within a boat length of your position. The prevailing southwesterlies make the fetch to Bermuda a tight reach. The compass bearing along the rhumb line is one hundred and seventy degrees. One of the biggest challenges is the Gulf Stream, which is a warm current coming up through the Florida Straits representing three to four knots of current strength, coursing northeasterly along the atlantic coast of the United States and then curving easterly toward the Elizabethan Islands south of Cape Cod such as Martha's Vineyard and Nantucket. The warm water of the Gulf Stream is why we enjoy the ocean as bathers along the eastern seaboard. North of Cape Cod where the Gulf Stream does not meander, the water is cold at around fifty degrees. Navigators begin to study the Gulf Stream six months before the start of the race, which occurs in mid-June when the oceans are calmest. Large eddies pinch off the stream, rotating both counter-clockwise (warm eddies) and clockwise (cold eddies). These eddies can be ten miles or one hundred and twenty miles wide. Picture a bicycle wheel rotating clockwise or counterclockwise. If your boat is on the outside border of the tire in the direction of Bermuda, your speed over the ground will be substantial. If, however, your boat is on the side of the wheel rotating toward Newport, your speed over the ground can even be negative.

A navigator must consider the downside of the boat's position relative to the Gulf Stream if the wind dies while crossing the stream. A yacht could be swept east of the rhumb line in a light breeze or in no breeze and when prevailing winds pick up you might have to tack to Bermuda. The extreme volatility of the Gulf Stream as it leaves Cape Hatteras complicates these tactical decisions as large eddies form unpredictably, much like you would see in a river breaking off each edge. The navigational dilemma and challenge is to position your yacht on the correct side of either a warm or cold eddy which is going toward your destination. Getting it wrong could mean facing short-term adverse current while competitors seize positive current resulting in a compounded velocity differential.

The Bermuda race was a crap-shoot.

Action at the 1988 Swan World Cup, Porto Cervo, Sardinia
Colt International foreground left

Exactitude upwind, 1986 Swan World Cup, Porto Cervo, Sardinia

Colt International heavy air spinnaker run in the Straights of Bonifacio between Corsica and Sardinia Swan World Cup, 1988

The Royal Bermuda Yacht Club, Newport to Bermuda Race 1986 (from left: Tom Glassie, Tony Chiurco, Toby Bull, Al Scalabrine, John Milburn, and Andrew Dunbar end right)

Tony Chiurco (right) receiving the trophy from Paul Buttrose
after winning The International 12-Metre North American
Championships, Newport, Rhode Island, 2004

American Eagle foreground, sailing upwind against *Weatherly*
Edgartown 12-Metre Regatta, Martha's Vineyard, 2011

Fazisi coming out of Direktor's yard Fort Lauderdale, Florida, 1991

The crew of *Fazisi* Miami Montego Bay Race, 1991

Tony Chiurco (left) with Ralph Mason, Porto
Cervo, Sardinia, Swan World Cup, 1986

Tony Chiurco at the helm of *Colt International* (note the "South" added
above Philadelphia on the transom) Porto Cervo, Sardinia, 1988

Aeolus port tacking the fleet. Swan North American
Championships Newport, Rhode Island, 1986

Tony Chiurco receiving The Seven Seas Trophy from Commodore Lawrence Huntington, The New York Yacht Club, 2006

Crew of *Exactitude,* Swan World Cup Porto Cervo, Sardinia, 1986 (left: Teddy Turner next to Tony Chiurco, standing second from left)

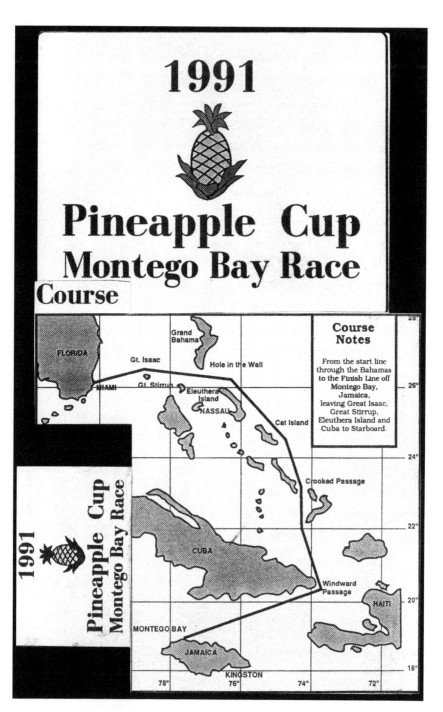

The Miami to Montego Bay Race, course through
the Caribbean Sea (The Pineapple Cup)

Vladislav Murnikov,
designer of *Fazisi*

Tony Chiurco inspecting
the rigging of *Fazisi* prior to
The Pineapple Cup, 1991

Tony Chiurco showing Eddie Chiurco fundamentals at the helm

Tony Chiurco concentrating at the helm of *Fazisi* with Peter Grimm, rounding Cuba in the Windward Passage at 22 knots boat speed under spinnaker. Miami to Montego Bay Race, 1991.

Tony Chiurco and Peter Vielbig, on-board chef

Aeolus christening day October 1982

Tony Chiurco (center), Bill Hardesty (center
right) christening day Annapolis, 1982

Tony Chiurco (left) with Paul Buttrose, April 1982

Aeolus on the edge of a broach, Swan North American
Championships, Newport, Rhode Island, 1983

In 1986, our class had a spinnaker start as the wind direction off the New England coast came from the north. We left Block Island to starboard. We rarely saw another boat after the first twenty-four hours. We fought occasional squalls staying west of the rhumb line. As we entered the Gulf Stream the wind died and we were swept east to the rhumb line when fortuitously the southwesterlies returned leaving us close hauled to Bermuda as we entered the Sargasso Sea. About twelve hours out of Bermuda I noticed a sweet scent in the air, almost perfume like—the smell of pine and spruce trees. I had caught the scent of our destination—the island of Bermuda. It was three o'clock in the morning when we approached Kitchen Shoals and suddenly it was as crowded as a bus station with tremendous number of yachts converging toward the finish line at St. David's Light. It was an exciting adventure which took us about four days as we arrived tired and with a sense of achievement, having placed again in the top third of boats for the overall finish. Because of the numerous shipwrecks at the bottom of Kitchen shoals, the magnetic direction of your compass can be inaccurate. When the sails came down, the crew began to celebrate and we motored to the dock at the Royal Bermuda Yacht Club. Sailing stories began to circulate around the bar and as we imbibed we celebrated not running onto the numerous reefs surrounding the finish line. Ultimately, your finish is a result of not only persistence, hard work, and homework, but also teamwork. The 2002 record of fifty-four hours set by Roy Disney's *Pyewacket* in 2002 was broken in June 2012 by George David's decade old, ninety-foot Rambler maxi yacht which lowered the course record by fourteen hours to thirty-nine hours, thirty-nine minutes, eighteen seconds, averaging over sixteen knots under perfect sailing conditions.

Being at sea for more than four days, the ground was moving up and down as I walked ataxic down the tree-lined streets of Bermuda.

In addition to distance ocean racing I raced in numerous Edgartown regattas at Martha's Vineyard, Block Island Race Week, as well as the North Atlantic Swan regattas held in Rhode Island Sound.

THE SWAN WORLD CUP:

Porto Cervo is the center of attraction of the Costa Smeralda, which means "Emerald Coast" in Italian. Costa Smeralda was developed in the 1960s by the Aga Khan, one of the world's wealthiest royals, along with the aristocracy of the Italian business community, such as Fiat chief Gianni Agnelli. The Aga Khan's father, Aly Kahn, was given his weight in diamonds by the Muslim sect he ruled over. (It is no wonder he was once married, among others, to Rita Hayworth, the famous American actress.) They put luxury hotels on these twenty miles of coastline on northeast Sardinia, overlooking spectacular mountains and pristine green water, making it a highly attractive vacation spot for the aristocracy of Europe. Yachting World Cups were hosted by the Yacht Club Costa Smeralda and attracted yachts owned by the wealthy of many nations. For my first World Cup in 1986, I arranged to charter a sixty-five-foot yacht called *Exactitude* from a Danish company. The Swan 651 designed by German Frers was a formidable yacht requiring a crew of eighteen to control such raw power, especially in high wind. I had never raced a boat that large, and there was excitement in the challenge among the crew as we embarked on the racecourse. We entered the racing division. The wind would blow so hard some days, we had to cancel racing because of mistral, a breeze that can rise to fifty knots, beyond gale-force strength. I believe mistral is caused by a gargantuan sea breeze as the continent of Africa heats up and sucks the air off the Mediterranean. We were one of only two American entries in the World Cup that year. That was the year Ronald Reagan bombed Libya, which is right across the Mediterranean from Sardinia. There was fear for terrorist retaliation against any Americans or boats flying the American flag. The only other American entry was the yacht *Zoom*, a Swan 65 owned by Dave Solomon, a real estate developer in New York. We finished fourth in the racing division, and I got the "Losers Trophy," a nice crystal vase, which still sits in my bookcase.

The Aga Khan held a dinner one night for the skippers of the yachts in the World Cup. I recall sitting directly across from him, and the two of us stared at each other because we sort of looked alike. He had the same male-pattern baldness and the same relatively weaker chin line. We chatted briefly, and it turned out he happened to be a classmate of Andrew Dunbar's father, Charles Dunbar, at Harvard. (Andrew took care of my boat and was part of my crew for that World Cup. Charles Dunbar was a career diplomat who spoke fluent Farsi and I subsequently learned reading *Time* magazine that he had negotiated the 'arms for hostages' deal with Iran.) This was an opulent banquet on the grounds of the Cala di Volpe Hotel in Porto Cervo, where the James Bond movie *The Spy Who Loved Me* had been filmed. Among historic architecture, landscaping and scenery around us, it was just spectacular. I sat next to a skipper from Australia who had produced and directed *The Thornbirds*.

Attending the lavish parties at the Cervo Tennis Club and the Yacht Club Costa Smeralda, I saw firsthand how the aristocracy of Europe lived. I observed it as someone who came up from South Philly and was lucky enough to experience a totally different culture. It made me realize how the upper one percent lived. You know, having a lot of money does not buy happiness — but you can sure have a hell of a lot of fun. And it certainly makes misery easier to bear. But if you like yacht racing, you need to have a lot of money — there is no way around it. This is not really a hobby for doctors. The men driving the big boats in the 1980s were real estate developers. When real estate markets tanked in the early '90s, they were gone. Now the ones driving the boats are from Goldman Sachs and other investment banks on Wall Street or entrepreneurs from the computer world.

An interesting anecdote occurred during our practice session the first day when I blew out my #4 headsail. In a favorite drinking spot later that evening I ran into the skipper of a large non-participating yacht called *Drum* lying in the harbor. The skipper was Johnny Le Bon, brother of Simon Le Bon of the English band Duran Duran. With slurring words as the evening wore on with Johnny, I mentioned my predicament and Johnny loaned me his #5 headsail from his eighty foot boat, which was perfect as a #4 on my sixty-five foot boat. *Drum* had just completed the Whitbread Round the World race and had turned upside down in the Solent off the Isle of Wight and U.K. frogmen rescued the crew. Johnny was terrific, especially as a drinking pal and I always regretted not taking him up on his invitation to visit Simon's nightclub in London.

After my first World Cup, I had such a burning desire to win that I returned to Sardinia in 1988. At that time, I chartered a tall rig Swan 59, *Colt International*, from John Baker and assembled an even better crew. Steve Colgate called the tactics. Unfortunately we finished seventeenth out of eighty-six yachts. Each day of the Cup was sponsored by a different vendor, and on Rolex Day *Colt International* was in the lead. We were flying downwind in a heavy air spinnaker run. A Swan 46, *Midnight Sun*, was riding our stern wave. She was crewed by the team who won the America's Cup on *Australia II* in 1983 from Dennis Connor and the New York Yacht Club, ending the longest possession of a trophy in the history of sports. This was a good example of the level of competition participating in the Swan World Cup. As we arrived at the leeward mark, where you drop the spinnaker and raise the jib sail, Billy Nettles jammed it in the feeder and he could not get the sail hoisted, so everybody went by us. At a party after, at the home of Stan Switlik (owner of the Switlik Parachute Co.), the crew gave me a fake Rolex to remember the race. I was disappointed not to win, but in reality anything can happen in a yacht race. The yacht *Evrika* won the World Cup that year with a stacked crew. Moose McClintock was driving with an America's Cup team on board, including Mike Toppa, etc. Because of my classic education I cannot help but mention *Evrika* is from the Greek meaning "I have found it"—the word allegedly yelled by Archimedes running naked down the streets of Athens after discovering the concept of specific gravity, proving that the King's crown was truly gold. It is dramatic that *Evrika's* owner died from a heart attack on the deck the day after winning the World Cup. But it is even more ironic that his son died in the same place on the deck when the boat was launched at the factory in Finland several years prior. *Evrika* was raced in his memory and then the father died in the same way in the same place.

I had a British crew, Rich Mason, who commented before the regatta started that he had seen *Evrika* hauled in the islands and that she carried a modified keel and that I should protest her to the race committee. The race committee sent a diver down to investigate and reported that it was a standard keel, which brings us to another ironic episode in my long career racing yachts.

ANTIGUA RACE WEEK:

Three years later, in 1991, I went down to Antigua to find a boat for Antigua Race Week. I traveled there during the week of the yacht charter show, and lo and behold what do I see? *Evrika*. I inquired about chartering the boat, and the French captain invited me on board for lunch. *Evrika* was then owned by Richard Wright, the keyboard player of Pink Floyd. There were multiple platinum albums on the bulkhead in the main salon. Wright bought the yacht from the Basel-Mavrites family of Virginia, who likely were glad to dispose of her following the family misfortune, which occurred on her deck. While we were eating, I said to him, "You know? I have heard that *Evrika* has a modified keel." And he told me, "Yes, it does. In fact, we were protested in Sardinia a few years ago. They sent a diver down, but they cannot tell."

I never told him that I was the one who protested!

The keel modification did not matter for the Caribbean yacht rating system, so I made a deal and chartered *Evrika* for Antigua Race Week, which is one of the great regattas in the world. The regatta is held at the end of April when yachts leave the Caribbean for summer in the Mediterranean. There were a dozen Swan 65s in our class. Talk about excitement: Rounding the marks with a dozen sixty-five-foot boats within a length or two of each other, with spinnakers and all the laundry up, is an amazing sight and simultaneously formidable. En route to the leeward mark I was passing a fifty-plus-foot boat to windward, taking a chance that the helmsman would not luff me because we were not racing in the same class. I kept my eye on him and was ready to put the helm down hard in case he did luff. At that moment he waved to me and with an ease of tension I waved back as we understood each other. I later learned that that helmsman was King Juan Carlos of Spain, an avid sailor. As we approached the mark I saw something I had never seen.

A sailor on the deck of a French Swan 65 called *Beja Flo* went up into the air and into the water. He must have had a sheet wrapped around his foot. So the boat had to come head to wind to pick him up. I had hired someone to videotape the mark rounding and recorded the entire event. Years later, I was walking in the harbor of Antibes, in the south of France, and I saw *Beja Flo*. I knocked on the hatch and found someone who spoke English, and explained that I raced against her when one of their crew went up in the air and into the water. The French sailor said, "Ohhh, oui! Qui était Freddy!" So I took his address and sent him a copy of the video.

In my thirty-plus years of racing, I have been very lucky that I never lost anyone. We had some broken bones, lacerations and head injuries, but no deaths. One year at Edgartown, a crew was struck in the head with the spinnaker pole and was seizuring on the deck. I went over to attend to him. He was crewing for Frannie Curran, one of my frequent competitors and the winner of the Newport-Bermuda race in his Swan 47. In 2011, I raced against Frannie's son, Skip Curran, in the twelve-meter class at Edgartown. When I got the trophy in the Edgartown Yacht Club, I said, "You know you're getting old when you're racing against an old archrival's son, thirty years later." In the same vein, in the 1988 Bermuda race a colleague Skip Peerless, a neurosurgeon from London, Ontario, Canada, experienced an accidental jibe in the middle of the night in high wind the boom struck a physician on board who subsequently expired. A similar event occurred in the Vineyard race several years ago on *Blue Yankee* and the crewman's body washed up on the Long Island shore several days later.

Danger is a part of yacht racing — it is not a benign sport.

THE MIAMI TO MONTEGO BAY RACE:

Memorable experiences continued as I entered the 1991 Pineapple Cup, which ran from Miami to Montego Bay, Jamaica, a 900-mile race through the Caribbean. In 1990, Teddy Turner, oldest son of Ted Turner, founder of CNN, invited me to come down to Charleston to sail with him on *Challenge America*, an eighty-foot yacht he had purchased. Teddy was the sailing mate at the Citadel of Billy Nettles and had crewed for his father from childhood and for me in the 1980s. I recall Teddy picking me up at the airport and telling me he had pledged his CNN stock to buy the boat from John Baker. His goal was to break every existing ocean racing record and he planned to start with the Miami Montego Bay race in early 1991. He told me that his father, Ted Turner, was going to skipper the boat for that race while bringing along his new companion, Jane Fonda, whom he had just started seeing and eventually married.

While Teddy and I were in Charleston, we had a match race in Charleston Harbor against a fire-engine-red, eighty-foot Russian yacht called *Fazisi*. *Fazisi* had a fractional rig, with a forestay that came to seven-eighths the height of the mast. She looked fast off the breeze and had a very low freeboard (the distance between the water and the top of the deck). She looked like she was going to be wet in any kind of sea. But I noticed she was definitely fast off the breeze (with the wind aft the beam). Knowing that Mo Bay was basically a downwind race I thought *Fazisi* could be very competitive. So I told Teddy, "I would like to give you a run for your money. If you're going to try to break the record, I want to race against you — we could push each other." The longstanding record of thirty-five years at the time was held by an eighty-foot yacht called *Windward Passage* of three days, three hours, forty minutes, and seven seconds.

Teddy then introduced me to Vladislav Murnikov, who was the architect and manager of *Fazisi*. Over dinner in a New York restaurant, Murnikov and I made a deal— half of the twenty-person crew would be American, and the other half of the crew would be Russian. As the race approached, I went down to Palm Beach to get *Fazisi* ready, where it was docked on the Intracoastal Waterway. I discovered the Russians had not done a thing to prepare the boat. There was no incentive. This was my first experience with Russians and people brought up in the Communist system. When there is no reward there is no incentive to work. I had to get my American crew down there to get that boat ready for the race. As race day arrived, Ted Turner — who had won the race three times — had to cancel his plan to skipper his son's boat because of the outbreak of Operation Desert Storm. He needed to oversee the work of CNN, the network he created, in its groundbreaking real-time coverage of the war in the Persian Gulf. Because of the danger, Turner made it voluntary for newscasters to stay in Baghdad. Who can forget Peter Arnett reporting live on the roof of a Baghdad hotel as United States cruise missiles struck their target. For the first time in history the world watched live the outbreak of war.

Teddy took over the skipper's duties in his father's absence, and he was working with a stacked crew, including a famous navigator named Peter Bowker. My crew was hot, too, including Steve Colgate, Mike Hobson, an English professional sailor, and some ex-America's Cup sailors from the Doyle sail loft in Fort Lauderdale. Among them Peter Grimm. I also hired the bowman from Bill Koch's maxi yacht *Matador*. The race went off, but unfortunately an existing front did not make it as far as Palm Beach depriving us of the needed wind to break *Windward Passage's* record. If the front had made it down to Palm Beach, there is no question one of us would have broken the record, which eventually was broken by *Zephyrus V* in 2003.

There was another Maxi boat in our class owned by Bevin Koeppel, a real estate developer in New York that was a Farr 80 called *Congere* (short for Connie and Gerry, two of his children). These races, despite their distance, were tight as we all set spinnakers within sixty seconds of each other when we rounded Cat Island in the Bahama chain. I was entered among three yachts in the maxi class (overall length eighty feet) and running third behind *Congere* and *Challenge America* as we approached the northeast coast of Cuba. Teddy was on the horizon seven miles ahead and had jibed toward the Jamaican coast in what is called the Windward Passage, where the wind howls thirty to thirty-five knots. *Congere* was not visible. I was trailing with a boat speed of twenty-two knots under spinnaker — it was exhilarating! I had never sailed that fast as very few have. Since I was the CW (check writer) I stayed at the wheel until I couldn't keep my eyes open. As we rounded Cuba, still trailing *Challenge America* and likely *Congere* I realized we were going to lose unless we changed our tactics or found better wind. I decided we needed to go along the shore of Cuba to pick up thermal breezes as the wind was dying. The crew was urging me not to do it, as a few years prior Cuban patrols had arrested sailors from the same race and held them in jail for weeks. This was still a significant risk as Castro was relentless in his paranoia of any foreign intrusion into Cuban waters. I decided, "Fuck it." I ordered the Russian flag up on the transom. I countered the crew's concerns by claiming that the Cubans would not interfere with a Russian yacht. So we put the Russian flag up and came right along the beach so close I could have pissed on the shore of Cuba. We picked up thermal breezes off the shore for a good half a day along the coast of Cuba (which, by the way, looked gorgeous). Then that night there were squalls, thunder and lightning, and I sailed the boat toward the squalls because that is where you find the wind.

By morning, I could see Teddy on the horizon toward the Jamaican coast, and he looked like he was pretty even with me. By the next morning, we crossed the finish line about twelve to fifteen minutes ahead of *Challenge America*, but about ten minutes behind *Congere*. We finished in three days and change — not enough to break the record — but it was nonetheless a fantastic race. I had my good friend Peter Vielbig learn to cook borscht and other Russian dishes so all of the crewmen could share meals and bond. ABC News wanted to come on the boat to film during the race, but I did not want the added weight so I turned them down. The front page headlines of *The Trenton Times* read, "Taking on Ted Turner in a high stakes sea race." *USA Today* did give us a front-page commentary because at the end of the Cold War this was the first occurrence in history of the United States and Soviets working together trying to win in a conjoined effort. This reflects Ted Turner's groundbreaking concept of the Goodwill Games—nations joining together in the bond of athletic endeavor.

After the race, I had rented a villa for the crew with a swimming pool, and it was great to see the camaraderie that developed between the American and Russian sailors. The crew bonded over their shared love of sailing. The Russians learned about the American culture and how we viewed life coming from a capitalist system, and we learned about their lives being raised with a Communist mentality.

An unfortunate incident occurred in Jamaica. In the middle of the second night with the crew still fairly exhausted from our one thousand-mile chase through the Caribbean, the Jamaicans surreptitiously entered the villa and stole most of the crew's money, watches, and whatever else of value or personal items they could purloin and abscond. Despite my complaints to the Commodore of the Montego Bay Yacht Club and to the police, nothing was done and the money was not recovered. The Russians had survived on selling red t-shirts with the Russian symbol of the hammer and sickle and that money was stolen as well. I had to finance the Russians' passage back to the United States. I have never returned nor will I return to the island of Jamaica.

THE INTERNATIONAL TWELVE-METER CLASS:

Prior to departure in the Miami Montego Bay Race, the Russians had requested that I give a crew position to a gentleman, David Matthews, who had helped them financially and who had sailed on *Fazisi* on the last leg of the Whitbread Round the World Race from Fort Lauderdale to Portsmouth, England. I was initially reluctant, but after meeting David Matthews we shared a sense of humor. I agreed to take him. When we arrived in Jamaica, my chest hurt from laughing with David all the way to the finish line. David was a real estate developer with his brother Bob in Connecticut. Their business failed when the real estate market turned in the early nineties and David became unemployed. We bonded during the race to Montego Bay, so David followed me back to Princeton. I suggested that he try to obtain a mid-career fellowship at the Woodrow Wilson School at Princeton University. David had gone to St. Michael's College, but I do not think he graduated. Through a good friend he knew from Utah, Senator Orrin Hatch, David was admitted to the Woodrow Wilson School for a one-year fellowship. After one year he was appointed Director of the Peace Corps in Kazakhstan. He subsequently went on to become the senior economic advisor in Iraq answering to General Petraeus. Around 2003, David phoned and asked if I would do tactics for a Twelve-Meter Regatta, which was part of the Opera House Cup in Nantucket where his brother, Bob, owned a home overlooking the harbor. Simultaneously, I had run into an old sailing friend, Paul Buttrose, who was president of the International Twelve Meter Association who encouraged me to try my hand at Twelve Meter Racing. He recommended the yacht *American Eagle* owned by Herb Marshall which was a McCurdy and Rhodes design built in the mid-1960s. As the racing season was winding down in 2003, I agreed to sail *American Eagle* in the Twelve Meter North American Championships at Newport, Rhode Island. Two weeks before the North Americans, I flew into Nantucket to do tactics for Bob Matthews on *Weatherly* at David's request. *Weatherly,* a Twelve Meter, which won the America's Cup in 1962, was racing in the same class as *American Eagle*. While on the dock prior to departure for the first race, Dave Matthews introduced me to his lifelong friend, Senator Ted Kennedy. Kennedy with his son had chartered *American Eagle* for the Opera House Regatta and when I met him I told Kennedy that I would be racing *American Eagle* in another two weeks in the North American Championships and I would like to know his opinion of the yacht after the regatta. I found Kennedy a jovial man and we shared a lot in common. He loved sailing, the ocean, and painting in oils. He was overweight and appeared like a manatee in a bathing suit. The irony of our conversation occurred when it drifted to neurosurgery. Kennedy asked me what the challenges were in my field after the usual small talk. I explained to him that the greatest challenge at that time in neurological surgery was the malignant brain tumor. I explained how I had been operating on and treating patients with glioblastoma for more than thirty years with minimal hope in sight. I went through the standard treatment including operative intervention, radical removal, radiation as well as chemotherapy, and explained that the average lifespan at that point in time remained nine months to a year after the diagnosis no matter what the intervention. The irony as most readers now know, was that four years later Ted Kennedy came down with a glioblastoma which was ultimately operated on at Duke University and his lifespan was as I recall a little more than a year following the diagnosis. I often wonder if the senator recalled our conversation of that day on the dock in Nantucket Harbor. Ted Kennedy was a good sailor and he shared the helm with his son. He would have won the classic Twelve Meter Class that day if he had not tacked into a header in the last race. As it turned out, *Weatherly* won the event.

This was the first time I had ever sailed on a Twelve Meter. The reader should know that Twelve Meter is not the length of the boat, but rather the result of a complex formula, which includes sail area, girth, draft, length at the water line, and overall length among other measurements.

$$\frac{L + B + G/3 + 3d + \sqrt{S}/3 - F}{2} \leq 12 \text{ metres}$$

Where
L= waterline length (LWL)
B= beam
G= chain girth
d= difference between skin girth and chain girth
S= sail area
F= freeboard

These beautiful sleek racing yachts measuring overall between sixty-five to seventy feet in length were used to defend and challenge for the America's Cup after World War II replacing the enormous J boat class which measured one hundred thirty feet in length and became not only obsolete and but unaffordable. The Twelve Meter class boats are probably best known for their use from 1958 to 1987 in the America's Cup. They are all sloop-rigged, with their masts typically being about eighty-five feet tall. The Twelve Meter yachts are referred to as "Twelves." Associated with the formula above is an extremely comprehensive set of rules that allow designers to adjust any of the variables in the formula influencing the boat's performance on certain points of sail which not only ensures competitive racing but attempts to produce a winner. Twelve Meter yachts were used for the last time in America's Cup held in Freemantle, Australia. All of the innovations in sailing come from America's Cup technology, such as the double grooved forestay allowing a sail change while the old sail was still functioning as the new sail was raised in the other groove. Coffee Grinders to rapidly wind in enormous headsails under extreme pressure from their sheer size, revolution in keel and hull design, sailcloth technology and on and on. Most of these innovations and advances came through America's Cup competition always looking for a technological edge to defeat the challenger or the defender. The evolution from canvas sails to carbon fiber technology has occurred over the past eighty years.

After the Twelve-Meter era, Michael Fay, a Kiwi, challenged the San Diego Yacht Club who held the America's Cup after Dennis Connor's loss to Australia in 1983 and winning it back in Perth, Australia in 1987 with *Stars and Stripes.* Connor was defending the cup for San Diego. Michael Fay of the Mercury Bay Boat Club, which allegedly was the backseat of a car, challenged with a 120-foot boat claiming that there was no rule in the deed of gift that stated that he had to challenge in a Twelve-Meter even though the Twelves had been the conventional yacht used in America's Cup Racing since 1958. Because the San Diego Yacht Club could not design, build and gain the sailing experience necessary in a 120-foot boat in time to defend, Dennis Connor decided to defend in a catamaran. A monohull is no competition for a catamaran and Michael Fay's syndicate was soundly defeated. This situation dragged through the courts in New York for several years before a decision came down in favor of Dennis Connor and the San Diego Yacht Club. Thereafter, all the nations in America's Cup competition came together and a new cup class was decided upon which was in fact called the America's Cup Class Yacht. These yachts were again stripped out racers measuring approximately ten-feet longer than a twelve-meter in overall length. The last series and one of the most exciting America's Cup events in its almost 200-year history occurred in Spain when Alinghi of Switzerland successfully defended her title. Switzerland and Bertarelli, the Serono Pharmaceutical heir, had hired all the Kiwi sailors, which had won the cup eventually from San Diego to then win the cup for Switzerland, a landlocked country. Thereafter, Larry Ellison of Oracle challenged in a catamaran which Bertarelli agreed to and the America's Cup moved on to the catamaran racing in which Ellison prevailed in their first meeting three years ago in Valencia, Spain. The next America's Cup will be defended on San Francisco Bay by the Oracle syndicate, but the racing has not drawn the interest of many traditional monohull sailors like myself who have minimal experience in catamarans which requires an entire new set of racing rules, completely different tactics, and boat handling. Although the attempt to make sailing more exciting to watch and generate more of a spectator fleet, and therefore, generate potentially more revenue, its ultimate success remains to be seen. It is certainly a far cry from the traditional America's Cup, which began after the yacht *America* won the Queen's Cup around the Isle of Wight in 1851.

A celebration of that event of 1851 occurred in 2001 at the 150th Anniversary of the America's Cup. The celebration was at the sight of the original race off the Isle of Wight at Cowes in UK. Many, if not most, of the surviving America's Cup challengers and defenders participated in a week-long regatta. The most beautiful boats racing at Cowes were the Twelve Meters, which rejuvenated the class and brings us to the present where many of the old Twelve Meter yachts, both Cup winners and defenders as well as challengers, were rehabilitated and form an active racing class known as the International Twelve Meter Class governed by the International Twelve Meter Association.

THE NORTH AMERICAN CHAMPIONSHIPS 2003, NEWPORT, RHODE ISLAND:

In 2003 I had not raced for several years after selling *Aeolus* in 1989 to an investment banker from Greenwich, Connecticut. I had moved down to smaller boats (after divorce court) and bought a J/22, which I raced on Sundays at the Toms River Yacht Club on Barnegat Bay. After several years I sold the J/22.

One day I received a call from Paul Buttrose, an Australian mate who used to run *Windward Passage* before selling ladies underwear. He enticed me to return to racing and suggested the Twelve Meter Class. Being interested, I needed a refresher course. I went down to Annapolis for a day and hired the team from J World Sailing School and tuned up for eight hours on Chesapeake Bay, sailing upwind and practicing tacking as well as jibing downwind with a spinnaker up. I felt I was now ready to race again.

At Newport, we assembled a good crew with some professional sailors, which are needed particularly on the foredeck with such a large sixty-eight foot boat since the forces on the sails are substantial and which precludes amateurs in crucial positions because of the risk involved. There were five yachts in our class, and I was pleased to see Teddy Turner returning to race *Onawa* which he had part ownership with John Walters doing tactics, both of whom used to crew for me in 1980s. We enjoyed a terrific tight series and going into the last race on day three, I was one point out of first place behind Weatherly sailed by Clay Deutsch with tactics by Jack Slattery from the North Sails loft in Marblehead, Massachusetts. After the start of the last race, I sailed into a header on the first windward leg after the start but was pinned by *Columbia*, another America's Cup winner and could not tack into the lift. This caused me to finish second behind *Weatherly* which if I had beaten I would have won the regatta, since in yacht racing whoever wins the last race if it ends in a tie wins the regatta. I took a second place.

"Losing is the first step toward winning." —*Ted Turner*

Twelve Meter Racing was so challenging I became intensely involved for the next ten years. I was an active participant helming *American Eagle* and enjoyed great success winning three North American Championships in 2004, 2006, and 2014, four New York Yacht Club annual regattas in the International Twelve-Meter Classic Division as well as several Edgartown Twelve-Meter Regattas, Rolex Race Week sponsored by the New York Yacht Club, the Newport Trophy, the Ted Hood Trophy for overall best seasonal performance several times, the Leukemia Cup helming Heritage in 2014 as well as the Museum of Yachting Annual Regatta and the Tiedeman Trophy. I experienced the elation of winning as well as the disappointment of losing, but overall retained fond memory of the thrill of competition, the camaraderie of the sailors, and the lifelong friendships, which endure. One of my memorable moments occurred in August 2011 when I won the International Twelve Meter Regatta at the Edgartown Yacht Club in Martha's Vineyard. This occurred a year after I underwent a craniotomy to remove a large brain tumor under my left frontal lobe. I received a standing ovation when I was awarded the trophy by the Edgartown Yacht Club Commodore. Most of the crews of the International Twelve Meter Association knew my medical history and the reason I missed the North American Championships the year before as my craniotomy occurred five days before that regatta. Ted Turner took *American Eagle* and was thrilled to sail his old boat again with Gary Jobson. It was a big comeback for me in 2011 — first I won the New York Yacht Club Annual Regatta in the Twelve Meter Classic Division and then the trophy at Edgartown. Turner wanted *American Eagle* again in the North Americans, so I did not compete once again in that seasonal finale.

At 1400 hours I made a decision that the least risk was to head *Aeolus* up in the lulls toward the Long Island Coast and I instructed each rotating helmsman to do so and to bear way in gusts over forty-five knots. It would be nightfall in five hours making identification of waves difficult. Our boat speed was ten to twelve knots and I determined we could make the Long Island Coast in four hours, which would put us in the lee of the land and subsequently diminished wind strength. Increased wave height in shallower water was a consideration I decided to ignore. Although conditions earlier in the afternoon still presented as confused seas, but later in the day the sea state seemed to settle into a more predictable pattern, which was somewhat reassuring when nightfall approached. *Aeolus* was pushed and shoved for several hours rising on the peaks of misting waves then falling with a deep boom into the troughs. Cold spray splattered our face and upper torso as large waves struck her hull just forward of the stern. The yacht had no rhyme or reason in her motion through the sea. As we headed up we were careful to avoid the oncoming waves striking the beam. A hard hit abeam could cause a broach. The hissing and roaring and slapping continued incessantly without an interlude. My fear was to try to make safe harbor before exhaustion and darkness. We were a functioning crew of three with Bucky impaired with his chest wall injury, later diagnosed as rib fractures by x-ray. Eventually with luck and tenacity we made Sheepshead Bay as darkness set in. We anchored in flat water as we were settled among tall buildings in front of a schoolyard. The sky was clear and there was a beauty in the quiet solitude of the safe harbor. The full moon was playing hide and seek with passing clouds. The gale force winds were diminishing with time, but the wind continued to whistle through the rigging. We secured anchorage with a quiet sense of accomplishment, resolution of anxiety, and cessation of pumping adrenaline. We immediately fell fast asleep, glad to be safe and happy to be alive.

Sailing was an outlet from the severe stress of neurosurgery. I saw many interesting places and it allowed me exposure to interesting people. All of us shared a common interest in the sea. Sailing allowed me to disperse the stress of my occupation, which is one of the most stressful in the world. It represented freedom.

I remember a day sailing offshore, rounding Cape May en route to Newport. It was a perfect sailing day—blue skies with high pressure and northwest winds at ten to fifteen knots. We were close reaching with the apparent wind angle at sixty degrees. *Aeolus* was gently heeled and the boat speed was eight knots. All you heard was the sound of the water against the hull generating the bow wave. The boat's stereo system was piping in a low background of Gordon Lightfoot's *The Wreck of the Edmund Fitzgerald* into the cockpit. I thought to myself, of all the dues I have paid in my life—working summers and vacations to pay tuition, struggling in school, never having the freedom in my youth—this moment made it all worthwhile. A perfect day with good friends on the water—it made me thankful for every ounce of effort I put into getting myself to that moment. I thought heaven does exist and it was right here on Earth and few experiences could surpass this moment in time.

CHAPTER XVI:
A BUSMAN'S HOLIDAY

"The doctor who treats himself has a fool for a patient..."

Following the Labor Day weekend in 2010, I was looking forward to my favorite time of the year. Fall in Princeton was just simply spectacular as it is in many places, but Princeton in particular with the ambience of a University town offered a particular nostalgia, perhaps reflecting most of my life in Universities prior to entering practice. Moreover, fall in New England was also spectacular and I anticipated the following week participating in the International twelve-meter Class North American Championships to be held in Rhode Island Sound off Newport. I had had a successful racing season with *American Eagle* and was looking forward to success in this seasonal finale.

On Wednesday, September 8th, 2010, I had been in the operating room earlier in the day and came home in late afternoon, had the usual dinner with Kim and the twins, read the newspapers, watched the news and then retired my usual time around 10:30 p.m. I was bothered by a frontal headache when I went to bed, which did not preclude falling asleep. However, the headache became intense enough around three in the morning to awaken me from a deep sleep. I was tossing and turning, not being able to get comfortable because of the dull persistent ache through the forehead and vertex of my cranium. I got out of bed and went into the bathroom and took an 800 mg Motrin tablet. Within half an hour, the Motrin seemed to allay the discomfort for me to get another few hours of sleep and I awakened at my usual time at 6:30 a.m. A dull ache did persist, but was not compromising. After breakfast, I drove my son,

Coleman, to Princeton Academy up the Great Road and then went to the office for my usual Thursday morning office hours, which commenced at 8:30 a.m. As I walked into building #4, I walked right into the wall by the elevator. I could not explain it. I walked around the corner of the elevator to the men's room because I felt nauseous. When I entered the men's room, I went into the toilet and started to retch, but no emesis occurred. I continually retched and then felt better. The headache was increasing. I took the elevator to the second floor rather than climb the steps, and as I entered the office, I noticed that my gait was ataxic and I tended to fall to the right. I did fall, leaning over twice into the wall of my office corridor. I went down to Judy, my office manager, and said to her that I did not feel well enough to have office hours and I suggested that she send everyone home as I had a "flu" and I was going home to rest. I walked back out to my car looking like I had just come from the neighborhood tap room having had too much to drink. I no sooner drove out of the parking lot onto Princeton Pike North, when I had to pull over and get out of the car to vomit. However, again, nothing came up, just continual retching. I was able to drive home, stopping one more time for a similar episode and then arrived home, went into the family room, and lied on the couch. My wife, Kim, was just finishing her session with Paul Edwards, a trainer who came early in the morning twice a week. She told me I did not look good, nor did I sound right, and wanted me to go to the emergency room. I was dismissive of her thoughts, but she insisted and had Paul Edwards help me up into the car and they both drove me to the emergency room at University Medical Center at Princeton on Witherspoon Street where I had served as Chief of Neurosurgery for more than thirty years. I entered the emergency room in a wheelchair, the memory of which is somewhat fuzzy. I do not recall being in a CAT scanner, but I do recall being in a little cubicle sitting in my wheelchair when the emergency room physician, Dr. Dan, said to me that I had better look at the film. Having been a neurological surgeon for almost forty years, I turned him away from Kim and I said, "Kimba (her nickname since childhood representing the white lion in Disney's Lion King), I have really enjoyed our relationship and marriage and I love you madly. Thank you for everything." In my mind, I felt with reasonable certainty that they were about to show me a CAT scan with a brain tumor that in a sixty-nine-year-old man with rapid onset of symptoms was a glioblastoma, which we have discussed in previous chapters in reference to Ted Kennedy. With trepidation, they wheeled me over to the computer screen by the emergency room clerk's desk. Interestingly, I was not at all nervous or anxious or upset. Why? Because I had such marked frontal lobe edema bilateral that it was comparable to having a frontal lobotomy after which operation you really do not give a shit about anything. When I glanced at the computer screen, I saw an enormous tumor measuring five cm in the left frontal lobe of my brain and with a significant shift of the midline structures measuring two cm, which was critical. I still was not upset. Perhaps the frontal lobe edema being so striking was the reason that I completely missed the diagnosis of myself walking into the office that morning thinking I had "the flu." I had the classic symptoms of increased intracranial pressure, namely severe headache and vomiting, which is pathognomonic of elevated intracranial pressure, but which diagnosis was not the sole cause since I have seen flu syndromes, especially gastroenteritis, produce similar symptoms. After almost forty years of neurosurgery, I missed the diagnosis! But not completely. I glanced at the handwritten preliminary report by the radiologist who said more likely than not, there were malignant characteristics representing with probability, a glioma. My immediate reaction to the preliminary report and viewing the computer screen was that the radiologist missed the diagnosis! It looked to me like a classic meningioma, a benign tumor arising from the coverings of the brain and typically as they enlarge, displace the brain and even invade into the brain, but not becoming part of neural tissue. As it turned out, I was right and the radiologist was wrong. Kim had summoned Frank Pizzi to come to the emergency room. Frank arrived as I was looking at the computer screen. Frank asked me what I wanted to do and I said, "Call Dave Andrews at Jefferson." I knew Dave, having worked with him and sharing mutual patients over many years. David Andrews was the tumor surgeon at Jefferson, my alma mater, and Professor of Neurological Surgery. I knew him to be a good solid technician and clinician. Frank got Dave on the phone and he handed the cell phone to me. I said, "David, I have a large meningioma with a two-cm shift and increased intracranial pressure." David said, "I would be glad to see the patient, what's the name?" and I answered, "Jesus Christ, David, it's me. I am the goddamned patient." David said, "Come on downtown, I will take care of you." They loaded me in the ambulance then I went to Jefferson.

I went back where I came from.

I have vague memories of the admission process and transportation up to intensive care unit. I do remember going into the MRI scanner sometime prior to my surgery the following morning. I arrived at Jefferson about 5:30 p.m. Thursday evening and my surgery occurred at 7:30 a.m. the next morning, as I was urgent with a two-cm. shift. As I recall my scan, the incisura or the cerebrospinal fluid pathway around my midbrain was still open and I did not have midbrain compression nor had I had significant diminished conscious level. I was lethargic, which is the onset of the beginning of decompensation of the brainstem, which starts in the diencephalon where consciousness lies. I recall being wheeled in the operating room that following morning and David saying something to me, which I cannot remember, and the rest was instant oblivion as the propofol took effect. The next thing I recall was lying in my bed in the intensive care unit with some dull ache in the left side of my forehead. I felt weak, but cognitive of what was around me and aware of my thought processes and visitors. I remember Kimba coming in the room and David visiting me, telling me that things went well and that I had a meningioma. I answered, "I knew that." About a year later, of interest, is the fact that I was having dinner with neurosurgical colleagues in Chic's in Hamilton Township, New Jersey. The neurosurgeons were from Capital Health, namely Erol Veznedaroglu, Ken Liebman, and Joe Scogna who practiced in Bucks County. Joe asked me how I felt and that he had spoken with David Andrews the night before my craniotomy. He surprisingly informed me that David Andrews himself thought that I had a malignant tumor and was quite concerned about my prognosis. I guess I was the only one who felt comfortable that I had a meningioma and that I would be curable. As a longstanding neurosurgeon having removed well over a hundred meningiomas, when I originally looked at my film and the location of the tumor, I felt in my mind, "No sweat - if I was doing this case, the patient should be fine." My original thought at that day in the emergency room looking at the film being the only one confident that my tumor was benign, was that I was happy the tumor was not sitting on the motor strip or pushing against the brainstem or at the foramen magnum pushing my medulla over or along the parasellar area, which is fraught with hazard in removal. As an experienced seasoned neurosurgeon, I have removed on multiple occasions, tumors of all sizes in all of these treacherous locations, but I felt that the location of my tumor should be a chip shot for a good solid technician like Dave Andrews. This is not to be dismissive of the risks involved in any craniotomy. The surgeon must be sure that he does not violate brain especially the dominant left frontal lobe. He has to ensure that he has burned the membrane of origin of the tumor to try to prevent recurrence. He has to be careful not to enter the frontal sinuses, which could lead to infection or pneumocephalus (intracranial air). Tumors along the floor of the skull such as the location of my meningioma adjacent to the olfactory groove, could potentially lead to cerebrospinal fluid rhinorrhea (spinal fluid draining from the nose and with a high risk of meningitis). One could lose the sense of smell if the olfactory nerve or tract is damaged. However, of more significant concern is cognitive function since the left frontal lobe contains not only personality, but the speech area is not far away in the posterior aspect of the left frontal lobe (Broca's area) as well as recent memory and orientation. I was aware of all of these variables going into the operation, but I really did not give a shit. Having frontal lobe swelling is wonderful—you feel like you just had a fifth of vodka, giving new meaning to the phrase "L'belle indifferance."

The meningioma is one of the most common classic benign brain tumors occurring commonly in middle-aged women and not uncommonly an incidental finding on brain scans and MRI scans done for other reasons. I have seen patients referred to the office following motor vehicle accidents after they were evaluated in the emergency rooms with CAT scans or MRI scans where small incidental meningiomas were present, typically along the sagittal sinus in the midline toward the vertex or over the convexity, which are not causing any problem. They are slow growing and do not necessarily evolve into problematic tumors. They can, however, cause seizures. Meningiomas arise from the arachnoid cell and can develop into enormous size. I have removed meningiomas from the intracranial compartment the size literally of a grapefruit. The typical meningioma coming to surgery is the size of a plum or an apple. Although they are benign tumors, about four percent are malignant. They most commonly occur over the convexity and then parasagittal along the sagittal sinus, but they can also occur commonly along the sphenoid wing, floor of the skull, posterior fossa including the petrous ridge, foramen magnum, and even parasellar around the cavernous sinus or on the diaphragma sellae where the pituitary stalk exits to join the pituitary gland in the sella turcica. The tentorium, which is a fold of dura on which the cerebral hemispheres sit and through which the brainstem exits, is another common location and dangerous for removal when the tumors lie along the tentorial edge against the brainstem, i.e. the midbrain or the pons. They can also occur in the spinal canal and compress the spinal cord.

I have removed all sizes of meningiomas from all of these locations mentioned above on numerous occasions in my career. What is completely astounding is that three months prior to my craniotomy, I performed flawlessly removal of a large pituitary tumor transsphenoidal, a ruptured brain abscess into the ventricle, a large epidural hematoma, and what is even more ironic, a large right frontal meningioma in the exact location where my tumor lay, only on the right side rather than the left. I even totally removed a five-centimeter acoustic neurinoma severely indenting the pons in a seventy-nine-year-old man. The tumor was so large that I placed a ventriculoperitoneal shunt for non-communicating hydrocephalus prior to opening his posterior fossa. All of these patients had excellent results and left the hospital with no neurological deficit except the patient with the acoustic tumor whose partial seventh nerve palsy was complete after surgery along with hearing loss in one ear. I felt that if I could perform flawless neurosurgery with the brain tumor the size that I was harboring and with the shift of the midline, then either I was lucky or neurosurgery was not that tough—or a combination of both. It did wonders for my ego.

On the day of surgery, I managed to drag myself out of bed when no one was looking in the ICU at Jefferson. I tried to find a mirror to see where my incision was, although I felt bandages on my forehead. Typically, as an older trained neurosurgeon, I might have been inclined to do a bicoronal incision from the front of one ear to the front of the other ear, which would put the incision behind the hairline for cosmetic reasons, then peel the scalp down and perform the frontal craniotomy, and then repair the bone and scalp. David had another idea, which I was extremely pleased with. David made the incision in my brow furrow, i.e., the normal wrinkle of one's forehead above the eyebrows from the middle of the right eyebrow to where the wrinkle ends past the left orbit. He spared my supraorbital nerve although I am still numb in the forehead and frontal scalp toward the bregma. I developed the anticipated periorbital ecchymosis (black and blue), bilateral, worse on the left, which is typical after an operation on the frontal skull. I felt weak, but having been up to that time rowing at least three miles every other day, I was in pretty good shape so much so that I left the hospital forty-eight hours following my craniotomy. My wife was at home. My daughter, Katie, who works in real estate investment banking for JP Morgan in London, had flown in with her husband, Emanuel, for the occasion. Katie and Emanuel loaded me in the car and we got some pastries and coffee at Starbucks and drove home. That evening, I had instructed Kimba to call all of our friends to the house for a party. We had a great time and my first drink when I arrived home was a martini despite my postoperative instructions. I was dancing a jig that my tumor was benign and that I escaped without any neurological impairment. Based on my premorbid personality when my friends heard that I had a brain tumor, the first comment was often, "Well that explains a lot," since I can be somewhat of a prurient comic at times. As the swelling in my brain gradually subsided, my insight and judgment became sharper. The following day, Monday morning, Dave Andrews called the house to see how I was doing. I answered him in my typical comical fashion, "I am glad you called Dave because I am in between cases. I left the hospital early and I am going back to do my second case." I do not know how amused David was, but my wife instantly knew that I was back to my old personality. David instructed me to taper off the Decadron, which is a potent steroid for brain swelling. I was also on anticonvulsants, which he instructed me to discontinue as well. Getting over my ordeal was not hard. The toughest part of all of it was missing the North American twelve-meter championships in Newport, which began five days after my craniotomy. Naturally, I could not sail that close to my ordeal. I was not missing any time at work, however, because I had scheduled that week as vacation knowing that I would be racing in Newport. So, there were no concerns about the practice.

I returned to work the following Monday, one week after being discharged from the intensive care unit at Thomas Jefferson University Hospital.

Although I did not operate for three weeks following my discharge from Jeff, I was seeing patients the week after I left the hospital, in the office and making rounds in the hospital and seeing consultations. My associate, Frank Pizzi, strongly suggested that in view of our high-risk field, it would be prudent if I underwent psychological testing to be sure I did not sustain significant brain damage or damage which could incriminate me in a medical liability suit if an undue complication occurred in my practice. I reluctantly agreed and scheduled complete neurocognitive testing at Jefferson by Dr. Joseph Tracy, the Head of Neuropsychology. This went on for an entire eight hours.

I passed with flying colors.

After receiving the green light from Joe Tracy, I resumed operating. As I realized in my youth that life in many ways is a matter of luck. I was lucky in spades. I was lucky to have a benign tumor in an accessible location without sustaining brain damage because I had an excellent surgeon. I did not have postoperative complications. I did not have postoperative seizures that can occur following removal of a meningioma. I did not develop hydrocephalus requiring a ventricular shunt, which occurs in small percentage of patients undergoing craniotomy. I did not develop a cerebrospinal fluid leakage. I did not lose my sense of smell. I did not sustain brain damage. I had full use of my extremities. I could immediately return to my practice and continue in my spare time with salacious thoughts.

I returned to the operating room and the joy of my profession.

CHAPTER XVII:
THE RISE OF WESTINGHOUSE
LIGHTING CORPORATION

"The American dream is alive and well for entrepreneurs who are willing to learn the hard lessons of the business of making money and willing to work and sacrifice long and hard to be successful..."

As I discussed in an earlier chapter, the Angelo Brothers Company (ABCO), founded by Uncles Stan and Tim Angelo, was a major part of my upbringing. Not only did I spend many hours working for ABCO, bagging washers and doing other jobs such as addressing annual Christmas catalogues, but also I unloaded supply trucks and conveyor belts as needed. Their example showed me how hard work and determination can overcome obstacles that are put in your path. These were the sons of immigrants, with no college or high school degrees, and not unlike my mother did not finish grade school. They built a business that eventually became one of the most successful light bulb producers in the world. They truly represent the American dream. Success was based on not only diligence and hard work, but innovation, tenacity, and determination. I remember Uncle Tim complaining that he did not have a place to park, which was difficult living in a row house in South Philadelphia when returning from a hard day of work. Only financial success could alleviate his problem—to move out of South Philly.

The Angelo Brothers founded the company in 1946 as a paint shop on Snyder Avenue, using $500 in savings from Stan's wife, my Aunt Rita, and a remortgage on Uncle Tim's house on 22nd Street. Customers would frequently come into the shop and buy a lamp, which Uncle Tim had constructed and placed in the window. He was very creative taking cut glass ashtrays, drilling a hole in the middle, and then using a glass flower vase placing it on top of the ashtray turned upside down, threading a pipe through the drilled hole, and securing it with a washer and bolt. He would then cap the vase, add a socket and chimney and a shade and presto there was a lamp. The customer would buy the final product with a bulb that Uncle Tim would give me to screw into a socket and document that the bulb worked before giving it to the customer. I was six years old. Customers wanted to know how he made such a beautiful lamp, and he explained to them how he constructed it with available parts. People wanted to buy the parts to make their own lamp, which was a "eureka" moment for Uncle Tim. They focused at first on lamp repair and replacement lamp parts. Eventually they began to buy and make lamp parts, which they sold to customers as well as other lamp stores and to antique dealers. To generate more interest in this growing part of the business, they created a beautiful catalog with hand-drawings of lamp parts by Uncle Emidio the artist, and began to enjoy a thriving mail-order operation. Lighting glassware was added to the product line in the 1950s. The company moved from the tight quarters of 20th and Snyder Avenue to Rittner Street in South Philly. After complaints from neighbors about the noise from cutting pipe for lamps they moved to Mascher Street in northeast Philadelphia. On Saturdays and holidays, as well as vacations, I would take the elevated train at 69th and Market Streets in west Philadelphia and ride the elevated to York and Dauphin Streets exit and walk to the Mascher Street facility. As they outgrew the latter, they moved to the old Robert Bruce Sweater Building, then vacant, on Allegheny Avenue. In addition to the lamp part business, the company added lighting showrooms and electrical distributors to its expanding customer base. As the company grew, other family members joined in the business, and Uncle Stan and Uncle Tim put together a profit-sharing plan so their employees could join in the company's success.

Uncle Rocky joined the company in 1958 leaving his show business career, which ended with Marty Allen as a comedy act playing all the major clubs in Las Vegas and around the country. He became vice president of marketing, and he made a major contribution by importing decorative light bulbs from Kashima Trading Company in Japan in the 1960s. This is the line of business for which I joined him on the trip to Tokyo in 1967. I recall visiting a factory with Rocky in Tokyo where at the end of the business day employees were carrying their work home in boxes to continue their job after hours. I vividly recall Rocky's comment in May 1967, that the Japanese people were so industrious that they "will conquer the world economically in twenty years." Rocky was prescient in his observation.

The year prior to my Japan excursion with Rocky, he took my cousin Stan — Uncle Stan's son, who eventually became CEO of the company — on a six-week trip to Japan to initiate him into that side of the business. Stan, whom we called as children "Baby Stanley," (in contradistinction to his father "Big Stanley") remembers the impact of that six-week excursion to Japan with Uncle Rocky:

"Oh, my wife loved that, after being married only two years! I went to see all the sources. When we got into the airport, there were some fifty people meeting us. Each one was a submaker, making a particular type of lamp in their home or in their garage. And there was one central company that would bring it all together and package it. You don't see that today. But with Rocky's personality, he just made everybody dance. He was a great negotiator — a real cool dude, smart and self-educated."

With the success of the decorative light bulb business, the Angelo Brothers Company (also known as ABCO) developed a slogan: "The House of a Million Parts ... The Home of Good Service." The company offered flexible service depending upon the needs of the customer. For example, lighting parts would be sold in paper bags to the lamp trade but packaged in polybags or cards for the retail trade. During the 1960s, the hardware trade was added to the list of customers. As the expense of having light bulbs made in Japan grew too high, the company moved onto suppliers in Korea and then Taiwan.

The 1970s were a time of rapid growth in the emerging home center industry, with more than one hundred regional chains throughout the United States. In the Northeast, for example, stores such as Rickels,

Channel and Hechinger's were thriving business at the time. My cousin Stan was named president of the company in 1971. Three years earlier, he devised an innovation that helped the company expand further, by packaging lamp parts to sell to home centers and hardware stores. Companies like Sears, Montgomery Ward, Ace Hardware, Cotter & Company (now True Value) all purchased the Angelo Brothers' line of packaged lamp parts. Angelo Brothers continued to add to its line of light bulbs, glassware and lighting accessories to keep up with the growing demand of its varied customer base. The growth opportunities on the West Coast prompted the company to open its second distribution in the Los Angeles area, and eventually warehouses were opened in Texas, Chicago and Atlanta. The company also outgrew its building in North Philadelphia and moved to the more open spaces of Northeast Philly.

In the 1980s, Angelo Brothers added lighting fixtures to the product line. The company was experiencing growth in all channels, but especially in the expanding home center channel. The company once again outgrew its building and moved farther north to its current location, 12401 McNulty Road in Northeast Philadelphia with 35,000 square feet of office space and several hundred thousand square feet of warehouse on twenty acres of land. By the 1990s, the company's continued growth led to a very unique opportunity. The ABCO brand of light bulbs represented one of the largest "non-branded" lighting companies in the country. For many years, the "Big Three" of lighting in the United States were General Electric, Westinghouse and Sylvania. But Westinghouse was a massive conglomerate, and by the 1980s and '90s had been selling off its commercial businesses — including selling its lighting operations in 1983 to the Belgian company Philips, which did away with the Westinghouse lighting brand in the United States in favor of its own.

A fateful moment occurred in 1997 that eventually would lead to the resurrection of the Westinghouse brand on the United States, and a new direction for the Angelo Brothers Company. Cousin Stanley explains:

"I'm in Hechinger's around Christmas of 1997, shopping for Christmas decorations, and I see Westinghouse Christmas tree lamps. And I said,

'What the hell?' At that point Westinghouse lighting products have been gone for almost fifteen years. I pick up the package, and there's licensing verbiage on there. I thought, 'They must just be licensing for Christmas trees, it can't be for all light bulbs.' So I bought the package, brought it to our in-house attorney at the time, and said, 'Please follow up on this.' Nine months later, we had a license for light bulbs and light goods, with the two marquee product lines of Westinghouse in the old days."

Stan started by acquiring a ceiling fan company and changing the name to Westinghouse. The company then started changing all its products from the ABCO brand to the Westinghouse brand. Stan, his brother John (executive vice president) and cousin Raymond (president) decided that instead of being the Angelo Brothers Company selling Westinghouse products, they should become Westinghouse Lighting Corporation. In 2002, they went to Pittsburgh to visit with CBS/Westinghouse Electric Company, which licensed the Westinghouse name, and struck an agreement to take the name as their own.

Some customers were upset by the changing of the company away from the family name, but as a business move it was propitious. This not only helped to solidify its business in the United States, but helped greatly to expand opportunities in international markets. The Westinghouse brand is well known around the world and has stood for quality and innovation for years. As Stan said in the corporate press release announcing the name change:

Westinghouse Lighting Corporation world
headquarters, Philadelphia, Pennsylvania

"This move will clearly identify us with the Westinghouse brand, while retaining the culture, reputation and expertise we've established at Angelo Brothers over the past fifty-seven years. We believe this powerful combination will help us change the face of our industry and expand our efforts to provide consumer and commercial customers with innovative, high-quality products on a global basis."

By the time of the name change, the company had grown to become an international leader in the lighting industry with hundreds of employees. When Raymond Angelo became President and CEO succeeding Stanley Angelo, he implemented in great part a vision to replicate the successful U.S. business model around the world while also adapting the company culture to be able to compete effectively in the rapidly changing global lighting market. This is a continuous work in progress incorporating higher levels of collaboration, system thinking, personal development and teamwork.

The current global distribution facilities (in Mexico, Panama, Canada, Germany and Hong Kong) with more than five thousand products are the first phase of the longterm strategy. Today, Westinghouse Lighting remains at the top of its field, and the humble business my uncles started with a little bit of savings and a lot of ambition is recognized around the world and stands as a model for success.

In 2009, my cousin Stan was named Entrepreneur in Residence by the Fox School of Business at his alma mater, Temple University, and was cited by the school's leaders as "a highly accomplished entrepreneur, an out of the box thinker, someone who has transformed his/her industry, and a highly personable executive."

Indeed, the rise of the company from the Angelo Brothers to Westinghouse Lighting represents the success that arose when, as the company states, "The American Dream Met an American Brand."

CHAPTER XVIII:
A LOVE OF ART

"Art is the only way to run away without leaving home..."
— Twyla Tharp

About two decades into my career as a neurosurgeon, I found myself learning to work with a new instrument: a paintbrush. Art had been an interest since I was a child, but in my early fifties, I began to pursue the craft in earnest. In many ways, painting is a natural outlet for someone in my field — as in neurosurgery, painting requires manual dexterity, attention to detail and intense concentration.

My interest in art stemmed from the fact that, in my family, there was always praise for my mother's oldest brother, Emidio. Uncle Midi, who was also known as Mike (after Michelangelo), was a renowned artist and cartoonist known throughout Philadelphia, as well as around the country, due to the success of his syndicated comic, *Emily and Mabel*. Through Uncle Midi's painting and Uncle Rocky's involvement in show business, art was always on the surface of family life when I was growing up. The Angelos were very creative people. They were fascinated by movies. Uncle Midi was the cinematographer for *Kidnap*, a black and white silent home movie that Uncle Rocky made with Uncle Tim and Burt Lancaster on the beach in Sea Isle City in the early 1940s, featuring my cousin Donna, Emidio's daughter, as a kidnapped baby and my father as a dour detective (a perfect role for him!). "In a gangland version of *Three Men and a Baby*, the kidnappers fell for the baby and decided to return her to her parents. Despite the change of heart, the kidnappers ended up serving thirty years in jail" (*Philly.com*) except for Lancaster's character, who was shot by the detective (my father) in the surf at the film's ending. Our summerhouse in Sea Isle City served as the location for the kidnappers' hideaway.

Emidio Angelo whose trademarks were a goatee and an easygoing manner did not believe in retirement and worked until his very last days. Emidio was the only one of the seven Angelo siblings who had a formal education. He studied at the Pennsylvania Academy of the Fine Arts, where he received two Cresson scholarships in 1927 and 1928 to study in Paris and Italy. After his studies in Europe, he came back to Philadelphia and started his career by painting portraits of wealthy WASPs on the Main Line. That did not last long, however, as he found it frustrating to deal with subjects who insisted that their portraits make them look decades younger than they really were.

Emidio turned his talents to cartooning to help pay the bills. It was a better fit for his jovial personality, and he was hired by *The Philadelphia Inquirer* in 1937 by Walter H. Annenberg, editor and publisher, to bring some levity into its pages. His early work included the *Uncle Dominick*

cartoon that ran with political columns by John Cummings, as well as a general panel called *Funny Angles*. Two recurring characters from that panel were twin sisters, unliberated spinsters named Emily and Mabel who were forever in search of a man. They wore the same upswept hairdos and long Victorian dresses. They were spun off to become the subjects of their own comic strip. *Emily and Mabel* became a favorite of Inquirer readers and, the 1940s and 50s, was syndicated in 150 newspapers around the country and gave Uncle Midi a national reputation. The characters were based on women he encountered while working at a soda fountain in South Philly as he earned money for art school.

Uncle Midi was always proud of the fact that President Harry Truman had requested a copy of one of his cartoons, which poked fun at Truman's famous use of off-color language. The cartoon depicts a mother washing her son's mouth out with soap, as she tells her husband, "Ever since you told him he might be President someday, he's been using that language." In addition to the *Inquirer*, Emidio also created cartoons for many magazines, including *The Saturday Evening Post, Life* and *Esquire*.

Emidio Angelo

Emidio Angelo, 1903-1990

As he gained renown as a cartoonist, Emidio continued to paint and produce sculptures. His brothers hired him to produce the Angelo Brothers' annual catalog, which came with a calendar that featured an original painting for each month of the year. Over the course of his career until he died in 1990, Emidio won many awards and mounted numerous exhibitions of his artwork. A couple of years ago, I stopped into the Newman Galleries on Walnut Street in Philadelphia and wound up in a conversation with the proprietor. I asked if he knew of my uncle. "Oh my goodness!" he said. "Emidio Angelo — he was a Philadelphia institution!"

Through Uncle Midi's influence, I had been interested in art since my youth, but it was not until I was in my early 50s that I began to seriously study painting myself. In the earlier years of my practice, I worked 15 to 18 hours a day, covering eight hospitals at once, which left little free time to pursue art. Once I found myself with the time to act upon my interest in painting, I called the Arts Council of Princeton for a recommendation for a private instructor, as my work obligations would not permit me to sign up for scheduled classes. I settled on Helen Bayley, a British artist with a studio in Kingston, New Jersey.

Helen Bayley was born in Great Britain and moved to America to attend the Rhode Island School of Design in Providence, Rhode Island and later Indiana University. Having obtained both undergraduate and graduate degrees in painting Helen remained in America teaching painting and drawing at the college level. The latter included Tyler School of Art and Temple University in Philadelphia. Throughout her career she exhibited in galleries in New York, Chicago, Washington DC, and Philadelphia. Her college studies brought her to Italy and fascination with the human figure. She loved the romantic aristocratic ladies of Sir Thomas Gainsbourough, but Italian figurative painting seemed more brutal and dramatic. Caravaggio and Artemisia Gentileschi became her immediate favorites along with more contemporary artists like Lucian Freud.

I began taking lessons with her on a weekly basis for roughly five years. She taught me oil painting and sketching techniques, and we frequently would hire models to come and pose. In addition to practicing the mechanics of painting, we discussed art history. We would review books featuring works of classic painters, and Helen would show me how the great masters positioned their figures. She taught me that the way to learn painting is through self-portraits and still life. So I would go home and paint down in my basement, as my home at that time had no room for a studio. Framed by a little bit of light from a small window, I would look in the mirror and paint myself over and over. In my first self-portrait, I looked like a murderer or rapist. It looked like one of the FBI's Top Ten Most Wanted posters. It took about a year or so for these self-portraits to actually start to look like me.

After that I started to sketch my friends while I was having coffee with them. I remember painting Ira Kasoff, a good friend and neurosurgical colleague who passed away in 2012, from a sketch over coffee and a picture he sent me via email. I was very pleased when he actually hung the painting—my first real viable work. Helen taught me to incorporate the subject's personality into the painting along with the relationship I may have with the subject.

I have found that I learn a lot just by looking at the works of others. If I am in a painting slump, I will go to New York and attend the museums and art galleries. I enjoy studying the works of the old masters, like Rembrandt and John Singer Sargent. I look at how they apply paint around the eyes and nose, how they highlight features. Lucian Freud, who died in 2011, was one of my favorite artists. I loved the way he put on paint for portraiture. He was to say the least, confrontational. His work is a profound exaggeration of light and dark, in terms of shadows on the face and body of his subjects. His 2001 portrait of Queen Elizabeth caused an uproar in England among those who felt it was unbecoming and insulting, while others hailed it as a masterpiece. I agree on the masterpiece. I actually painted my surgeon, Dave Andrews at Jefferson, from his photo in the alumni magazine, and I used Freud's work as my inspiration. Dave loved the way it came out! (I hope).

Winston Churchill, who actually was an accomplished watercolor artist, famously said that painting chased away the "black dog," which was his expression for depression. I, too, found that painting takes me completely away from everything — I become absorbed in trying to get the work right, especially when I am painting people. I learned that if you exaggerate someone's features, you have a better chance of capturing their countenance.

If the subject has a long pointed nose, for example, if you exaggerate the nose even further, it more looks like the person. Even-featured people are more difficult to paint than someone who has a big nose or prominent lips. A painter comes to these realizations through trial and error. You have to be tenacious in your endeavor, and sooner or later, you'll see some results. When you are painting someone, you try to capture the subject's character and personality, which is the most difficult thing to do. I have three rules with portraiture: 1) I am not Rembrandt. 2) It is not a photograph, it is a likeness. 3) I will never know if my painting is in your basement.

Burt Lancaster (left) with Rocky Angelo aka Rex Dale filming the movie *Kidnap* in Sea Isle City, NJ, *circa* 1948

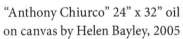

"Anthony Chiurco" 24" x 32" oil on canvas by Helen Bayley, 2005

"Tony Chiurco in a Single Shell" self-portrait 48" x 60" oil on canvas, 2003

"Emidio Angelo" 18" x 20" oil on canvas
By Anthony Chiurco, 2001

"After the Jump" 48" x 72" oil on canvas
Kim Jingoli Chiurco and Cameron by Anthony Chiurco, 2012

"American Eagle at the Leeward Mark" 60" x 72"
oil on canvas by Helen Bayley, 2006

Ben Weiss, Founder, Bai
Brands 24" x 36" oil on canvas
by Anthony Chiurco, 2011

"The Tactician" 18" x 20"
oil on canvas, Robert Goff
by Anthony Chiurco, 2006

Stanley Angelo, Jr., CEO Westinghouse Lighting Corporation
24" x 36" oil on canvas by Anthony Chiurco, 1998

"Desperate Housewife" 48" x 72"
oil on canvas portrait of Kim
Jingoli Chiurco by Anthony
Chiurco, *circa* 2004

"David Andrews, MD"
18" x 24" oil on board
by Anthony Chiurco, 2012

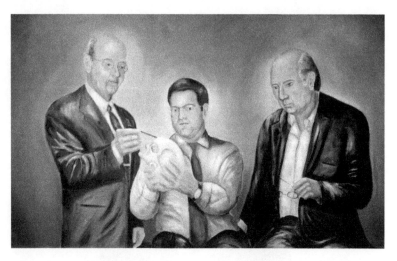

NeuroGroup: (left) Francis Pizzi, MD, (right) Anthony Chiurco, MD, (center) student, 48" x 72"oil on canvas by Anthony Chiurco, *circa* 2002

Painting provided a tremendous sense of fulfillment comparable to performing a technically flawless operation, such as removing a tumor or clipping an aneurysm. When the patient awakens alert and neurologically intact it is like viewing a work of art that you created. Great art occurs in the operating rooms around the world by great artists skillfull with instruments analogous to the paintbrush. In my field there are technicians who are masters with their hands, like the great masters of painting.

Over the years, I have done nearly one hundred paintings of still life and portraits of my family and friends. I have provided photos of some of these paintings for the reader to view.

Helen Bayley subsequently moved on and currently lives in Florence, Italy teaching at the Florence Academy, the mecca for painting in the world. She continues to exhibit her work in Italy and America.

CHAPTER XIX:
EPILOGUE

"Fair is where pigs win ribbons..."

For more than twenty years, on Saturday morning, I enjoyed coffee with a neurosurgical colleague, Dr. Ira Kasoff, who practiced during his life in New Brunswick, New Jersey. He grew up on the Lower East Side of Manhattan and we shared a similar view of the world. Our conversations would range from politics, religion, and ethnicity to books, movies, and sociopolitical activity, domestically as well as globally. Ira Kasoff was trained by Eben Alexander, Sr. at Bowman Gray School of Medicine and completed a fellowship in cerebrovascular surgery under Sir Charles Drake of London, Ontario, Canada — the foremost aneurysm surgeon of our era. Ira Kasoff was a solid neurosurgeon and like myself was intensely devoted to his profession. Our discussions would often be heated arguments over management of clinical issues and surgical approaches. These confrontational discussions were on a level of scientific inquiry in a learned profession. There was never anger or hostility, but rather a reflection of a fondness for our work. Ira was well read. We both enjoyed *The New York Times* crossword puzzles, which historically become more difficult as the week progresses. Whereas I flourished Monday through part of Thursday, Ira did not start the puzzles until Thursday because he found that puzzles earlier in the week were too easy. Ira did *The New York Times* crossword puzzles in ink.

One Saturday morning, I called Ira to confirm our rendezvous when he told me he did not feel well and thought he had the "flu" (sound familiar?). He canceled our meeting. On Monday morning, forty-eight hours later, I received a call from Terry, his office manager, informing me that Ira drove himself over to the emergency room at St. Peters University Hospital in New Brunswick on Saturday and was diagnosed with a myocardial infarction (heart attack). He was not clinically well and immediate coronary angiography revealed an occlusion of a major coronary artery. He then underwent an emergency triple bypass procedure. On the second postoperative day, he expired. I did not go to visit him at the hospital, the day he expired because I was told he was poorly responsive and I thought he would likely not appreciate my presence although I certainly would have gone if I knew what was about to happen. This occurred about 1 year after the demise of one of my previous associates, Dr. Fred McEliece, who failed to arise one morning and was found expired in bed by his wife. Although certainly mortality increases with age, but in my opinion the demise of my two colleagues at around age seventy reflects the severe stress of a life in neurological surgery. In my early years of practice in Mercer County, three neurosurgeons who practiced in Somerset County had all expired before age fifty-five mostly from cardiac disease with one carcinoma of the pancreas. I recently listened to Dr. Ben Carson, the noted pediatric neurosurgeon, from Johns Hopkins on the air claiming that he was about to retire because he wanted to live a little longer. His neurosurgical colleagues as well were experiencing a diminished lifespan.

The stress in neurosurgery is overwhelming.

With advancing age, one becomes more sensitive to mortality. If life was a round of golf, I am playing the back nine and I can see the clubhouse. I often wonder how did life go by so fast and I ask myself what it was all about? I cannot go back and change things. It was not a dress rehearsal. Like most people, I made my share of mistakes in many instances and exercised good judgment in others. Life is like the weather, fronts and storms come through and you have to reef your mainsail and secure the hatches. Other days are sunny with high pressure, gentle wind and a cloudless sky. The lessons I have learned as I expressed somewhat in this book certainly reflect that life in many ways is a matter of luck. I was more or less a product of affirmative action. Despite my mother's education up to the third grade and my father's limited income, I was able to play well the hand I was dealt. I was fortunate to have been able to study in a chosen profession and be successful in that profession, but in the end as in many instances luck played a major role. This does not preclude that hard work does not reap rewards. You do reap what you sow. When you have lived the plethora of human tragedy in neurological surgery, you cannot help but feel fortunate to be alive and well.

I have made certain conclusions about life. The first has to do with human nature, which I have concluded is basically selfish. Although capable of altruistic endeavor, man is to the core selfish. I have also concluded that a major problem with the world is the maldistribution of wealth. And lastly, it is my opinion that, in great part, the maldistribution of wealth may be due to the maldistribution of intelligence based on both the unfairness of evolution as well as heredity.

And then there is democracy. Winston Churchill once commented, "Democracy is the worst form of government with one exception, everything else." The words of Churchill could not be more lucid. Democracy began in ancient Greece, propelled forward by ancient Rome as mankind emerged from the dark ages. In recent years, America is a poor example of how ideally a democracy should work. This reflects the dysfunctional nature of our legislative process. Resolution of the gridlock of bipartisan confrontation, routine in our legislative process, could in great part be resolved if term limits were implemented. If all representatives in both the house and senate served one term whether four or six years, the legislative process would reflect the votes of each representative's ideology but more importantly it would be about the American people and not about the next election.

Our central government reeks of incompetence. To allow twelve million illegals to enter the United States is one issue, but to invade another country preemptively on the basis of false intelligence represents even greater incompetence and the greatest foreign policy blunder in my lifetime causing the death of thousands of our young men and women in the military and the catalyst for several hundred thousand civilian deaths.

Lastly, to run up a twenty trillion dollar deficit through uncontrolled spending while at the same time passing Obamacare when Medicare and social security are jeopardized reflects ongoing concern. Look at the record of Medicare. In 1965 Congressional budgeters said that it would cost $12 billion in 1990. Its actual cost that year was $90 billion. The hospitalization program alone was supposed to cost $9 billion, but in the end cost $67 billion. The rate of increase in Medicare spending has outpaced overall inflation in nearly every year (up 9.8 percent in 2009), so a program that began at $4 billion now cost $428 billion. This is nearly always the case with government programs because their entitlement nature — accepting everyone who meets the age or income limits—means there is no fixed annual budget (*The Wall Street Journal*, October 20, 2009, "Review and Outlook — Health Costs and History"). On the other hand, kudos to President Obama for attacking health insurers for making excessive profits, paying excessive bonuses, spreading misinformation about the actual cost of health insurance, and manipulating how to avoid covering people while enjoying a privileged exemption from our anti-trust laws.

The public option was defeated as a down payment on single payer healthcare. It is unfortunate that the public option is unaffordable because it would evaporate the private insurance market. Unfortunately for the physician work force, limited income would result in less qualified practitioners in my opinion because government pays so much below costs. More than twenty-five percent of the current work force does not participate in Medicare and that number is climbing.

Free market capitalism is the optimal path to prosperity. A society with increasing socialism and entitlement will lead to economic decline, loss of initiative and entrepreneurship - all the things, which made America great. The economies of socialist countries in Europe are a prime example where socialism and entitlement, when excessive, have endangered European financial markets. If it was not for the driving force of the economy of Germany, the Euro and Euro zone could collapse. I believe that low taxation allows economic expansion and increasing employment especially if entwined with lowering the corporate tax rate. I believe in the Laffer Curve. I believe in closing "tax loopholes" on corporations and individuals. Everyone should pay a fair share. Punishing the achiever with high taxation on individuals with higher incomes may be popular political rhetoric, but would not make a dent in treasury reserves or pay the interest on a week of national debt.

During my years in Winnebago, Nebraska, the American Indian Reservation of the Omaha and Winnebago tribes, I soon realized the deleterious effects of government entitlement. Entitlement when excessive creates detrimental complacency, removal of initiative and desire to achieve. I realized as a young man that hard work was the only means to success. This is reflected in my life after medical school; I never took a vacation that lasted more than seven days. After a major operation such as a craniotomy and removal of a brain tumor, I was back to work one week after discharge from the hospital. I continue to perform neurosurgery past age seventy without intention of retirement. And then, I view a socialist country such as France where according to *The London Financial Times* more than one-half of the work force is retired after age fifty. The hand of socialism in France has fingers in job creation, retirement, wage control, as well as the hiring and firing of workers and excessive taxation. It restricts entrepreneurship and becomes a wart on the ass of progress. As the individual becomes more dependent upon government loss of individual freedoms evolves, now experienced in the socialist countries of Europe. Friedrich Hayek's classic work *The Road to Serfdom* is paved through Western Europe and is now breaking ground on our shores.

America has a third of our population on some type of government entitlement whether food stamps, social security disability, or welfare. This does not include social security or Medicare. It is not to say that some social policies are not needed or beneficial. It is the degree of entitlement, which requires prudent restraint and fiscal responsibility. As more of our population becomes dependent upon central government, we are moving down the road to serfdom.

The recent economic collapse of 2008 precipitated by the real estate fiasco began with a social policy where minorities were "entitled" to own homes they could not afford, implemented by an incompetent interest rate and an inadequate down payment, followed by fraud and corruption on Wall Street where investment banks sold mortgage-based securities doomed to failure and which in fact they even bet against—the height of unethical behavior and fraud. This was followed by dishonesty and fraud of the rating agencies, such as Standard and Poor, Moody's, and others who graded these mortgage-based securities as AAA. I am still awaiting this type of criminal behavior to undergo due process in the criminal justice system. And don't forget AIG, the major insurer bailed out by the Federal Government, thanks to our illustrious Treasury Secretary, Henry Paulson. Paulson was a former CEO of Goldman Sachs. Is there any consideration that AIG owed Goldman Sachs multibillions from insuring the crap that Goldman had in its portfolio doomed to fail? So that AIG could make good on the credit default swaps of Goldman Sachs, Paulson ensured government bail out. And then, there is the incompetence in the auto industry rewarded by the Obama administration bailing them out and allowing the unions to reap the benefit. As a result of all of these machinations, the stock market lost more than half of its value with the Dow Jones industrial average plummeting to under 7,000. Hard working citizens watched their life savings become devalued to the point of abandoning retirement and going back into the workforce if they could find a job. All of the above was clearly a result of the lack of government regulation in the real estate market and the irresponsibility of the Bush Administration, warned of the potential catastrophic consequences. Moreover, an entitlement program out of control coupled with fraud and deception, and the incompetent lending policy of Alan Greenspan led to Armageddon in American financial markets, which resonated globally.

I do not wish to leave this discussion without bringing in our Supreme Court. In medicine, we err on the side of patient safety. For example, if the patient has possible meningitis but not probable, antibiotics will more often than not be given to ensure that the worst possible consequence is avoided. When I read the Second Amendment, it is my opinion that it could be interpreted as guns for militia only not for private citizens. The Supreme Court has failed to rule on the side of citizen safety in the interpretation of the Second Amendment. Look at the catastrophic consequences—the number of gunshot-inflicted deaths in America is astronomical. Guns also play a key role in suicide, which number of deaths, more than thirty-eight thousand annually, has now exceeded the number from motor vehicle accidents. The Supreme Court found a way to validate Obamacare by viewing the penalty of a citizen who fails to acquire health insurance as a tax, thereby allowing this major healthcare legislation. And they cannot do the same for the Second Amendment being more strict and responsible in the interpretation of the Second Amendment wording? The gun violence in America is an absolute disgrace. Our legislators and the Supreme Court are abominable and should be subject to the most severe criticism for allowing the multitude of gun violent deaths of our children in schools, laborers in the workplace, and innocent victims of robbery and criminal behavior. The fact that the NRA can have that much political influence is disconcerting to say the least. The Supreme Court continues in its irresponsibility with the recent ruling that corporations can be viewed as individuals and thereby have unlimited funding to an individual's campaign further fanning the fire of money influencing public policy as relates to American business. And the lobbying effort needs no words. The health insurance industry likely spent close to a billion dollars, if not more, lobbying healthcare legislation in Washington to be sure they protect their profiteering and fraudulent practices.

Socialist practices and the lack of regulation were the catalysts for allowing indiscriminate lending in the real estate market and the subsequent collapse of financial markets. The way democracy works is like the pendulum on a clock. It will swing to the left and then to the right and back to the left and so forth appeasing in each direction the constituents on each side of the aisle. The swinging pendulum maintains the timepiece of social rest preventing a restive citizenry. Free market capitalism remains the optimal choice for maintaining our individual freedom in a democracy and offers the optimal path to prosperity. We live in the greatest nation ever created on Earth. Most of the world's great innovations have come from America based on our system of free market capitalism. This reflects the genius of our founding fathers who created and constructed the Constitution and a way of life allowing our individual freedoms which must be preserved. Milton Freidman once said that greed has driven business since the beginning of commerce. Without greed and a political structure which fosters entrepreneurship, however, we would not innovate. We would not have televisions, computers, airplanes, iPhones, iPads, cell phones, etc. We must take the good with the bad.

The creation of a cognitive elite and the maldistribution of wealth are related and only the swinging pendulum can help resolve the unfairness of evolution. Some degree of socialism is necessary. Government should ensure equal opportunity for employment, regardless of race, religion, or sex. It should ensure the opportunity for access to competent healthcare for every citizen regardless of an individual's financial resources. And lastly, it should ensure that every citizen has the opportunity to pursue education.

Around 1980, an old army buddy of Uncle Rocky, Tony Scalese, was lying on the beach in Atlantic City. A familiar face and figure jogged by and the recognition was immediate. It was Burt Lancaster. Lancaster was on location filming the well-known movie *Atlantic City,* for which his leading role as Lou Pascal received numerous awards and a nomination for an Academy Award. This fortuitous meeting with Scalese prompted Lancaster to request a reunion with the Angelo family. Subsequently, I received a phone call from Uncle Tim who requested that I arrange a dinner with Lancaster at Cous' Little Italy since I was very friendly with Cous Pilla, the chef we described in a previous chapter. Cous, the greatest southern Italian chef on the eastern seaboard, arranged a private dinner at his restaurant. It was a wonderful reunion of Burt Lancaster with Angelo family members. Cous provided the very best of Italian cuisine. Years later, however, unfortunately Cous' Little Italy was closed by the Internal Revenue Service for alleged money laundering. Uncle Tim later confided that Lancaster had acquired enormous wealth and offered to financially support Angelo Brothers to implement their global expansion of products, especially light bulbs. The Angelo brothers politely demurred.

As Burt Lancaster had achieved fame and fortune as a Hollywood icon and Academy Award winner, Rocky took another path. His increasing alcohol abuse led to divorce from his wife, Geri, and four lovely children. It also led to his divorce from Angelo Brothers, a company, which he substantially contributed to with the creation of the light bulb line which became the main stalwart of company products, generating enormous income. I recalled our trip to Japan when Rocky would drink scotch and milk because of his peptic ulcer. His golf partner, Dr. Jerry Silvestri subsequently performed a hemigastrectomy and vagotomy which took away the stomach pain allowing Rocky a more comfortable access to alcohol. He became alcoholic. While Burt Lancaster received an Academy Award for Elmer Gantry, Rocky was drying out in Carrier Clinic.

Burt Lancaster enjoyed another decade of life after that Angelo family reunion, but he was compromised with atherosclerosis and underwent a quadruple bypass in 1983. In 1990, he suffered a severe stroke leaving him densely hemiparetic and with an expressive aphasia (unable to speak). He died in his Los Angeles apartment after his third myocardial infarction (heart attack) on October 20, 1994 at the age of eighty.

Like other Angelo brothers, Rocky sustained metastatic carcinoma of the lung from a lifetime of cigarette smoking. I visited him in his apartment in Northeast Philadelphia a few weeks before his demise. He jokingly said, "Doc, you've gotta come to the funeral and have a great time. You're gonna come, aren't you?" Rocky maintained his charisma and unrivaled sense of humor to the very end. He never did speak to Burt Lancaster right up to the day he quietly walked off stage July 14, 1990.

Anthony A. Chiurco, MD

Circa 1988

CPSIA information can be obtained
at www.ICGtesting.com
Printed in the USA
BVHW031817131218
535575BV00001B/25/P

9 781489 701459